Instructor's Manual to Accompany

AN INTRODUCTION TO POETRY

Instructor's Manual to Accompany

AN INTRODUCTION TO POETRY

Sixth Edition

X. J. Kennedy

Dorothy M. Kennedy

Little, Brown and Company

Boston   Toronto

ISBN 0-316-48909-3

9 8 7 6 5 4 3 2 1

DON

Published simultaneously in Canada
by Little, Brown & Company (Canada) Limited

Printed in the United States of America

PREFACE

USING THIS MANUAL

Here are notes--background information, classroom strategies, capsule summaries of comment by critics, pigheaded personal interpretations--for every poem in the book. Well, almost every. Eight brief poems, given in the book as illustrations, didn't seem to require any. It has been a special pleasure to include the suggestions and teaching experiences of several instructors who cared to contribute them.

As in the past, the arrangement of this manual follows the order of the book itself. To help you quickly find a note to go with a poem, page numbers appear at the tops of pages in this manual. These correspond to the page numbers in the parent book.

Every time An Introduction to Poetry is revised, so is its manual. Notes for the poems still kept in the book are enlarged and updated, while new notes are supplied for all new poems. We hope to keep serving all instructors, even those who hold that all an instructor's manual is good for is to swat flies. At least, we trust, this manual will supply some crushing weight, without pretending to be a crushing authority.

RENOVATIONS

This manual has two brand new features:

1. A thorough list called "Poems Arranged by Subject and Theme" (covering the entire book). We commend it to instructors who wish to break out of the organization of the book and to teach poetry thematically.

2. Another thorough list called "Poems in the Anthology Section, Arranged by Elements." This should help you find more poems to illustrate a certain element of poetry--imagery, irony, technical language, symbolism, myth, or what you will. The list also directs you to poems of similar feather: blank verse, sonnets, ballads.

As explained in the book's Preface ("Changes in This Edition"), this edition of the parent book has undergone a shakedown to try to make it closer to what instructors have been telling us are their hearts' desires. One universal, burning desire seemed to be for fewer graphic poems and poems in funny shapes. Fewer songs was another. Still another wish was for more good poems that exhibit imagery, while several instructors asked for a slightly fuller anthology.

The book's most radical repacking has been the combination of what used to be two separate chapters, "Telling Good from Bad" and "Knowing Excellence," into a new one, "Evaluating a Poem." Many find that, with all else there is to do, the problem of evaluation can be given less time, if any at all.

The book feels an obligation to reflect contemporary poetry, and among recent poets new to this edition you will find Olga Broumas, Christopher Bursk, Fred Chappell, Amy Clampitt, Lucille Clifton, Norman Dubie, Dana Gioia, Michael Hogan, Garrett Kaoru Hongo, Donald Justice, Carolyn Kizer, Brad Leithauser, Sharon Olds, Mary Oliver, Robert Phillips, Paul Ruffin, Gjertrud Schnackenberg, Bettie Sellers, Stephen Shu Ning Liu, Louis Simpson, Timothy Steele, and Robert Wallace. Most of the poems by these writers have not been in textbooks before, but we trust this manual will be of some help in introducing them.

Woman poets of the past are better represented with the addition of work by Louise Bogan, Emily Brontë, Maria Lowell, Charlotte Mew, and Christina Rossetti. Contemporary woman poets, too, are more numerous this time.

A few standard favorites are now added (or restored): de la Mare's "The Listeners," Frost's "The Wood-Pile," Robinson's "How Annandale Went Out," Donne's "The Flea," Ben Jonson's "On My First Son," Raleigh's "The Nymph's Reply to the Shepherd," Vaughan's "The Retreat," Updike's "Ex-Basketball Player."

For work by poets who speak for minorities in America, see the selections by Gwendolyn Brooks (three poems), Lucille Clifton, Countee Cullen, James Emanuel, Robert Hayden, Garrett Kaoru Hongo, Langston Hughes (two poems), James C. Kilgore, Etheridge Knight, N. Scott Momaday, Dudley Randall, Stephen Shu Ning Liu, Gary Soto, Jean Toomer, Richard Wright, the anonymous "Scottsboro," and all poems by contemporary male poets.

REPRESENTATION

This edition includes 433 whole poems, including translations, haiku, and clerihews: by coincidence, exactly the same number it had the last time. (Every effort has been made not to let the size of this book inflate greatly.) There are 286 poems in the body of the text, 146 in the Anthology section, 3 in the Supplement.

In case you wish to teach a poet's work in greater depth than a single poem affords, these are the poets most heavily represented (listed by number of poems):

Yeats	11	
Dickinson	10	
Hardy	10	(Counting the 5 "Satires of Circumstance")
Frost	9	
Blake	8	
W. Whitman	8	
W. C. Williams	8	
Donne	7	

Besides, there are now three poems apiece by Bishop, Brooks,
Cunningham, Jarrell, Jonson, Lawrence, Levertov, Milton, Plath,
Pope, Rich, and James Wright.

PLAN OF THE BOOK

There is one, but you are under no obligation to follow it.
Chapters may be taken up in any sequence. Many instructors find
that a surefire chapter to begin with is "Imagery." If, because
you skip around in the book, students meet a term unknown to them,
let them look it up in the Index of Terms. They will be directed
to the page where the term first occurs, and is defined and
illustrated.

So that parts of the book may be taught in any order, the
sections called "For Review and Further Study" do not review the
whole book up to that moment; they review only the main points of
the chapter. These sections provide extra material for the
instructor who wants to go further into a certain element of
poetry. Most contain poems a little more difficult than those in
the main body of the chapter.

The assumption behind the book is that appreciation of poetry
cannot be created, but may be increased. Without trying to usurp
the right of instructors to teach poetry in ways after their own
hearts, the book offers short discussions of the elements of
poetry, which students may read for themselves, freeing class time
for the study of poems.

TEXTS

Spelling has been modernized (rose-lipped for ros-lip'd) and
made American, unless the sound of a word would be changed. But
the y has remained in Blake's strange "Tyger" and Whitman has kept
his bloom'd on the conviction that bloomed would no more resemble
Whitman than a portrait of him in a starched collar would.
Untitled poems, except for those that have titles assigned by
custom ("The Twa Corbies"), are identified by their first lines.
Chaucer's "Your ÿen two wol slee me sodenly" is given as edited by
F. N. Robinson; the poems of Emily Dickinson, as edited by Thomas
H. Johnson.

GLOSSES

It would have been simpler to gloss no word a student could find in a desk dictionary, on the grounds that the rummaging of dictionaries is good moral discipline; but it seemed best not to require the student to exchange text for dictionary as many as ten times in reading a single poem. Glosses have been provided for whatever seemed likely to interfere with pleasure and understanding.

ORTHOGRAPHY

The spelling of rime is used instead of rhyme, on the theory that rime is easier to distinguish from rhythm.

LIVE POETS

Now that there is a guidebook to poets' whereabouts, there seems no point in trying to include data setting up poetry readings in this manual. Anyone who wants to order a live poet is advised to send for A Directory of American Poets and Fiction Writers from Poets and Writers, Inc., 201 West 54 St., New York, NY 10019. The price of the 1985-86 edition is $14.95.

CREDITS

Besides the many instructors who contributed to this manual and whose names appear in the acknowledgments in the book itself, we wish to thank Sally Stickney and Susan M. S. Brown for helping us make more sense.

XJK and DMK

CONTENTS

POEMS ARRANGED BY SUBJECT AND THEME

    This list sorts out and classifies most of the poems in the entire textbook. Besides subjects or themes, it includes some genres (i.e., Elegies, Pastoral Poems, poems of spring and other seasons).
    How to Use This Information. May a browse through this list reveal poems worth teaching side by side. This list will be particularly helpful to the instructor who wishes to organize a whole poetry course quite differently from the way the book is structured: to teach poetry not by the elements of poems, but by themes. But, however you prefer to organize your course, you will find this list a ready source of possible writing assignments.
    For Writing Topics. You might have students read three or four poems in a group (say, those in the category "Apocalypse," or a few of your choice from "Coming of Age"), then ask them to reply, in a page or two, to the question, What do these poems have in common? Or, How do these poets differ in their expressions of a similar theme?
    What follows is thorough, but not exhaustive. We have left out some categories that sounded unpromising. Would you have cared that the book has four locomotive poems (by Dickinson, Stillman, Walt Whitman, and William Carlos Williams) and three (by Cunningham, Davison, and Tichborne) about three persons literally or figuratively decapitated? Not all these themes and subjects are central to their poems, but all will be fairly evident.

Apocalypse

Frost	Fire and Ice, 69
MacLeish	The End of the World, 167
Yeats	The Second Coming, 217

Art

Auden	Musée des Beaux Arts, 279
Pastan	Ethics, 6
Stevens	Anecdote of the Jar, 212
Wilbur	Museum Piece, 375
W. C. Williams	The Dance, 178

Beast and Bird

Blake	The Tyger, 282
Clampitt	The Cormorant in His Element, 291
Clare	Mouse's Nest, 45
Hall	Names of Horses, 310
Hopkins	The Windhover, 320
Kinnell	Saint Francis and the Sow, 329
Kizer	The Intruder, 329
Layton	The Bull Calf, 332
R. Lowell	Skunk Hour, 334
Smart	For I will consider my cat Jeoffry, 359
Taylor	Riding a One-eyed Horse, 37
Tennyson	The Eagle, 83

Belonging to a Minority (see also Black Experience)

Hogan	Spring, 318
Hongo	The Hongo Store, 318
Momaday	The Delight Song of Tsoai-talee, 338
Olds	The One Girl at the Boys Party, 341
Sellers	In the Counselor's Waiting Room, 31
Shu Ning Liu	My Father's Martial Art, 367
Soto	Black Hair, 362
Stafford	At the Klamath Berry Festival, 363

Black Experience (see also Belonging to a Minority)

Anonymous	Scottsboro, 58
Brooks	The Rites for Cousin Vit, 284
Brooks	Sadie and Maud, 284
Brooks	We Real Cool, 144
Clifton	to the unborn and waiting children, 292
Cullen	For a Lady I Know, 11
Emanuel	The Negro, 54
Hayden	Those Winter Sundays, 6
Hughes	Dream Deferred, 323
Hughes	Subway Rush Hour, 324
Kilgore	The White Man Pressed the Locks, 98
Knight	For Black Poets Who Think of Suicide, 101
Randall	Ballad of Birmingham, 347

Books and Reading

Bradstreet	The Author to Her Book, 12
Keats	On First Looking into Chapman's Homer, 326
Larkin	A Study of Reading Habits, 331
Wallace	The Girl Writing Her English Paper, 415

Boredom, Boring Life-styles

Eliot	The Boston Evening Transcript, 202
Simpson	The Boarder, 209
Stevens	Disillusionment of Ten O'Clock, 64

Faith and Doubt (see also Clerics, Glory Be to God)

Fame

Families (see also Fathers and Children, Mothers and Children)

Farm and Country (see also Pastoral Poems)

Lust and Concupiscence

Magic and Vision

Marriage

Old Age

Pastoral Poems   (see also Farm and Country)

Protest Poems

Sports

Time and Aging (see also Carpe Diem)

War

A Woman's Identity (see also Mothers and Children)

Instructor's Manual to Accompany

AN INTRODUCTION TO POETRY

1

READING A POEM

The aim of this chapter is to assure the student that reading
poetry is not going to be entirely different from reading prose.
He or she will learn a few ways in which poetry _is_ different, and
how to cope with it.

A. E. HOUSMAN, Loveliest of trees, the cherry now, page 3

Not part of the rough poem Housman began with, the second
stanza was added last. Lines 9-10 originally read: "And since to
look at things you love / Fifty times is not enough." What can be
said for Housman's additions and changes? (These and other
manuscript variations are given by Tom Burns Haber in The Making of
"A Shropshire Lad" [Seattle: Washington P, 1966].)

ROBERT HAYDEN, Those Winter Sundays, page 6

This brief poem, simple in the word's best sense, has a depth
that rewards close reading. That the speaker is a boy is a safe
inference: most grown-ups do not lie abed while their fathers
polish their shoes. Besides, evidently years have intervened
between the speaker today and his previous self--the observing
child. Now the speaker understands his father better, looks back
on himself, and asks, "What did I know?"
The poem states its theme in its wonderful last line (worth
quoting to anyone who distrusts abstract words in poetry).
Students can miss Hayden's point unless they understand its
vocabulary. Austere can mean stern, forbidding, somber, but it can
also mean (as it does here) ascetic, disciplined, self-denying. To
rise in the freezing house takes steely self-discipline. That the
father's life is built on austerity we get from his labor-worn
hands. What is an office? A duty, task, or ceremony that someone
assumes (or has conferred on him): the tasks of shining shoes, of
stirring banked fires in a furnace (or a coal-burning stove?).
James Wright, a keen admirer of Hayden's poem, has spoken of it in
an interview:

The word offices is the great word here. Office, they say in
French. It is a religious service after dark. Its formality,
its combination of distance and immediacy, is appropriate. In
my experience uneducated people and people who are driven by

1

brute circumstance to work terribly hard for a living, the
living of their families, are very big on formality.

(The Pure Clear Word: Essays on the poetry of James Wright, ed.
Dave Smith [Urbana: U of Illinois P, 1982] 10.)
Perhaps the "chronic angers" belong to the father: the boy
gets up slowly and fearfully, as though in dread of a tongue-
lashing. Yet this reading does not seem quite in keeping with the
character of the father as he emerges: stoic, patient, long-
suffering, loving. Hayden does not invest these angers in the
father exclusively. Perhaps any tenant of this bitterly cold house
has reason to dread getting up in it.
When read aloud, the opening stanza reveals strong patterns of
sound: the internal alliteration of the k-sound in blueblack,
cracked, ached, weekday, banked, thanked (and, in the next stanza,
in wake, breaking, chronic)--staccato bursts of hard consonants.
Rather than using exact rime at the ends of lines, Hayden
strengthens lines by using it internally: banked/thanked (line 5),
wake/breaking (6); perhaps off-rime, too: labor/weather (4),
rise/dress (8). Alliteration and assonance occur in clothes . . .
cold (2), weekday weather (4). If you assign this poem early in
your investigation of poetry, probably it matters more that
students hear and respond to the rich interplay of repeated sounds
than that they be able to give these devices labels.
"Those Winter Sundays" is the most often reprinted poem of
Robert Hayden. The poet, a black who grew up in Detroit and who
for many years professed English at the University of Michigan, has
written other poems apparently drawn from childhood and memory,
among these "Obituary," another moving tribute to his father.
Hayden's posthumous Collected Poems (New York: Norton/Liveright,
1985) belongs, we think, in every library.

LINDA PASTAN, Ethics, page 6

As a student, the narrator, like others in her class, found
her teacher's ethical puzzler irrelevant. Now the mature woman
pondering the "real Rembrandt" in the museum finds the question
still remote from her vital concerns, but for different reasons.
The approach of her own old age has shown her that nothing lasts,
that with the onflow of years our choices, whatever they may be,
fade into insignificance. Is the theme of the poem carpe diem?
No, for the poet seems not to believe in day-seizing. Is the theme
ars longa, vita brevis est? No, for both art and life are piti-
fully brief and temporary. The point, rather, is that all things
pass away despite our efforts to hold on to them. In its moving
statement of thoughts and feelings, the poem seems essentially
lyric rather than narrative. One thing about its story puzzles us
though: how many times did the speaker have to repeat that ethics
course? She had to sit through the same lesson plan every fall?
In reply to question 4, Pastan's language is perceptibly more
musical than prose. In particular, she makes beautiful use of
alliteration and assonance. Read out loud the poem's last two

2

sentences. Central to "Ethics" is an immense metaphor: old woman, season, earth, painting, and poet become one--all caught in time's fire.

First printed in Poetry for December 1979, "Ethics was chosen by the poet to represent her in The Poet's Choice, an anthology of poets' own favorite poems edited by George E. Murphy, Jr. (Green Harbor: Tendril Magazine, 1980).

ROBERT FRANCIS, Catch, page 7

Putting a spin on his poem-baseball, hurling high ones and sometimes grounders, the pitching poet keeps the catching reader on his toes by creating little difficulties, yet once in a while supplies an instant reward. Most students (though they may paraphrase it differently) will find this much of Francis's comparison easy to catch. How does a poet "outwit the prosy"? Playing with swagger and style, the poet doesn't want to communicate in a dull, predictable way, but (being a magician on the mound) will do anything to surprise, to make poetry a game in which both poet and reader take joy.

If you skip the chapter "Reading a Poem," or don't discuss "Catch at this moment, the poem can be especially useful later in teaching metaphor, or tone.

ANDREW MARVELL, To His Coy Mistress, page 8

1. There's a grain of truth to this paraphrase, rude though it be. We might question, however, whether Marvell's speaker is trying to hoodwink his loved one. Perhaps he only sums up the terrible truth he knows: that time lays waste to youth, that life passes before we know it. He makes no mention of "romance," by the way--that's the paraphraser's invention. A more nearly accurate paraphrase, taking the three divisions of the poem one by one, might go like this:

Lines 1-20: If we had all the room in the world and if we were immortal, then our courtship might range across the globe. My love for you could expand till it filled the whole world and I could spend centuries in praising your every feature (saving your heart for last). After all, such treatment is only what you deserve.
Lines 21-32: But time runs on. Soon we'll be dead and gone, all my passion and all your innocence vanished.
Lines 33-46: And so, while you're still young and willing, let's seize the day. Let's concentrate our pleasure into the present moment. Although we can't make the sun stand still (like Joshua in the Bible), we'll do the next best thing: we'll joyously make time fly.

Now, obviously, any such rewording of this matchless poem must seem a piddling thing. But if students will just work through Marvell's argument part by part, they may grasp better the whole of it.

2. To point out the approximate location of the Humber and the Ganges on a globe (or a simple circle drawn on a blackboard) can drive home the fact that when the poet says world enough, he spells out exactly what he means. A little discussion may be needed to show that in defining "enough" time, Marvell bounds it by events (the conversion of the Jews), numbers the years, and blocks out his piecemeal adoration. Two hundred years per breast is a delectable statistic! Clearly, the lover doesn't take the notion of such slow and infinitely patient devotion seriously.

3. Both Marvell and Housman in "Loveliest of trees" (page 3) are concerned with the passage of time; they differ on what needs to be done about it. Marvell urges action; Housman urges filling one's youth with observed beauty. Of these two expressions of the carpe diem theme, Housman's seems the more calm and disinterested.

4. In lines 37-44, Marvell, Marvell's point seems to be that time works a gradual, insidious violence. It is like a devouring beast (slow-chapped), holding us in its inexorable jaws. Some students will find the imagery odd, even offensive in a love poem: birds of prey (who want to eat, not be eaten), the cannonball of strength and sweetness that batters life's iron gates. Violence is not the speaker's counsel, but urgency. His harsh images lend his argument intensity and force.

5. This fifth question presents an easy dichotomy, but of course Marvell's speaker is both playful and serious. In making clear the tone of the poem, a useful poem for comparison is Marlowe's "Pas- sionate Shepherd" (page 335). What are the two speakers' attitudes toward love? Marvell's seems more down-to-earth, skeptical, and passion-driven: a lover in a fallen world, not (like Marlowe's shepherd) a lover in a pastoral Eden.

If later on, in teaching figures of speech, you want some great lines for illustrations, turn back to this inexhaustible poem. There's hyperbole in lines 7-20, understatement ("But none, I think, do they embrace"), metaphor, simile, and of course the great personification of chariot-driving time.

Telling a class that Marvell was a Puritan usually shakes up their overly neat assumption. Some may be surprised to learn that one can be a Puritan and not necessarily be puritanical.

Defending the poem against charges that its logic is fallacious, a recent critic, Richard Crider, has shown that "the speaker's appeal is not merely to the lady's passion, . . . but to a more inclusive and compelling value--completion and wholeness." A good student of Aristotle's logic as well as Aristotle's ethics, Marvell's speaker calls on his listener to exercise all her human powers, among them reason. "Although no single net will capture all the resonances of the final couplet, near the heart of the passage is the thought of living life completely, in accordance with natural law" ("Marvell's Valid Logic," College Literature [Spring 1985]: 113-21).

2

LISTENING TO A VOICE

TONE

THEODORE ROETHKE, My Papa's Waltz, page 10

Jay Parini would disagree. In his Theodore Roethke: An American Romantic (Amherst: U of Massachusetts P, 1980), he finds that in "My Papa's Waltz" the boy "clings to his father for dear life, terrified by his physical power." "Which is to miss the point completely," protests John Lucas, reviewing Parini's book in the Times Literary Supplement for 6 February 1981. For the mature poet, looking back,

> recognizes how his timidity of spirit must have been a kind of death to his father, a terrible drag on his vitality. "Such waltzing was not easy." In substituting the trite phrase about clinging on for dear life for Roethke's finely judged one about hanging on like death, Parini quite fails to note how, for once at least, Roethke makes good use of cliché rather than being used by it.

As Alan Seager discerns in his biography of Roethke, The Glass House (New York: McGraw, 1968) 23, the mature Roethke seems to have felt a certain guilty resentment against his father, a sense of how (as an awkward, chubby, bookish, and sensitive child) the young poet had failed to make the old man proud of him.

"My Papa's Waltz" may have had its genesis in a wish-fulfilling dream. After his father's death, Roethke wrote a memoir (calling himself "John"): "Sometimes he dreamed about Papa. Once it seemed Papa came in and danced around with him. John put his feet on top of Papa's and they'd waltz. Hei-dee-dei-dei. Rump-tee-tump. Only babies expected dreams to come true" (qtd. in Seager 24).

COUNTEE CULLEN, For a Lady I Know, page 11

From Cullen's first book, Color (1925), this is one of a series of twenty-nine epitaphs. Compare it with another brief poem that makes a biting social comment: Sarah N. Cleghorn's "The Golf Links" (page 26). Cleghorn's poem seems angrier; the tone of Cullen's poem seems to be wry amusement at stupidity.

Cullen's early biography is sparsely documented. Raised by his grandmother until he was eleven, he was then adopted by the Reverend Frederick A. Cullen, pastor of a Methodist church in Harlem, who gave the future poet not only a name but a new life of books and conversation. Famed as the leading poet of the Harlem Renaissance, Cullen suffered a decline in reputation when militant black critics of the 1960s reevaluated his work and found it wanting in anger and social consciousness. But his wit can bite, as it does in "For a Lady I Know"; and Houston A. Baker has rightly called much of his work an "ironical protest . . . against economic oppression" in his short study of Cullen, A Many-colored Coat of Dreams (Detroit: Broadside, 1974).

ANNE BRADSTREET, The Author to Her Book, page 12

The "rags" (line 5) worn by this bastard brat of a book may have been the first edition's abundance of typographical errors. Although Bradstreet patiently revised her work, she did not live to see her "brat" appear in better dress. This poem prefaced the Boston edition published in 1678, six years after the poet's death.
Robert Hutchinson, in the introduction to his edition of Poems of Anne Bradstreet (New York: Dover, 1969), gives a concise account of the book's publication. Evidently the author's family, proud of her poetry, felt that it deserved more notice than New England could then give. The Reverend John Woodbridge, Bradstreet's brother-in-law, took with him to England the manuscript of the collection. London at the time had sixty printers; New England, one--and so it must have been difficult, even then, to print poetry in America. "The fact," notes Hutchinson, "that Herrick's Hesperides had just appeared in England while the latest venture of Samuel Green, the Cambridge, Massachusetts, printer, was a revision of The Bay Psalm Book to rid it of its crudities, gives an indication of the intellectual distance between the two countries."

WALT WHITMAN, To a Locomotive in Winter, page 13

EMILY DICKINSON, I like to see it lap the Miles, page 14

Though both of these great nineteenth-century Americans take almost the same subject, in tone and in form the two poems differ as sharply as opera differs from chamber music. (Some students might argue that the mutual subject isn't a moving locomotive, but the poets' praise of it. While seeing a real similarity, they would be missing the distinction between subject and tone.) Whitman addresses his machine in awe and exultation. In lines 14-19 he practically prays to it (almost like Henry Adams on bended knees before the dynamo in Education). Dickinson is evidently more playful in her affectionate view of the locomotive as a great beast. It is horselike in that it neighs and has a stable, but it isn't quite a horse: it crawls and hoots. Both poets, incidentally, see not only a locomotive, but a whole train.

Dickinson's seeing it "chase itself" suggests cars trying to catch
their locomotive as they roll downhill. Dickinson's allusion to
Boanerges means no more, I think, than that the locomotive is a
servant, and is thunderous.

Whitman's poem is full of diction from music: <u>recitative</u>,
<u>beat</u>, <u>ringing bell</u>, <u>notes</u>, <u>chant</u>, <u>harp</u>, <u>piano</u>, <u>trills</u>. The
locomotive embodies poetry, too, in its <u>metrical</u> pant and roar, and
in its ability to serve the Muse. The word <u>recitative</u> indicates
the form the poem will be cast in. In Italian opera, to which
Whitman was devoted, Rossini had introduced the use of the full
orchestra to accompany the recitative, the passage of half-sung,
half-spoken declamation; and it may be that, as Robert D. Faner has
argued, such recitative was a basic model for Whitman's poetry.
"The recitative, highly rhythmic and emotional, punctuated by
instrumental accompaniment with thrilling effect, and in its
chanted delivery giving the impression of the rhythms of speech, he
found well adapted to the bulk of his work, which he thought of as
a sort of bardic chant" (<u>Walt Whitman & Opera</u> [Carbondale: Southern
Illinois UP, 1951] 234).

JOHN MILTON, On the Late Massacre in Piemont, page 15

Sorrow, wrath, and hatred seem mingled in this powerful
sonnet. Milton sees the Waldenses as true primitive Christians.
They had broken with Rome in the twelfth century, refusing to
accept rituals and dogmas which, they thought, had been too
recently decreed. Protestant Europe was outraged at the massacre.
As Cromwell's secretary, Milton was instructed to write letters of
protest to the heads of state. His own indignant prayer to a
wrathful God has, as William Riley Parker has said, "the awesome
sound of a great wave pounding against a wall."

THE PERSON IN THE POEM

TRUMBULL STICKNEY, Sir, say no more, page 16

The death at age 30 of the brilliant Stickney, scholar of
Greek and recipient of the only doctorate in letters that the
University of Paris had granted to an Anglo-Saxon, silenced one of
the finest lyric voices in American poetry. One of his sonnets,
"Near Helikon," ends:

> To me my troubled life doth now appear
> Like scarce distinguishable summits hung
> Around the blue horizon: places where
> Nor even a traveller purposeth to steer,--
> Whereof a migrant bird in passing sung
> And the girl closed her window not to hear.

16-19 (text pages)

Indispensable to anyone who wishes to read further is The Poems of Trumbull Stickney, ed. Amberys R. Whittle, with a foreword by Edmund Wilson (New York: Farrar, 1972).

RANDALL JARRELL, A Sick Child, page 17

Lonely and bored, the child is tired of his own imaginings. He longs for something colossal and unthinkable to take him by surprise. He wishes that creatures from another world would arrive and make him their pet--the very wish of grown-up Gottfried Rosenbaum in Jarrell's novel Pictures from an Institution (1954), as Suzanne Ferguson points out in The Poetry of Randall Jarrell (Baton Rouge: Louisiana State UP, 1971).

In the imaginary conversation, the mailman seems ashamed that his game of make-believe has been spurned, but he hasn't understood the child's terrible longing to be surprised. By understanding the child, by so perfectly detailing the child's mental games, by conveying the child's longing in simple language that bursts into a kind of desperate outcry at the end, Jarrell clearly shows his own profound sympathy.

WILLIAM WORDSWORTH, I Wandered Lonely as a Cloud, page 17

To point out the distance between art and reporting, it may be helpful to read Wordsworth's poem aloud--at least parts of it. In their rhythm, lines such as "fluttering and dancing in the breeze" and "Tossing their heads in sprightly dance" make the motion of the daffodils come alive. By comparison, Dorothy Wordsworth's record of the incident ("the rest tossed and reeled and danced") seems merely excellent prose.

Actually, Wordsworth's sister was a distinguished poet in her own right, as Hyman Eigerman demonstrates in The Poetry of Dorothy Wordsworth (New York: Columbia 1940), an anthology of passages from her journals arranged into formally open verse.

EDWIN ARLINGTON ROBINSON, How Annandale Went Out, page 19

Robinson unfolds his little horror story with tongue-in-cheek understatement ("the sight was not so fair"), and leaves it to the reader to imagine a coup de grace administered in the last line. A doctor who considers himself Annandale's friend tells a single listener (addressed as "yourself"--perhaps a judge or investigator?) how he injected his patient with a fatal sedative. In the last line's ellipsis, he demonstrates how ("Like this . . .") he delivered one quick thrust of a hypodermic needle. In self-justification, he calls the tormented wreck that used to be Annandale an "it," no longer a man.

Some will argue that the poet approves of this mercy killing. He clearly implies that the doctor is a kindly liar, given to con- cealing the truth from his suffering charge; a man of whom no one

can cite previous bad behavior (line 11). The speaker expects the
listener does not want to hang him, and his listener condones his
deed.

Yet the poem seems (for us) ambivalent; the poet's own
attitude, deliberately concealed. In most dramatic monologues
(Robert Browning's "My Last Duchess" [page 286] and "Soliloquy of
the Spanish Cloister" [page 288], Tennyson's "Ulysses" [page 367])
the reader is given to understand, without quotation marks, that a
character is speaking. Why, then, is this poem enclosed in
quotation marks? asked David Lynch, copyeditor for this edition of
An Introduction to Poetry. Perhaps, sensitive to the protests of
readers who don't think physicians ought to do in patients,
Robinson carefully dissociates himself from the doctor's words by
making the whole poem a quotation--as if to say, "Don't think these
words are mine!" The doctor is not the poet, however we may
suspect the poet of being on his side.

Louis O. Coxe finds this a melodramatic "trick" poem with an
O. Henry plot, a regrettable backslide to the Robinson of "Richard
Cory"--in Edwin Arlington Robinson: The Life of Poetry (New York:
Pegasus 1969). To discuss: How does "Annandale" resemble "Richard
Cory" (page 108)? Is there a good word to be said for either poem?

The ruined Annandale's past hardly matters, but students who
care to read more of Robinson's work may be steered to an earlier
(1902) narrative poem, "The Book of Annandale," in which we find
that Annandale's first name is George, that his young wife had died
after a short happy marriage, and that he had originally wanted to
marry somebody else.

XJK notes: I had quite forgotten this tremendous old
class-rouser until three instructors, asked to suggest poems to add
to this edition, reminded me of it. I would be grateful to hear
how it fares with your students today, when mercy killing continues
to be a lively controversy.

PAUL ZIMMER, The Day Zimmer Lost Religion, page 20

Paul Zimmer writes usually comic, sometimes touching poems
featuring a central character who bears his own last name. If
Zimmer in this poem is the poet and not a fictitious character,
then the speaker may be the mature Zimmer, looking back through his
own younger eyes. The "old days" mentioned in line 8 would seem an
even earlier time when, as a schoolboy, Zimmer assisted at Mass.
Now (as an adolescent?) he has come to doubt--but he still takes a
boyish view, expecting Christ, "like the playground bully," to pun-
ish him. The last two lines seem the mature Zimmer's view. Only
the grown-up are ready for Christ. Without knowing the actual
Zimmer's present convictions, we can assume that the mature poet
speaks either as a believer or as one with a deepened respect for
belief.

For more Zimmer poems, see The Zimmer Poems (Washington:
Dryad, 1976). The world in which the character Zimmer moves often
seems dreamlike.

20-21 (text pages)

RICHARD HUGO, In Your Young Dream, page 20

Unless you were ever a traveling basketball player who loved a woman now married to someone else, the <u>you</u> in the poem isn't you. It may well be the poet. But by relating this dream in the second person (and in the present tense) Hugo gains for his poem a certain immediacy.

What makes this narrative convincingly dreamlike? Years drop away. The other player is "vaguely seen." With the precipitous haste and defiance of space that characterize dreams, the woman--at the will of "you"--is suddenly transported to "your room." (But she is "surrounded by children"--hardly a situation that invites seduction!)

A question which may be useful even if the class has yet to grapple with symbols is: What do the missing nets suggest? (The central character's feelings of emptiness and frustration, perhaps?)

For more of Hugo's "you" poems, see his collection from which "In Your Young Dream" is taken: <u>31 Letters and 13 Dreams</u> (New York: Norton, 1977). Its contents are reprinted in Hugo's collected poems, <u>Making Certain It Goes On</u> (New York: Norton, 1984).

WILLIAM CARLOS WILLIAMS, The Red Wheelbarrow, page 21

Evidently many readers have found it easy to admire this poem without feeling a need to know the circumstances in which it was written. For a fairly recent appreciation, see Louis Untermeyer, <u>The Pursuit of Poetry</u> (New York: Simon, 1969) 25. Untermeyer views the poem as a kind of haiku that makes us aware of glories in commonplaces. A more sharply critical estimate is that of Roy Harvey Pearce in his fine essay "Williams and the 'New Mode'" in <u>The Continuity of American Poetry</u> (Princeton: Princeton UP, 1961) 335-48. Pearce charges the poem with sentimentality: "At its worst this is togetherness in a chicken-yard." However, in Pearce's view, the poem also has a better aspect: what "depends" is the poet's vocation as a poet. He needs common objects in order to write poems, and the objects in turn need him to imagine them into poetry.

If the librarian is right about the situation in which the poem was written (see page 32), "The Red Wheelbarrow" seems a better poem than we had realized: a kind of prayer, a work of compassion. However, that the poem fails to give us an intimation of the reasons for the poet's feelings (and of why we ought to share them) does expose it to Pearce's accusation that it is sentimental. Whatever the instructor's opinion, the merits and demerits of the poem can be a lively topic for class discussion.

IRONY

ROBERT CREELEY, Oh No, page 22

"What interests me most about 'Oh No' is its tone," Cynthia
Edelberg remarks in an interview with the poet. "How would you
describe it?" Creeley replies that he sees it as wry irony, the
poem being "self-parody," a comment on his feelings at the time.
"As Joel Oppenheimer said, that would qualify me to be a Jew. He
really liked that poem. It's that kind of humor" (Edelberg's
Robert Creeley's Poetry: A Critical Introduction [Albuquerque: U
of New Mexico P, 1978] 168).

W. H. AUDEN, The Unknown Citizen, page 23

For making students better aware of irony, Auden's familiar
satire remains as dependable as any poem we know. Little seems to
have dated in it, other than the praise of the citizen for adding
five children to the population. Students are usually good at
seeing that, unlike the unknown soldier, the citizen is all too
thoroughly identified; and that, nevertheless, his true nature and
inmost wants remain unknown. Meaty questions for discussion
naturally arise: What are the premises of such a society? It
seems dedicated to the proposition that to conform to a norm is the
highest virtue--any individual traits, of course, being an
annoyance to statisticians. What is a "Modern Man"? One with
animal needs, but no aspirations. The epitaph, often overlooked,
is worth dwelling on: it tells us at once that the unknown citizen
is only a number, and that bureaucrats keep track of him--and,
incidentally, like the rest of the poem, the epitaph is in rime.
"The Unknown Citizen" is one of six poems in this chapter in
which we hear a voice obviously not the poet's. (The others are
the ones by Jarrell, Robinson, Betjeman, Stephens, and Blake.)

JOHN BETJEMAN, In Westminster Abbey, page 24

Cadogan Square was an especially fashionable London address
around the turn of the century, and the fact that the speaker owns
stocks (line 30) also indicates her style of life. Her mind,
however, is ordinary: her ideals seem bounded by drugstore novels
and by plumbing that works properly.
Students usually have a fine time picking out the easy
contradictions in the lady's beliefs: that the Lord may allow
bombs to hit German women, but not English women; that He protects
whites more dutifully than blacks; that it is all very well for the
"gallant blacks" to die, but let the Empire remain united; that
democracy and class distinction go hand in hand.
The speaker's attitude seems to be: "Let God wait upon my
convenience." To call His word a "treat" reduces Scripture to the
importance of candy. That Betjeman first printed this ironic blast

24-26 (text pages)

at smug, hate-mongering chauvinism in the midst of World War II
strikes us as a brave and large-minded plea for genuine Christian
charity.

SARAH N. CLEGHORN, The Golf Links, page 26

   What a great epigram!--no verbal irony in it, just matter-
of-fact notation of a social condition that seems ironic in the
extreme. As Robert Frost said, in his introduction to Cleghorn's
autobiography, Threescore (1936), "There is more high explosive for
righteousness in the least little line of Sarah Cleghorn's poem
about the children working in the mill . . . than in all the prose
of our radical-bound-boys pressed together under a weight of
several atmospheres of revolution." (The conservative Frost didn't
like Marxists, but he called Cleghorn "a saint and a reformer"
anyway.) For a more recent tribute, see Irving Dilliard, "Four
Short Lines," The Nation 222 (10 Apr. 1976): 444-45.
   In Stanley Kunitz and Howard Hayward's Twentieth Century
Authors (New York: Wilson, 1942), in an article on Cleghorn that
she apparently helped write, there is an explanation for the twenty
years that intervened between her early books and her later ones.
"This was caused by the fact that her socialism and pacifism made
editors and publishers reluctant to use her later writing, and
partly by the fact that in middle age she became a teacher." Among
her other works is a novel, The Spinster (1916), and a last
collection, Poems of Peace and Freedom (1945).

THOMAS HARDY, The Workbox, page 26

   Dramatic irony is present in the discrepancy between the
carpenter's limited knowledge and the reader's growing conviction
that the wife knew John much better than she cares to admit. Her
phrase "mere accidental things" contains verbal irony, and in
general the whole speech in lines 25-28 is a verbal irony. Cosmic
irony may be operating too (and one is sure that it is, knowing
Hardy) in the Fate or chance that caused the carpenter to select a
piece of poor John's coffin out of all pieces of wood in the world.
   To us, the situation in the poem had seemed like that in James
Joyce's "The Dead": the wife, by remembering a young man who died
of love for her, has a bleak realization that she might have known
a joyous life had she married him instead. However, Albert
Furtwangler and his students at Mount Allison University found
other possible levels of irony, as he kindly wrote to report. For
Professor Furtwangler, "The Workbox" is marred by an excess of
irony that runs too deep: "it remains fascinating in the long run
more as a puzzle than as a clear disclosure of character." Among
other readings he considered the two following, which he thinks
overingenious and yet consistent with the poem.
   The husband, aware of his wife's past, has contrived his
present as a cunning torture for her. "He seems to offer it in

12

love, but takes pleasure in drawing out his wife's confused replies
. . . thus trapping her in her own hypocrisy."
    The husband knows his wife's history; and she knows that he
knows it. "But they coexist uneasily with each other by exercising
an elaborate fiction of ignorance."
    What will you and your students decide?
    J. O. Bailey sees in this poem the "ballad-like theme of the
lover who died of grief when his beloved married another." Like
traditional English and Scottish ballads, the poem has a question-
and-answer structure and ends in a surprise. (See The Poetry of
Thomas Hardy [Chapel Hill: U of North Carolina P, 1970].) Compare
"The Workbox" in these respects with "Bonny Barbara Allan" (page
110) and "Edward" (page 271).

FOR REVIEW AND FURTHER STUDY

Exercise: Telling Tone, page 27

RICHARD LOVELACE, To Lucasta, page 27

WILFRED OWEN, Dulce et Decorum Est, page 28

    "To Lucasta" may refer to an actual parting. During the
Puritan Revolution of 1642-45, Lovelace fought in the service of
Charles I. Students will readily see the poet's theme that Honor
(duty to God and King) takes priority over duty to Lucasta; the
tone of the poem may give them greater difficulty. The closing
line makes a serious affirmation: Honor for Lovelace is not an
"old Lie," but a creed. Neither grim nor smug, the poem also has
wit and loving tenderness. The witty second stanza seems almost
comic in its figures of speech: having renounced Lucasta's nunlike
chastity and calm, the speaker will now go whet his sword upon the
body of someone wilder.
    Owen's theme is apparent: death in battle is hideous, no
matter what certain ignorant poets say about it. For us, there
seems irony in the fact that Owen himself was to be killed in
action in France. Although in a wartime letter he called himself
"a conscientious objector with a very seared conscience," Owen in
this poem does not question that to die for one's country may be
necessary. His attitude is overpowering disgust--with the butchery
of war, with those who idealize it.

JAMES STEPHENS, A Glass of Beer, page 28

    The high regard of the Irish for the magical powers of speech
has given them a long and glorious tradition of poetic cursing. In
the ancient tales of the Ulster sage, we read of kings who wouldn't
go to battle without an accompanying druid: a poet-priest charged
with pronouncing magnificent metrical curses upon the enemy. Who
knows?--in the pubs of Stephens's native Dublin, curses like the
one in "A Glass of Beer may well have seemed ordinary, even mild.

28-30 (text pages)

    Although the speaker--some frustrated drinker hard up for
cash--is in a towering rage at the barmaid who denied him, the tone
of the poem is not anger but high amusement. There is irony, too,
in the obvious contrast between the speaker's stupendous hyperboles
and the puny occasion for them. Save this poem, if you like, for
teaching figures of speech.
    There is hardly a better modern poem, however, for reminding
students that the feelings expressed in poetry aren't always
positive. A poem may be written in rage or chagrin, as well as in
love or joy. This seems an essential truth, and one that XJK has
tried to demonstrate at some length in Tygers of Wrath: Poems of
Hate, Anger, and Invective (Athens: U of Georgia P, 1981), an
annotated anthology showing the tradition of dark emotion in
British, Irish, and American poetry from the Middle Ages to the
present. Naturally, in this tradition, "A Glass of Beer" holds an
honored place.
    "A Glass of Beer" is a free translation from the Irish of
Dáibhí Ó Bruadair (c. 1625-98). The original with a translation by
Thomas Kinsella ("A Shrewish, Barren, Bony, Nosey Servant") is
given by Seán Ó Tuama and Kinsella in An Duanaire: An Irish
Anthology (Philadelphia: U of Pennsylvania P, 1981) 116-17.

JONATHAN SWIFT, On Stella's Birthday, page 29

    Swift's playfully tender birthday gift kids Stella about her
size, but artfully turns a dig into a compliment. Imagining her
split in two, he declares that even half of her would surpass any
other whole woman. For most students, the only difficult lines
will be 7-8. Swift's argument seems to be that, while Stella has
lost much of the slender beauty she had at sixteen, she hasn't
greatly declined in total worth, for an increase in her mental
gifts (among them wit) has amply compensated.

A. E. HOUSMAN. Epitaph on an Army of Mercenaries, page 30

HUGH MacDIARMID, Another Epitaph on an Army of Mercenaries, page 30

    In a poem that reads like a translation from the Greek
Anthology, Housman expresses wry admiration for these honest
heroes. He likens them to Atlas, condemned to stand and shoulder
the sky. Apparently the mercenaries sustained, along with a
government, a whole religion ("heaven," "the sky") and an entire
civilization ("earth"). The speaker assumes that these hirelings
died in a just cause. To Housman's mind, the British army of World
War I was an army of mercenaries; he once agreed with a comment to
this effect (letter of 14 November 1927, Letters, Harvard UP, 1971)
255.

    MacDiarmid's retort seems a blunt, commonsense protest against
most mercenary armies in recent times. But thugs hired to fight

14

for unjust causes aren't Housman's subject, and to curse his poem as a damned lie seems simple-headed.

BETTIE SELLERS, In the Counselor's Waiting Room, page 31

Evidently this student has been referred to the college psychologist. "Home soil" implies that the mothers have been plowed and planted and made to bear, a condition their daughters appear to be resisting.

Still, this "terra cotta" girl is the product of her soil. Unconsciously, her toes furrow the rug as if she is plowing it. Like the mothers, she seems to be one with the earth; but unlike them, she now (in the mothers' view) holds no promise of procreation. In this discrepancy lies the poem's main irony. (Other mildly ironic discrepancies: that a farm girl from a Bible-reading background now studies existentialism; the girl's guilt feelings juxtaposed with existential anguish over the nature of the universe.)

Because the flat-footed girl is the subject, because we witness her unease (toes furrowing the rug as she clutches the comfortless book on existentialism), certainly she receives the larger share of the poet's--and our own--sympathy. She may be an awkward rustic, but she has found love and can't help loving. Sellers regards both student and mothers with (I think) affectionate humor: the girl with her "big flat farm feet," the mothers so eager to see their daughters reproduce that they weep over the prospect of a crop failure.

Yet clearly the understands the feelings of both generations. Without taking sides, she sets forth their conflict with wonderful brevity. Students who see her poem as an editorial for or against gay/lesbian rights will be reading into it.

WILLIAM BLAKE, The Chimney Sweeper, page 31

Set next to Cleghorn's "Golf Links" (page 26), Blake's song will seem larger and more strange; and yet both poets seem comparable in their hatred of adults who enslave children. "The Chimney Sweeper" resembles Jarrell's "A Sick Child" (page 17) mainly in its child's-eye point of view. Though Blake is not a child, he obviously shares Tom Dacre's wish that the chimney sweepers be freed from their coffinlike chimneys, washed clean, and restored to childhood joys. The punning cry "'weep! 'weep! 'weep!" is the street cry of the sweepers, sent through London to advertise their services. Compare the tone of this poem to that of Blake's "London" (page 62); the anger is similar, but in "The Chimney Sweeper," a poem also touching and compassionate, anger is not stated outright, but only implied.

Music to "The Chimney Sweeper" has been supplied by Allen Ginsberg, who sings the resulting song on Songs of Innocence and Experience (MGM recording FTS 3083), assisted by Peter Orlovsky.

3

WORDS

LITERAL MEANING: WHAT A POEM SAYS FIRST

Why a whole section on literal meaning? The need first oc-
curred to XJK in a conversation with Robert Reiter and David
Anderson of Boston College. Professor Reiter, who had been using
the book in a previous edition, averred that, while it was well to
encourage students to read poetry for its suggestions, his students
tended to go too far in that direction, and sometimes needed to
have their attentions bolted down to the denotations of words on a
page. Early in a poetry course, the problem seemed especially
large--"I try not to let them look for any symbols until after
Thanksgiving!" Mr. Anderson had felt the same difficulty. In
teaching Donne's "Batter my heart" sonnet, he had had to argue with
students who couldn't see how, in a poem of spiritual aspiration,
Donne possibly could be referring to anything so grossly physical
as rape. They needed to see the plain, literal basis of Donne's
tremendous metaphor, that they might then go on to understand the
poet's conception of sanctifying grace.
With these comments in mind, the publishers sent a
questionnaire to more than one hundred instructors who had used the
book, asking them (among other questions) whether they felt the
need for more emphasis on denotation. All who replied said that
they would welcome such an emphasis (in addition to the old
emphasis on connotation)--all, that is, except for one instructor
(God help him) who reported that he couldn't persuade his students
ever to rise above the level of the literal, if indeed he could get
them to rise that far.
Most instructors like to discuss imagery fairly early. They
will find nothing to hinder them from taking the chapter on imagery
ahead of this one. Another procedure would be to defer "Imagery"
until after having discussed both denotation and
connotation--taking in sequence the present chapter, "Words," and
Chapter 4, "Saying and Suggesting."

WILLIAM CARLOS WILLIAMS, This Is Just to Say, page 35

Williams once recalled that this poem was an actual note he
had written to his wife--"and she replied very beautifully.
Unfortunately, I've lost it. I think what she wrote was quite as
good as this" (conversation with John W. Gerber and Emily M.

Wallace in <u>Interviews with William Carlos Williams</u>, ed. Linda Wel-
shimer Wagner [New York: New Directions, 1976]).
   For parodies of this famous poem, see Kenneth Koch's "Variations on a Theme by William Carlos Williams" in <u>Contemporary</u>
<u>American Poetry</u>, ed. A. Poulin (Boston: Houghton, 1980) and other
anthologies.

KNUTE SKINNER, The Cold Irish Earth, page 37

   Skinner is an American poet who lives most of each year in
Killaspuglonane (pronounced the way it looks, with the accent on
POOG), a village of about 200, near Liscannon Bay in the west of
Ireland. This poem is one of several recollections of Irish
country life in his book <u>A Close Sky over Killaspuglonane</u> (Dublin:
Dolmen, 1968); 2nd ed., St. Louis: Burton, 1975). The Hag's face
is a rock formation in the Cliffs of Moher (or Mohee), in whose
crevices members of the IRA once hid from the British.
   The familiar phrase, of course, is "to become wet to the
bone." Every image in the poem indicates that it is to be taken
literally.

HENRY TAYLOR, Riding a One-Eyed Horse, page 37

   Henry Taylor comments in a letter: "I like the question about
the one-eyed horse; the answer is of course, both."
   The poem was first published in <u>Practical Horseman</u>.

ROBERT GRAVES, Down, Wanton, Down!, page 38

   This poem can be an astonisher, especially if students haven't
read it in advance. One freshman group XJK sprang it on provided a
beautiful gamut of reactions: from stunned surprise to hilarity.
At first, most didn't know quite what to make of the poem, but they
soon saw that its puns and metaphors point to details of male and
female anatomy; and, in catching these, they found themselves
looking to literal meanings. After further discussion, they
decided that the poem, however witty, makes a serious point about
the blindness of lust. To get at this point, students may be asked
to sum up the contrast Graves is drawing between Love and Beauty
and the wanton's approach to them.
   The title (and opening line) echo a phrase from Shakespeare in
a passage about eels being rolled into a pie (<u>King Lear</u>, 2.4.118-
23):

      <u>Lear</u>: O me, my heart, my rising heart! But down!
      <u>Fool</u>: Cry to it, nuncle, as the cockney did to the eels when
         she put 'em i' th' paste alive. She knapped 'em o' th' cox-
         combs with a stick and cried, "Down, wantons, down!" 'Twas
         her brother that, in pure kindness to his horse, buttered
         his hay.

37-40 (text pages)

One instructor at a community college in New Jersey has
reported an embarrassing experience. One morning, not having had
time to prepare for class, he introduced this poem without having
read it first. "What's it about?" he queried, and someone in the
class replied, "An erection." "WHAT?" he exploded. "Come on, now,
let's look at it closely. . . ." But as he stared at the poem
before him, a chill stole over him. Luckily, he was saved by the
bell.

PETER DAVISON, The Last Word, page 39

The tangible side of Davison's central metaphor--that to part
with a lover is to chop off her head--is plainly enforced by lines
9-13: painful physical actions that end with the k-sound of an
abrupt crack in nick . . . creak . . . block.

DAVID B. AXELROD, Once in a While a Protest Poem, page 39

The crucial word in this disturbing poem is silicone, a substance injected into flat bosoms to make them buxom, in order to
put up a false front--like those sympathies we merely pretend to
feel. Carefully cropped by someone in an advertising agency, the
breast of the starving woman (like a breast treated with silicone)
is artificially changed and becomes abstract. Although the photograph is supposed to rouse our sympathies (and our contributions),
it often has the opposite effect of making us callous. To the
poet, it seems meant to "toughen us" (as silicone toughens the
bosoms of Playboy bunnies?); it seems meant to "teach us to
ignore."

MILLER WILLIAMS, On the Symbolic Consideration of Hands and the
Significance of Death, page 40

Living hands being so often on the move, the mourners asso-
ciate dead hands with the motions of life, and so can't believe the
evidence in front of them. But the nuns, who have to look long and
intently at each lifeless bone to carve rosaries, have no such
illusions. Williams announces his poem with a deliberately long,
gaseous title, and then, as if to twit readers who expect the poem
to be full of large abstractions too, chooses words as simple as
possible (all but ten of them monosyllables). Implied in the poem,
maybe, is the advice that if we (like the nuns) want to know
reality, we had best believe our eyes, and switch off our symbol-
izers.

JOHN DONNE, Batter my heart, three-personed God, for You, page 40

On Donne's last line: the literature of mysticism is full of
accounts of spiritual experience seen in physical terms; and any
students who wish to pursue the matter might be directed, for

instance, to the poems of St. John of the Cross (which have been splendidly translated by John Frederick Nims).

John E. Parish has shown that Donne's poem incorporates two metaphors, both worn and familiar: the traditional Christian comparison of the soul to a maiden and Christ to a bridegroom, and the Petrarchan conceit of the reluctant woman as a castle and her lover as an invading army. Donne brilliantly combined the two into a new whole. In lines 1-4, the sinner's heart is like a walled town, fallen to Satan, the enemy. Now God the rightful King approaches and knocks for entrance. But merely to knock won't do--the King must break open the gates with a battering ram. The verbs in these lines all suggest the act of storming a citadel, "and even blowe may be intended to suggest the use of gunpowder to blow up the fortress" ("No. 14 of Donne's Holy Sonnets," College English 24 [Jan. 1963]: 299-302).

"The paradox of death and rebirth, the central paradox of Christianity" is (according to A. L. Clements in another comment) the organizing principle of the poem. To illustrate the paradox of destroying in order to revive, Donne employs two sorts of figurative language: one, military and destructive; the other, marital and uniting ("Donne's 'Holy Sonnet XIV,'" Modern Language Notes 76 [June 1961]: 484-89).

Both the Clements and the Parish article are reprinted, together with the four other discussions of the poem, in John Donne's Poetry, edited by Clements (New York: Norton, 1966).

It is hard to talk for long about rhythm in poetry without citing the opening lines of "Batter my heart." Both in meter and in meaning, they must be among the most powerful lines in English poetry.

THE VALUE OF A DICTIONARY

RICHARD WILBUR, In the Elegy Season, page 42

Rich with imagery, this early Wilbur poem makes a revealing companion piece to Keats's "To Autumn" (page 328). But unlike Keats, the speaker in Wilbur's poem accepts the season neither with mind (which gazes backward, remembering summer) nor with body (which strains ahead, longing for spring). The poem is also wealthy in allusions. Perhaps the "boundless backward of the eyes" echoes Shakespeare's Tempest: "the dark backward and abysm of time." The goddess heard climbing the stair from the underworld is Persephone. I am indebted to Donald Hill's reading of the poem in his study Richard Wilbur (New York: Twayne, 1967).

A brief glossary of etymologies:

potpourri: rotten pot (denotation: an incongruous mixture)
revenance: a return (denotation: the return of a spirit after death)
circumstance: condition that surrounds

> inspiration: a breathing in
> conceptual: taking in (denotations: perceived, apprehended, imagined)
> commotion: co-motion, moving together (a wonderful word for what a bird's wings do!)
> cordial: pertaining to the heart (cor in Latin) (denotations: friendly, stimulating)
> azure: lapis lazuli

Exercise: Catching Allusions, page 43

CID CORMAN, The Tortoise, page 44

J. V. CUNNINGHAM, Friend, on this scaffold Thomas More lies dead, page 44

HERMAN MELVILLE, The Portent, page 44

JOHN DRYDEN, Lines Printed Under the Engraved Portrait of Milton, page 45

LAURENCE PERRINE, Janus, page 45

Corman's allusion to the Aesop fable has to be caught, if students are to see his metaphor. Inexorable time is the tortoise that keeps plodding onward. The hare is haste--or, more specifically, a man trying to win his race with time, but given to fits of delay and laziness.

Cunningham's epigram also states a metaphor: it likens two famous separations decreed by Henry VIII. Separation of the Body (the Church of England) from the Head (the Pope) is like the decapitation of More, who had opposed it. A possible original for Cunningham's epigram, a Latin epigram by John Owen (1606), has been discovered by Charles Clay Doyle:

> Abscindi passus caput est a corpore Morus;
>   Abscindi corpus noluit a capite.

In 1659 Thomas Pecke rendered it into English:

> What though Head was from Body severed?
> More would not let Body be cut from Head.

Doyle remarks that in fact More played down the role of the Pope as "head" of the Church, preferring the allegorical view (derived from Paul) of Christ as head upon the Church's body. "Whether the 'head' of Cunningham's or Owen's second line is identified as the Pope or as Christ, the emphasis remains upon More's concern for the unity of the 'body,' the Church" ("The Hair and Beard of Thomas More," Moreana 18, 71-72 [Nov. 1981]: 5-14.

Melville's symbolic poem also refers to an execution: the hanging of John Brown on 2 December 1859, for seizing the arsenal at Harpers Ferry, where the Shenandoah River meets the Potomac. Captured by Robert E. Lee, Brown suffered a wounded scalp, concealed by a cap he wore to the gallows. Melville, seeing the swinging corpse with its long beard as a comet with a streaming tail, refers to the ancient belief that comets and meteors are omens of war or catastrophe--as students may recall from Shakespeare's Julius Caesar. Melville's recognition of the portent proved right, of course: Union troops were soon to go into battle singing "John Brown's Body."

According to Dryden, Homer plus Dante equals Milton. The rightness of the equation comes from the fact of all three having been the authors of epics, or (if The Divine Comedy isn't an epic) poems of enormous scope.

In "Janus," this two-faced husband is, to be sure, named for the Roman god who looks in opposite directions at once. Perrine, poet and textbook author, taught English at Southern Methodist University from 1946 until his retirement in 1981. This epigram appeared in Poetry for June 1984.

JOHN CLARE, Mouse's Nest, page 45

The connection between the final couplet and the rest of the poem is one of metaphor. Small trickles of water that "scarce could run" are newborn mice; "broad old cesspools," their mother.

Milton Klonsky has praised the poem in his anthology of graphic and pictorial poetry, Speaking Pictures (New York: Harmony, 1975). He admires "the cinematic flow of Clare's imagery, with each picture flashing by to be replaced by the next before its own afterimage has completely faded." This comment might be discussed --do students agree that Clare's poem seems cinematic and contemporary?

A few facts of Clare's heartbreaking life might interest students. Born into grinding poverty, the son of a field laborer in Northamptonshire, Clare enjoyed brief fame for his Poems Descriptive of Rural Life (1820). Lionized by Coleridge and other London literati as an untutored genius, he was then forgotten. The latter half of his life was spent in lunatic asylums, where he wrote some remarkable lyrics and (under the delusion that he was Lord Byron) a continuation of Don Juan. Theodore Roethke, whose work shows a similar delight in close-up views of living creatures, has paid tribute (in his poem "Heard in a Violent Ward") to "that sweet man, John Clare."

LEWIS CARROLL, Jabberwocky, page 46

"Jabberwocky" has to be heard aloud: you might ask a student to read it, alerting him or her in advance to prepare it, and offering tips on pronunciation. ("The i in slithy is like the i in slime; the a in wabe, like the a in wave.")

Although Carroll added <u>chortled</u> to the dictionary, not all his odd words are invented. <u>Gyre</u> of course means "to spin or twist about"--it is used as a noun in Yeats's "Sailing to Byzantium" (page 250) and "the Second Coming" (page 217). <u>Slithy</u> (sleazy or slovenly), <u>rath</u> (an earthen wall), <u>whiffling</u> (blowing or puffing), and <u>callooh</u> (an arctic duck that winters in Scotland, so named for its call) are legitimate words, too, but Carroll uses them in different senses. <u>Frabjous</u> probably owes something to <u>frab</u>, a dialect word meaning "to scold, harass, or nag"--as Myra Cohn Livingston points out in her anthology <u>O Frabjous Day!</u> (New York: Atheneum, 1977).

Writing in 1877 to a child who had inquired what the strange word meant, Carroll replied:

> I am afraid I can't explain "vorpal blade" for you--nor yet "tulgey wood"; but I did make an explanation once for "uffish thought"--it seems to suggest a state of mind when the voice is gruffish, the manner roughish, and the temper huffish. Then again, as to "burble": if you take the three verbs "<u>b</u>leat," "<u>mur</u>mur" and "war<u>ble</u>," and select the bits I have underlined, it certainly <u>makes</u> "burble": though I am afraid I can't distinctly remember having made it that way.

(<u>Uffish</u> suggests <u>oafish</u>, too.)

Students can have fun unpacking other portmanteau words: <u>gimble</u> (<u>gamely</u>, <u>gambol</u>); <u>frumious</u> (which Carroll said is <u>fuming</u> plus <u>furious</u>); <u>vorpal</u> (<u>voracious</u>, <u>purple</u>); <u>galumphing</u> (<u>galloping</u> in <u>triumph</u>), and so on. Some of these suggestions come from Martin Gardner, who supplies copious notes on the poem (as well as translations of it into French and German) in <u>The Annotated Alice</u> (New York: Bramhall, 1960).

WALLACE STEVENS, Metamorphosis, page 47

A possible meaning of <u>metamorphosis</u> is a sudden change undergone by an insect or a tadpole in the process of maturing. But we think Stevens implies by the falling sky (dead and lying with the worms) and the hanged street lamps that the year is decaying, not changing for the better, but undergoing (as <u>Webster's New World Dictionary</u> puts it) "a transformation, especially by magic or sorcery."

Language is, in a sense, also decaying rapidly. The name of the month of October is transformed, too, into a birdcall. <u>Niz--nil--imbo</u> is a corruption of <u>November</u>. It contains the words <u>nil</u> (nothingness) and <u>limbo</u>.

The first definition: "a sudden twist, turn, or stroke." The season makes such a sudden turn, and so does language. A worm is a "pretty quirk" in that it is physically twisted; also, it happens to appear unexpectedly (in flesh suddenly dead, or fall fruit become overripe).

WORD CHOICE AND WORD ORDER

JOSPEHINE MILES, Reason, page 50

Only the reference to Gary Cooper's horse at all dates this
concise story-poem, a thing of lasting freshness. "The real
characters in this story are the fragments of slang, not the
speakers," Lawrence R. Smith has noticed. "Their absence is
emphasized by the absence of personal pronouns at the beginning of
each line. In place of the pronouns, we simply have 'Said.' This
is a poem of pure language" ("Josephine Miles: Metaphysician of the
Irrational," A Book of Rereadings, ed. Greg Kuzma [Lincoln, Pebble
and Best Cellar, 1979] 29).

HUGH MacDIARMID, Wheesht, Wheesht, page 51

MacDiarmid, the most eminent twentieth-century poet to write
in Scots, is often compared with Burns; and for another brief love
lyric at least partly in dialect, students might be asked to compare "John Anderson my jo, John" (page 245).

THOMAS HARDY, The Ruined Maid, page 52

In a London street, an innocent girl from Dorset encounters a
friend who has run away from life on the farm. Now a well-paid
prostitute, 'Melia calls herself ruined with cheerful irony. That
this maid has been made, it would seem, has been the making of her.
Hardy, of course, is probably less stricken with awe before
'Melia's glamorous clothes than is the first speaker. As the ain't
in the last line indicates, 'Melia's citified polish doesn't go
deep.
For a sequel to "The Ruined Maid," see "A Daughter Returns" in
Hardy's last collection of poetry, Winter Words. With "Dainty-cut
raiment" and "earrings of pearl," a runaway daughter returns to her
country home, only to be spurned by her father for having lost her
innocence.

E. E. CUMMINGS, anyone lived in a pretty how town, page 53

Trained in the classical languages, Cummings borrows from
Latin the freedom to place a word in practically any location within a sentence. The first two lines are easy to unscramble: "How
pretty a town Anyone lived in, with so many bells floating up [and]
down." The scrambling is artful, and pedestrian words call
attention to themselves by being seen in an unusual order.
The hero and heroine of the poem are anyone and noone, whose
names recall the pronoun-designated principals in Cummings's play
Him--hero Him and heroine Me. Are they Everyman and Everywoman?
Not at all: they're different, they're strong, loving individuals
whom the poet contrasts with those drab women and men of line 5,

"both little and small," who dully sow <u>isn't</u> (negation) and reap <u>same</u> (conformity). Unlike wise noone and anyone, the everyones and someones of line 17 apparently think they're really somebody.

   In tracing the history of anyone and noone from childhood through their mature love to their death and burial, Cummings, we think, gives a brief tour through life in much the way that Thornton Wilder does in <u>Our Town</u>. But not all readers will agree. R. C. Walsh thinks that, in the last two stanzas, anyone and noone do not literally die but grow into loveless and lifeless adults, whose only hope of rejuvenation is to have children (<u>Explicator</u> 22 [May 1964]: item 72). But it seems unlike Cummings to make turncoats of his individualists. Bounded by the passage of the seasons, the rain, and the heavens, the mortal lives of anyone and noone seem concluded in their burial. But in the next-to-last stanza they go on sleeping in love and faith, dreaming of their resurrection.

JAMES EMANUEL, The Negro, page 54

   <u>The-ness</u> is the white viewing the black as a stereotype (some of whose features are illustrated in the second stanza). <u>A-ness</u> is the view that hasn't prevailed: of the black as an individual.

RICHARD EBERHART, The Fury of Aerial Bombardment, page 55

   Dr. Johnson said that technical language is inadmissible to poetry, but in the case of Eberhart's poem, it is hard to agree. We do not need to know the referents of "belt feed lever" and "belt holding pawl" in order to catch the poet's meaning. Indeed, he evidently chooses these terms as specimens of a jargon barely comprehensible to the unlucky gunnery students who failed to master it. At a reading of his poems in public, Eberhart once remarked that he had added the last stanza as an afterthought. The tone (it seems to me) remains troubled and sorrowful but shifts from loftiness and grandeur to matter-of-fact. This shift takes place in diction as well: from the generality of "infinite spaces," "multitudinous will," "eternal truth," and "the Beast" in man's soul down to "Names on a list," "lever," and "pawl." The poem is a wonderful instance of a poet's writing himself into a fix--getting snarled in unanswerable questions--and then triumphantly saving the day (and his poem) by suddenly returning with a bump to the ordinary, particular world.

<u>Exercise</u>: Different Kinds of English, page 56

ANONYMOUS, Carnation Milk, page 56

A. R. AMMONS, Spring Coming, page 56

WILLIAM WORDSWORTH, My heart leaps up when I behold, page 57

WILLIAM WORDSWORTH, Mutability, page 57

JOHN MALCOLM BRINNIN, The Ascension: 1925, page 57

ANONYMOUS, Scottsboro, page 58

Students won't need much help to see that "Carnation Milk" is unschooled speech; that Ammons combines technical terms with colloquial speech (nice); that Wordsworth's diction in "My heart leaps up" is plain and unbookish (except for natural piety), while his language in "Mutability" is highly formal--not only in diction, but in word order ("Truth fails not"); and that "Scottsboro" is a song in the speech of a particular culture (and, by the way, wonderful in its power to express).

Brinnin's "The Ascension: 1925" may need closer inspection. Playfully, this deft comic poem tours the levels of English. Aunt Alice and Uncle Lester speak a vulgar brand of vulgate; hit the highway and on the nose (line 13) are colloquial; line 12 is formal and literate; ship of air for airship or balloon seems a slightly highfalutin poeticism. Stark contrast of tone and of language may be drawn between these two sonnets (Brinnin's and Wordsworth's famous "Mutability"). Only the lovely abstract line "In strict submission to the absolute" would seem at home in Wordsworth's company.

On the difficult "Mutability" (in case anyone cares to read it for its sense): "the tower sublime" may refer to the Bastille, suggests Geoffrey Durant in his excellent discussion of the poem in Wordsworth and the Great System ([Cambridge: Cambridge UP, 1970] 82-5). For other poems with the theme of mutability, see Shelley's "Ozymandias" (page 253), Shakespeare's "That time of year . . . " (page 365), Auden's "As I Walked Out One Evening" (page 277), Thomas's "Fern Hill" (page 369), and (in this same chapter) Cummings's "anyone lived in a pretty how town."

About A. R. Ammons: Compare Eberhart's The Fury of Aerial Bombardment" (page 55) in its use of terms from science. Try applying to Ammons's poem the observation by Samuel Johnson (referred to in question 2 under Eberhart). What might Johnson have thought of "Spring Coming"? (Probably: "Sir, Ammons has written in no language, and no man can utter it.")

Repercussions from the Scottsboro case lasted long. In October 1976 the state of Alabama finally granted full pardon to Clarence Norris, last survivor of the nine "Scottsboro boys," after he had spent sixteen years in prison, five on death row, and thirty-one years as an escaped fugitive. In 1976, following the televised showing of a dramatization, "Judge Horton and the Scottsboro Boys," both alleged rape victims unsuccessfully brought suit against NBC for libel, slander, and invasion of privacy. The last of these suits was dismissed in July 1977.

4

SAYING AND SUGGESTING

JOHN MASEFIELD, Cargoes, page 61

   Much of the effect of Masefield's contrast depends on rhythms
and word-sounds, not just on connotations. In stanza 2, the poet
strews his lines with dactyls, producing ripples in his rhythm:
diamonds, emeralds, amethysts, cinnamon. In the third stanza,
paired monosyllables (salt-caked, smoke stack, Tyne coal, road-
rails, pig-lead, firewood) make for a hard hitting series of
spondees. Internal alliteration helps the contrast, too: all
those m-sounds in the dactyls; and in the harsher lines "Dirty
British coaster with a salt-caked smoke stack, / Butting," all the
sounds of the r, the t, and the staccato k.
   "Cargoes" abounds with lively, meaningful music--and yet Masefield is generally dismissed nowadays as a mere balladeer--a
jog-trot chronicler of the lives of the poor and unfortunate. In
naming him poet laureate, George V (it is said) mistakenly thought
him a hero of the working class; and, unluckily for his later fame,
Masefield, like Wordsworth, enjoyed a long senility.

WILLIAM BLAKE, London, page 62

   Blake at first wrote, "I wander through each dirty street, /
Near where the dirty Thames does flow." For his equally masterful
revisions of the poem's closing lines, see page 228 in Chapter 14,
"Alternatives."
   Tom Dacre's dream has a basis in reality: in Blake's time,
sweeps were often sent up chimneys naked, the better to climb
through narrow spaces (and thus saving the expense of protective
clothing). Martin K. Nurmi points out this fact in his essay,
"Fact and Symbol in 'The Chimney Sweeper' of Blake's Songs of
Innocence" (Bulletin of the New York Public Library 68 [April
1964]: 249-56). "Naked immersion in soot, therefore, is Tom's
normal state now, and naked white cleanliness is its natural
opposite."
   If Blake were to walk the streets of an American city today,
would he find any conditions similar to those he finds in "London"?
Is this poem merely an occasional poem, with a protest valid only
for its time, or does it have enduring applications?

WALLACE STEVENS, Disillusionment of Ten O'Clock, page 64

Stevens slings colors with the verve of a Matisse. In this
early poem, he paints a suggestive contrast between the pale and
colorless homeowners, ghostlike and punctually going to bed at ten
and, on the other hand, the dreams they wouldn't dream of dreaming;
and the bizarre and exotic scene inside the drunken head of our
disreputable hero, the old seafarer. Who in the world would wear a
beaded sash or ceinture? (A Barbary pirate? An Arabian harem
dancer?) Ronald Sukenick has made a terse statement of the poem's
theme: "the vividness of the imagination in the dullness of a
pallid reality" (Wallace Stevens: Musing the Obscure [New York:
New York UP, 1967]). Another critic, Edward Kessler, has offered a
good paraphrase: "Only the drunkard, the irrational man ('Poetry
must be irrational' [Opus Posthumous 162]), who is in touch with
the unconscious--represented here, and often elsewhere, by the
sea--can awake his own passionate nature until his blood is
mirrored in the very weather" (Images of Wallace Stevens [New
Brunswick: Rutgers 1972]).

While they will need to see the contrast between pallor and
color, students might be cautioned against lending every color a
particular meaning, as if the poem were an allegory.

Stevens expressed further disappointment with monotonous
neighbors in a later poem, "Loneliness in Jersey City," which seems
a companion piece to this. In Jersey City, "the steeples are empty
and so are the people," who can't tell a dachshund from a deer.
Both poems probably owe some of their imagery to Stevens's days as
a struggling young lawyer, living in rooming houses in East Orange,
New Jersey, and Fordham Heights, in New York City.

SAMUEL JOHNSON, A Short Song of Congratulation, page 65

"You have heard in the papers how Sir John Lade is come to
age," wrote Dr. Johnson to his friend Mrs. Thrale in 1780. "I have
enclosed a short song of congratulation, which you must not shew to
anybody." Lade, Mrs. Thrale's nephew, was to fulfill Johnson's
expectations. After a seven-year binge, he married a courtesan,
Laetitia Darby, and ran through the rest of his fortune. He is the
same Lade who (according to Mrs. Piozzi's Anecdotes of Dr. Johnson)
once called across a drawing room, "Mr. Johnson, would you advise
me to marry?" only to be told, "I would advise no man to marry,
Sir, who is not likely to propagate understanding."

TIMOTHY STEELE, Epitaph, page 65

"Silence is golden"--but Sir Tact is obviously a coward,
afraid to speak his mind. This epigram is included in Steele's
first collection of poems, Uncertainties and Rest (Baton Rouge:
Louisiana State UP, 1979).

66-67 (text pages)

RICHARD SNYDER, A Mongoloid Child Handling Shells on the Beach,
page 66

Snyder elaborates his metaphor with beautiful economy: the
"unbroken children," those without handicaps, are like surf at the
sea's edge, also like seabirds that skim the beach and the water.
Bright as they are, there is something superficial about them, in
contrast to the mongoloid child. Slow and deliberate as deep ocean
currents, she is both "broken" (like the shells she fondles) and at
the same time whole. As she hums her return message to the sea,
she is calm and serene, possessing a sober happiness.
To discuss: Should the poem now be retitled "A Child with
Down's Syndrome Handling Shells on the Beach"? Would that be as
effective?

GEOFFREY HILL, Merlin, page 66

There is an incantatory quality to this poem that seems to
indicate it is Merlin speaking; but then, nearly all of Hill's
richly suggestive and highly formal poems tend to sound this way.
The dead who might "come together to be fed" recall the souls
encountered by Odysseus in the underworld, to whom he fed blood.
Once, the towers of Camelot sheltered Arthur and his associates;
now, only the pointed tents of piled-up cornstalks (or perhaps
growing cornstalks, flying their silklike pennants) stand over the
city of the dead.

WALLACE STEVENS, The Emperor of Ice-Cream, page 67

Choosing this poem to represent him in an anthology, Stevens
once remarked, "This wears a deliberately commonplace costume, and
yet seems to me to contain something of the essential gaudiness of
poetry; that is the reason why I like it." (His statement appears
in Fifty Poets: An American Auto-Anthology, ed. William Rose Benét
[New York: Diffield, 1933].)
Some students will at once relish the poet's humor, others may
discover it in class discussion. Try to gather the literal facts
of the situation before getting into the poem's suggestions. The
wake or funeral of a poor old woman is taking place in her own
home. The funeral flowers come in old newspapers, not in florists'
fancy wrappings; the mourners don't dress up, but wear their usual
street clothes; the refreshments aren't catered but are whipped up
in the kitchen by a neighbor, a cigar-roller. Like ice-cream, the
refreshments are a dairy product. Nowadays they would probably be
a sour cream chip-dip; perhaps in 1923 they were blocks of Philadelphia cream cheese squashed into cups for spreading on soda
crackers. To a correspondent, Stevens wrote that fantails refers
not to fans but to fantail pigeons (Letters [New York: Knopf, 1966]
341). Such embroidery seems a lowbrow pursuit: the poor old
woman's pathetic aspiration toward beauty. Deal furniture is

cheap. Everything points to a run-down neighborhood, and to a woman about whose passing nobody very much cares.

Who is the Emperor? The usual guess is Death. Some students will probably see that the Emperor and the muscular cigar-roller (with his creamy curds) suggest each other. (Stevens does not say that they are identical.) Ice cream suggests the chill of the grave--and what besides? Today, some of its connotations will be commonplace: supermarkets, Howard Johnson's. To the generation of Stevens, ice cream must have meant more: something luxurious and scarce, costly, hard-to-keep, requiring quick consumption. Other present-day connotations may come to mind: sweetness, deliciousness, childhood pleasure. Stevens's personal view of the ice cream in the poem was positive: "The true sense of Let be be finale of seem is let being become the conclusion or denouement of appearing to be: in short, ice cream is an absolute good" (Letters 341). An absolute good! The statement is worth quoting to students who have doubts about the poet's attitude toward ice cream--as did an executive of the Amalgamated Ice Cream Association, who once wrote to the poet in perplexity (see Letters 501-02). If ice cream recalls sweet death, still (like curds) it also contains hints of mother's milk, life, and vitality.

On a visit to Mount Holyoke, XJK was told that, as part of an annual celebration, it is customary for the trustees and the seniors to serve ice cream (in Dixie cups) to the freshman class at the grave of Mary Lyon, founder of the college. In a flash he remembered Stevens's poem, and embraced Jung's theory of archetypes.

WALTER DE LA MARE, The Listeners, page 68

This much-loved old chestnut, once a favorite of anthologists, still seems a wonderful demonstration of the value to poetry of hints. The identity of the listeners is by no means clear: the more literal-minded will probably think of bats, mice, and crickets, while others will think of ghosts. The latter theory gains support from the poem: these listeners are phantom (line 13), not of the world of men (16), strange and mute (21-22). If the Traveller is "the one man left awake" (32), are the Listeners men who have fallen asleep (in death)?

In line 5, turret suggests a fortress or castle; but as line 14 makes clear, the scene is a house. Which to believe? Perhaps the scene is a sort of Loire Valley château: a mansion with castlelike touches.

Attempts to guess what happened before "The Listeners" opens may well be irrelevant, but if students will try, they may find themselves more deeply involved with the poem. This much seems clear: The Traveller has accepted some challenge to visit the house; he has given his promise to someone (more than one person, and someone other than the Listeners, whom the Traveller charges to convey his message to "them"). Perhaps this act is one of the deeds required to lift a curse from a kingdom, as in a fairy tale;

68-69 (text pages)

or as in the Arthurian story of Sir Percival (or Parsifal), who
must spend a night in the terrifying Chapel Perilous.

ROBERT FROST, Fire and Ice, page 69

     In his first line, Frost probably refers to those who accept
the Biblical prophecy of a final holocaust; and in his second line,
to those who accept scientists' forecasts of the cooling of the
earth. We admire that final suffice. A magnificent
understatement, it further shows the power of a rime to close a
poem (as Yeats said) with a click like a closing box.

5

IMAGERY

EZRA POUND, In a Station of the Metro, page 70

Pound recalled that at first this poem had come to him "not in speech, but in little splotches of color." His account is reprinted by K. K. Ruthven in A Guide to Ezra Pound's Personae (1926) (Berkeley: U of California P, 1969). Students might like to compare this "hokku-like sentence" (as Pound called the poem) with the more suggestive Japanese haiku freely translated on pages 76-77.

For a computer-assisted tribute to this famous poem, see the curious work of James Laughlin and Hugh Kenner, reported in "The Mixpoem Program," Paris Review 94 (Winter 1984): 193-98. Following Laughlin's suggestion that the five nouns of "In a Station of the Metro" might interestingly be shuffled, Kenner wrote "a Little program in Basic" that enabled a computer to grind out 120 scrambled versions of the poem, including these:

The apparitions of these boughs in the face;
Crowds on a wet, black petal.

The crowd of these apparitions in the petal;
Faces on a wet, black bough.

Kenner then wrote a program in Pascal that would shuffle eight words and produce 40,320 different versions. We don't know what it all demonstrates, except that Pound's original version still seems the best possible.

TANIGUCHI BUSON, The piercing chill I feel, page 70

Harold G. Henderson, who translates this haiku, has written a good terse primer in An Introduction to Haiku (Garden City: Anchor, 1958). Most of Henderson's English versions of haiku rime like this one; still, the sense of the originals (as far as an ignorant reader can tell from Henderson's glosses) does not seem greatly distorted.

72 (text page)

THEODORE ROETHKE, Root Cellar, page 72

Probably there is little point in spending much time dividing imagery into touches and tastes and smells; perhaps it will be enough to point out that Roethke's knowledgeable poem isn't all picture-imagery. There's that wonderful "congress of stinks," and the "slippery planks" are both tactile and visual. Most of the language in the poem is figurative, most of the vegetation is rendered animal: bulbs like small rodents, shoots like penises, roots like a forgotten can of fishing worms. Roethke doesn't call the roots lovely, but obviously he admires their tough, persistent life.

ELIZABETH BISHOP, The Fish, page 72

This poem is made almost entirely of concrete imagery. Except for wisdom (line 63) and victory (66), there is no very abstract diction in it.

Obviously the speaker admires this stout old fighter. The image "medals with their ribbons" (line 61) suggests that he is an old soldier, and the "five-haired beard of wisdom" (line 63) suggests that he is a venerable patriarch, of whom one might seek advice.

The poor, battered boat has become magnificent for having the fish in it. The feeling in these lines is joy: bilge, rust, and cracked thwarts are suddenly revealed to be beautiful. In a way, the attitude seems close to that in Yeats's "Sailing to Byzantium" (page 250), in which the triumphant soul is one that claps its hands and louder sings for every tatter in its mortal dress. The note of final triumph is sounded in "rainbow, rainbow, rainbow!" (line 75). The connotations of rainbow in this poem are not very different from the connotations often given the word by misty-eyed romantic poets such as Rod McKuen, but I think we believe Bishop because of her absolutely hard-eyed and specific view of the physical world. (She even sees the fish with X-ray imagination in lines 27-33.)

Anne Stevenson says in Elizabeth Bishop (New York: Twayne, 1966):

It is a testimony to Miss Bishop's strength and sensitivity that the end, the revelation or "moment of truth," is described with the same attention to detail as the rest of the poem. The temptation might have been to float off into an airy apotheosis, but Miss Bishop stays right in the boat with the engine and the bailer. Because she does so, she is able to use words like "victory" and "rainbow" without fear of triteness.

Because the fish has provided her with an enormous understanding, the speaker's letting it go at the end seems as act of homage and gratitude.

Compare "The Fish" with the same poet's richly imaged "Filling Station" (page 280).

The poet reads this poem on a recording, The Spoken Arts Treasury of 100 Modern American Poets, vol. 10, SA 1049.

JEAN TOOMER, Reapers, page 74

This ominous poem, with its contrasts between sound and silence, possibly contains a metaphor. The black field hands are being destroyed by something indifferent and relentless, much as the trapped rat is slain under the blade. (Or, as in "Scottsboro" [page 58], as a cat stalks a "nohole mouse"?)

A grandson of P. B. S. Pinchback, the black who served for a short time during Reconstruction as acting governor of Louisiana, Toomer had only a brief public career as a writer. His one book, Cane (1923), which experimentally combined passages of fiction with poetry, helped to spearhead the Harlem Renaissance. "Reapers" is taken from it.

GERARD MANLEY HOPKINS, Pied Beauty, page 75

Sumptuously rich in music (rime, alliteration, assonance), this brief poem demands to be read aloud.

Some students might agree with Robert Frost's objection that the poem "disappoints . . . by not keeping, short as it is, wholly to pied things" (1934 letter to his daughter Lesley in Family Letters of Robert and Elinor Frost [Albany: State U of New York P, 1972] 162). But, as question 4 tries to get at, Hopkins had more in mind than dappled surfaces. Rough paraphrase of the poem: God is to be praised not only for having created variegation, but for creating and sustaining contrasts and opposites. In lines 5-6, tradesmen's tools and gear, like the plow that pierces and cuts the soil, strike though the surfaces of raw materials to reveal inner beauty and order that had lain concealed.

For a convincing argument that Hopkins in "Pied Beauty," like Dickens in Hard Times, complains about a drab, mechanical, industrial-age uniformity in Victorian England, see Norman H. MacKenzie, A Reader's Guide to Gerard Manley Hopkins (Cornell UP, 1981) 85-86. Few students will crave to fathom the poet's notions of instress and inscape, but if you do, see John Pick's unsurpassed Gerard Manley Hopkins, Priest and Poet, 2nd ed. (Oxford UP, 1966) 53-56.

The point of question 5 is that if the images of the poem were subtracted, its statement of theme also would disappear.

Hopkins discovered the form of "pied Beauty" and called it the curtal sonnet (curtal, riming with turtle: "crop-tailed"). But, remarks MacKenzie, such sonnets are like a small breed of horse: "compressed, not merely cut short." Instead of two quatrains, the form calls for two tercets; then, instead of a sestet four lines and a brief line more. (Other curtal sonnets by Hopkins: "Peace" and, even more closely cropped, "Ashboughs.")

ABOUT HAIKU

Basho's frogjump poem (page 77) may well be the most highly prized gem in Japanese literature; in Japanese there exists a three-volume commentary on it.

For an excellent discussion of the problems of teaching haiku, and of trying to write English ones, see Myra Cohen Livingston's When You Are Alone / It Keeps You Capone: an approach to creative writing with children (New York: Atheneum, 1973) 152-62. Livingston finds it useful to tell students a famous anecdote. Kikaku, a pupil of Basho, once presented his master with this specimen:

Red dragonflies--
Tear off their wings
And you have pepper pods.

As a haiku, said Basho, that's no good. Make it instead:

Red pepper pods--
Add wings
And you have dragonflies.

A moment of triumph, such as all teachers of poetry hope for but seldom realize, has been reported in a letter to XJK from Professor Maurice F. Brown, Department of English, Oakland University, Rochester, Michigan:

Last year, teaching W. C. Williams in an "invitational" course for a week, I began with "Red Wheelbarrow" . . . and a student hand went up (class of 100): "That's not a poem! That's junk. What if I say, 'Here I sit looking at a blackboard while the sun is shining outside.' Is that a poem?" It was one of those great teaching moments . . . and I did a quick count and wrote it on the board:

Here I sit looking
    At a blackboard while the sun
is shining outside.

Not only a poem . . . a perfect haiku.

A thorough new guide to this rocky acre of poetry has lately appeared: William J. Higginson with Penny Harter, The Haiku Handbook: How to Write, Share, and Teach Haiku (New York: McGraw, 1985).

RICHARD BRAUTIGAN, Haiku Ambulance, page 77

This is a Zen poem poking fun at overly thoughty attempts to write Zen poems. Its satire does not seem in the least applicable

to the successful haiku-in-English of Paul Goodman, Gary Snyder,
and Raymond Roseliep.

FOR REVIEW AND FURTHER STUDY

JOHN KEATS, Bright Star! would I were steadfast as thou art,
page 78

　　Unlike Petrarchan poets, Keats isn't making the star into an
abstraction (Love); he takes it for a visible celestial body, even
though he sees it in terms of other things. His comparisons are so
richly laden with suggestions (star as staring eye, waters as
priestlike), that sometimes students don't notice his insistent
negations. The hermit's all-night vigil is not what Keats desires.
He wants the comfort of that ripening pillow, and (perhaps aware of
his impending death) envies the cold star only its imperishability
--oh, for unendurable ecstasy, indefinitely prolonged! Compare
this to Keats's "To Autumn" (page 328) in which the poet finds
virtue in change.
　　Many readers find the last five words of the poem bothersome.
Students might be asked, Does Keats lose your sympathy by this
ending? If so, why? If not, how would you defend it? We can't
defend it; it seems bathetic, almost as self-indulgent as Shelley's
lines in "Indian Serenade":

　　　Oh, lift me from the grass!
　　　　I die! I faint! I fail!
　　　Let thy love in kisses rain
　　　　On my lips and eyelids pale.

　　Thomas Mauch, of The Colorado College, intelligently disagrees, and suggests how "or else swoon to death" may be defended.
The or, he thinks, is what grammarians call an inclusive or, not an
exclusive.

　　　　I believe that the speaker is saying, not that if he
　　can't be forever in the close company of the beloved he would
　　rather be dead--sort of like what Patrick Henry said about
　　liberty--but rather that, given the closeness to the woman,
　　dying in that condition would be just as good as experiencing
　　it forever, since in either case he would not undergo a
　　separation from her (and still retain his consciousness of
　　it). I think it is the same point he makes in the "Ode to a
　　Nightingale":

　　　　Now more than ever seems it rich to die,
　　　　　To cease upon the midnight with no pain,
　　　　　　While thou art pouring forth thy soul abroad
　　　　　　　In such an ecstasy!

The poem, Mr. Mauch concludes, illustrates the kind of closure that
Keats admired when he affirmed that a poem should "die grandly."

35

CARL SANDBURG, Fog, page 78

Like Pound's "In a Station of the Metro" (page 70), Sandburg's celebrated minipoem is all one metaphor, all imagery. Not closely detailed, it seems vague when set next to Eliot's agile fog-cat in "Prufrock" (page 303). Eliot can depict even fog without vagueness; evidently cats are right up his alley. Students also might enjoy a look at his Old Possum's Book of Practical Cats.

Experiment: Writing with Images, page 79

To write a poem full of images, in any form, is probably easier for most students than to write a decent haiku. (On the difficulties of teaching haiku writing, see Myra Cohn Livingston, cited under "About Haiku.") Surprisingly, there is usually at least one student in every class who can't seem to criticize a poem to save his neck, yet who, if invited to be a poet, will bloom or at least bud.

WALT WHITMAN, The Runner, page 79

Try reading "The Runner" without the adverbs lightly and partially. Does the poem even exist without those two delicate modifiers?

T. E. HULME, Image, page 79

Hulme's poems seem always to have been brief. In his own collection Personae, Ezra Pound took two pages to include "The Complete Poetical Works of T. E. Hulme" (in which "Image" does not appear). Pound remarked, "In publishing his Complete Poetical Works at thirty, Mr. Hulme has set an enviable example to many of his contemporaries who have had less to say."

WILLIAM CARLOS WILLIAMS, The Great Figure, page 79

Is the figure a symbol? It looks like one--such intent concentration upon a particular. In an otherwise static land-scape, only the 5 moves. It's the one moving thing as in the eye of the blackbird in Stevens's "Thirteen Ways" (page 180). As far as we can see, however, the 5 has no great meaning beyond itself. Williams just rivets our attention on it and builds an atmosphere of ominous tension. The assumption, as in "The Red Wheelbarrow," is that somehow the figure has colossal significance. But "The Great Figure" is a much more vivid poem than "Wheelbarrow" (page 21) and it contains no editorializing ("so much depends"). Like the poems in the section "Literal Meaning," it's useful for discouraging students from spelling out colossal significances.

ROBERT BLY, Driving to Town Late to Mail a Letter, page 79

No doubt the situation in this poem is real: Bly, who lives
in frequently snowbound Minnesota, emits hundreds of letters.
Compare this simple poem to Frost's "Stopping by Woods on a Snowy
Evening" (page 307), which also has a speaker who, instead of going
home, prefers to ogle snowscapes.

GARY SNYDER, Mid-August at Sourdough Mountain Lookout, page 80

In brief compass, Snyder's poem appeals to the mind's eye
(with smoke haze, pitch glows on fir-cones, rocks, meadows, and the
imagined vista at the end), the sense of moisture (after five days
rain), of hot (three days heat) and of cold (snow-water from a tin
cup). The swarms of new flies are probably both seen and heard.
For more background to this poem and to Snyder's work in
general, see Bob Steuding, Gary Snyder (Boston: Twayne, 1976). A
fictional portrait of Snyder appears in Jack Kerouac's novel The
Dharma Bums (New York: Viking, 1958).

H. D. [HILDA DOOLITTLE], Heat, page 80

Heat becomes a tangible substance in this imagist poem, whose
power resides mainly in its verbs, all worth scrutiny. Compare
this poem and Snyder's: how does each convey a sense of warmth?
H. D.'s work has enjoyed a recent surge of critical attention.
For a concise, insightful comment on the lyrics and their
originality, see Emily Stipes Watts, The Poetry of American Women
from 1632 to 1945 (U of Texas P, 1977), 152-58.

JAMES PRESTON, Sunfish Races, page 80

Is there an artist in the class? If there is, just to
demonstrate how this haikulike poem appeals to the mind's eye, why
not invite him or her to step up to the blackboard and sketch what
this poem calls to mind?

MARY OLIVER, Rain in Ohio, page 81

Much of the strength of this poem, from Oliver's 1984
Pulitzer-winning collection, American Primitive, derives from its
images: the sounds of bird cries, the sights of the halted
blacksnake, and the white sky with its whirling storm clouds. But
much also derives from metaphors: the thunderheads seen as horses,
the snake's "long ladder of muscle," its body seen as a pourable
fluid. In this poem, metaphors are stated in images: the two
elements seem happily inseparable.
The images aren't constructed from thin air; Mary Oliver knows
Ohio. Born in Maple Heights, near Cleveland, she attended Ohio

81-82 (text pages)

State University and has taught as a visiting professor at Case
Western Reserve. Among her earlier collections is The River Styx,
Ohio, and Other Poems (1972).

6

FIGURES OF SPEECH

WHY SPEAK FIGURATIVELY?

ALFRED, LORD TENNYSON, The Eagle, page 83

For a hostile criticism of this poem, see Robert Graves, "Technique in Poetry," On Poetry: Collected Talks and Essays (New York: Doubleday, 1969) 402-05. Graves finds Tennyson's fragment unable to meet the minimal requirement that a poem should make good prose sense. He complains that if the eagle stands on its hands then its wings must be feet, and he ends up by rewriting the poem the way he thinks it ought to be. Though his remarks are fascinating, Graves reads the poem too literally.

A recent critic has suggested that this poem is a product of Tennyson's hopeless nearsightedness. Celebrating the eagle's 20-20 zoom-lens vision and ability to see a fish from high up, Tennyson yearns for a goal he could not attain: "optical inclusiveness." (See Gerhard Joseph, "Tennyson's Optics: The Eagle's Gaze," PMLA 92 [May 1977]: 420-27.

WILLIAM SHAKESPEARE, Shall I compare thee to a summer's day?, page 83

HOWARD MOSS, Shall I compare thee to a summer's day? page 84

Shakespeare's original--rich in metaphor, personification, and hyperbole--means more, of course, than Moss's tongue-in-cheek desecration. The only figure of speech in Moss's rewrite is the simile in line 1, and even that is denegated ("Who says?"). Moss manages to condense 115 great words to 78, a sonnet to a mere thirteen lines. It took a poet skilled in handling rimes to find such dull ones.

Shakespeare's nautical metaphor in line 8 may need explaining: a beautiful young person is a ship in full sail; accident or age can untrim the vessel. Compare this metaphor to "bare ruined choirs where late the sweet birds sang" ("That time of year," page 355).

METAPHOR AND SIMILE

RICHARD WILBUR, A Smile for Her Smile, page 86

Despite the title, it may be necessary to point out that the detailed and extended comparison that occupies Wilbur's poem isn't between the smile and the approach of a riverboat, but between the latter and the speaker's experience of his loved one's smile, or his anticipation of it, or his memory of it.

The graceful ingenuity of this poem, in which the simile is made so explicit, recalls earlier metaphysical poetry. Compare Wilbur's simile with Donne's figure of the two parted lovers in "A Valediction: Forbidding Mourning," (page 299), or to Edmund Waller's central metaphor in "On a Girdle" (page 95).

ALFRED, LORD TENNYSON, Flower in the Crannied Wall, page 86

Why does Tennyson say "what God and man is" instead of "what God and man are"? Apparently, this isn't faulty grammar, but higher pantheism. God and man are one.

SYLVIA PLATH, Metaphors, page 87

Students usually are prompt to see that the central fact of the poem is the speaker's pregnancy. The speaker feels herself to be a walking riddle, posing a question that awaits solution: What person is she carrying? The "nine syllables" are like the nine months of gestation. All the metaphors refer to herself or to her pregnancy, except those in lines 4-5, which refer to the unborn baby: growing round and full like an apple or plum, seeming precious as ivory (and with ivory skin?), fine-timbered in sinew and bone like a well-built house.

The tone of the poem is clear, if complicated. Humor and self-mockery are evident in the images of elephant and strolling melon. In the last line, there is a note of wonder at the inexorability of gestation and birth: "The train there's no getting off."

A lively class might be asked to point out any possible connection between what the poem is saying about the arbitrary, fixed cycle of pregnancy and its form--the nine nine-syllable lines.

As Plath records in her Boston journal for 20 March 1959, the pregnancy she had hoped for ended in a miscarriage. Grieving and depressed, she went ahead and finished this poem, then explicitly called "Metaphors for a Pregnant Woman" (Journals, New York: Ballantine, 1983) 298-99.

JANE KENYON, The suitor, page 87

   This economical poem moves from simile to simile: (1) "like
the chest of someone sleeping" (steadily rising and falling); (2)
"like a school of fish" (flashing their pale bellies); and (3)
"like a timid suitor" (hesitant, drawing back, reluctant to
arrive).
   Kenyon lives in Danbury, New Hampshire. "The Suitor" is from
her first collection, From Room to Room (Cambridge: Alice James,
1978).

EMILY DICKINSON, It dropped so low-in my Regard, page 88

   The whole poem sets forth the metaphor that someone or
something the speaker had valued too highly proved to be like a
silver-plated item (a chafing dish? a cream pitcher?) that she had
mistaken for solid silver. Its smash revealed that it was made of
cheap stuff.
   In another version, lines 5-6 read: "Yet blamed the Fate that
fractured--less / Than I reviled myself." Students may be asked
which version they prefer, and why they prefer it. (Personally, we
much prefer reviled to denounced because of its assonance--the
sound of the i--and its alliteration--the l in reviled and self.
Besides, fractured seems a more valuable word than flung: it gets
across the notion of something cracked or shattered, and its r sets
up an alliterative echo with the words entertaining, Wares, and
Silver.)

RUTH WHITMAN, Castoff Skin, page 88

   Apparently "crawled away" means that the old woman died,
leaving her body behind as a snake sheds a useless skin. "Paper
cheek" seems a fine evocation of snakeskin. The simile in line 2
("small as a twig") also suggests stiffness and brittleness.

DENISE LEVERTOV, Leaving Forever, page 89

   The man seems glad to go: "stones rolling away" suggests the
shedding of some great weight, or possibly even a resurrection (an
echo of the rolling away of the stone from the Easter tomb?). But
in the woman's view the mountain seems like someone rejected and
forlorn. The woman's view, expressed in a metaphor and given force
by coming last, seems stronger than the man's simile.
   Another question: is the poet right to repeat away, way,
away, away? The sound reverberates with a terrible flat monotony,
it is true--but apparently that is the effect necessary.

89-91 (text pages)

PETER WILLIAMS, When she was here, Li Bo, page 89

Li Bo's lines supply Williams with methods for both parts of
his poem. First he gives similes and metaphors to show what the
lover's presence was, then adds more similes: terms for her
absence. She was beautiful, sensuously appealing, and she afforded
her lover satisfaction; her absence is like depressing,
standardized food and drink and pop music, like a then-mediocre
football team.
        In the first part, most students will be more familiar with
the term quadraphonic than with the name of Gustav Mahler (1860-
1911). What "custardy honey from the old art books" might the poet
mean? (Rubens's nudes seem more beefy than custardy.
Botticelli's? Manet's?)
        In the last lines, the poet alludes to a popular "process
cheese food" spread, smeared on standard white bread; to singer and
TV-show host Bobby Vinton (one of whose hits was "La, La, Chicken
Cacciatore, My Memory of Love"), and to an NFL team noted for its
checkered career.
        The wry, comic tone of Williams's poem--communicated by its
hilarious, self-deprecating similes--clearly differs from that of
Li Bo's lines. Evidently, the Chinese poet is completely serious.

Exercise: What Is Similar? page 90

        Let us suggest that this exercise be run through rapidly. We
wouldn't give students much time to ponder, but would briskly call
on people, and if anyone hesitated for long, would skip to someone
else. Give them time to cogitate about these items, and they are
likely to dredge up all sorts of brilliant, reached-for
similarities in each pair of things--possibly logical, but having
nothing to do with the lines. Immediate flashes of understanding
are the goal of this exercise, not ponderous explication. Do this
one for fun, and so it might be; do it slowly and seriously, and it
could be deadly.

OTHER FIGURES

        On the subject of puns, students familiar with Hamlet and
other classics of the Bard may be asked to recall other puns of
Shakespeare (besides the celebrated lines about golden lads and
girls, quoted on page 94). If such a discussion prospers, Dr.
Johnson's well-known observation in his preface to Shakespeare's
works may provide an assertion to argue with:

        A quibble is to Shakespeare what luminous vapors are to the
        traveler: he follows it at all adventures; it is sure to
        lead him out of his way, and sure to engulf him in the mire.
        . . . A quibble is the golden apple for which he will always
        turn aside from his career or stoop from his elevation. A
        quibble, poor and barren as it is, gave him such delight that

42

he was content to purchase it by the sacrifice of reason,
propriety, and truth. A quibble was to him the fatal
Cleopatra for which he lost the world, and was content to lose
it.

JAMES STEPHENS, The Wind, page 91

As a birthday present to Stephens, James Joyce once translated
this poem into five other languages (French, German, Italian,
Latin, and Norwegian). These versions are reprinted in Letters of
James Joyce, ed. Stuart Gilbert (New York: Viking, 1957) 318-19.

Exercise: Paradox, page 93

CHIDIOCK TICHBORNE, Elegy, Written with His Own Hand, page 93

"One must admit the possibility that these verses were written
by some other poet, rather than by the protagonist himself," note
J. William Hebel and Hoyt H. Hudson in Poetry of the English
Renaissance (New York: Appleton, 1929). Set to music by a later
composer, the "Elegy" was sung as a madrigal.

GEORGE HERBERT, The Pulley, page 94

The title may need clarification. Man's need for rest is the
pulley by which eventually he is drawn to rest everlasting. The
pulley Herbert has in mind is probably not horizontal (like the one
with a clothesline), but the vertical kind rigged to hoist a heavy
weight. Despite the puns, the tone of the poem is of course
devoutly serious, Herbert's concern in it being (in the view of
Douglas Bush) "to subdue the wilful or kindle the apathetic self."
Lines 2-10, on the "glass of blessings" and its contents, set
forth a different metaphor. As Herbert's editor F. E. Hutchinson
(Works [Oxford: Oxford UP, 1941]) and others have remarked, "The
Pulley" seems a Christian version of the story of Pandora. At her
creation Pandora received gifts from all the gods, mostly virtues
and graces--though Hermes gave her perfidy. In some tellings of
the myth, Pandora's gift box (or vase) held not plagues but further
blessings. When she became curious and opened it, they slipped
away, all except the one that lay at the bottom--hope.
Herbert's poem, in its fondness for the extended metaphysical
conceit, invites comparison with Donne's metaphor of the compasses
in "A Valediction: Forbidding Mourning" (page 299). if the
instructor cares to discuss metaphysical poetry, "The Pulley" may
be taken together with Herbert's "Redemption" (page 207) and "Love"
(page 316). ("Easter Wings" [page 193] raises distracting
considerations and may be left for a discussion of concrete or
graphic poetry.) Other metaphysical poems by Waller and Roethke
immediately follow "The Pulley" in this chapter. (See note on
Roethke's poem.) Other poems of Donne and of Dickinson can be

mentioned. For recent poems that contain extended conceits, see
Wilbur's "A Simile for Her Smile," also in this chapter, and Alan
Dugan's "Love Song: I and Thou" (page 301).

It is a problem, of course, how deeply to become embroiled in
metaphysical poetry, if one wants to do so at all. One might try
to encourage students to see that poets of the seventeenth century
had certain habits of thought strikingly different from our own;
but that some of these habits--like the fondness for startling
comparisons of physical and spiritual things--haven't become
extinct. Perhaps the closest modern equivalent to the conceits of
Herbert and Donne may be found in fundamentalist hymns. Two
earlier twentieth-century illustrations:

    If you want to watch old Satan run
    Just fire off that Gospel gun!

and

    My soul is like a rusty lock.
    Oh, oil it with thy grace!
    And rub it, rub it, rub it, Lord,
    Until I see thy face!

(The first example is attributed to a black Baptist hymn writer;
the second, to the Salvation Army, according to Max Eastman in
Enjoyment of Laughter [New York: Simon, 1936] 79.) An even more
recent illustration, probably influenced by fundamentalist hymns,
is a country-and-Western song recorded in 1976 by Bobby Bare,
"Dropkick Me, Jesus" ("through the goalposts of life").

EDMUND WALLER, On a Girdle, page 95

Another way to enter this poem might be to ask:

1. In what words does the poet express littleness or con-
striction? (In the "slender waist," the rime confined/bind, "pale
which held," "narrow compass," bound.)
2. In what words does he suggest vastness and immensity?
(With any luck, students will realize that the entire poem demonstrates the paradox stated in lines 9-10.)
There may be another pun in line 6: deer.
What is the tone of "On a Girdle"? Playful and witty, yet
tender. You can have fun with this poem by asserting an overly
literal-minded reading: somewhere in the world, isn't there
probably some ruler who wouldn't abdicate just to put his arms
around her? If the speaker rejects all the sun goes round, where
will that put him and his loved one? If students have trouble
objecting to such quibbles, remind them of the definition of a
figure of speech. That should help. An overstatement isn't a lie,
it's a means of emphasis.
Compare this to another love poem full of hyperbole: Burns's
"Oh, my love is like a red, red rose," at the end of this chapter.

THEODORE ROETHKE, I Knew a Woman, page 96

   Both outrageous puns occur in line 15. In question 2, the
three lines quoted contain overstatement or hyperbole. The
speaker's reference to his whole being as "old bones" is synecdoche. "Let seed be grass, and grass turn into hay" are not
metaphors, but literal events the speaker hopes for--unless you
take the ripening of the grass to be the passage of time. Metaphors occur also in the sickle and the rake, and in calling
lovemaking mowing.
   "I Knew a Woman" shows Roethke's great affection for metaphysical poetry in its puns, its brief conceits (sickle and rake),
and its lovely image out of geometry--"She moved in circles, and
those circles moved." Two metaphysical poets of the seventeenth
century come immediately before Roethke in this chapter: Herbert
and Waller. Here's a good chance to dwell on metaphysical poetry,
or at least to mention it. (See the notes on Herbert's "Pulley.").
   For more outrageous puns, compare Robert Graves's "Down,
Wanton, Down!" (page 38).

FOR REVIEW AND FURTHER STUDY

ROBERT FROST, The Silken Tent, page 97

   Although the word as in the opening line might lead us to
expect a simile, "The Silken Tent" is clearly an immense metaphor,
comparing woman and tent in a multitude of ways. What are the
ropes or cords? Not merely commitments (or promises to keep) to
friends and family, but generous sympathies, "ties of love and
thought," on the part of a woman who cares about everything in the
world.
   While paying loving tribute to a remarkable woman, the poem is
also a shameless bit of showing off by a poet cocksure of his
technical mastery. Managing syntax with such grace that the poem
hardly seems contrived, Frost has sustained a single sentence into
an entire sonnet. "The whole poem is a performance," says Richard
Poirier, "a display for the beloved while also being an exemplifi-
cation of what it is like for a poem, as well as a tent or a
person, to exist within the constrictions of space ('a field') and
time ('at midday') wherein the greatest possible freedom is
consistent with the intricacies of form and inseparable from them"
(Robert Frost: The Work of Knowing [New York: Oxford UP, 1977]
xiv-xv). Poirier points out, too, that the diction of the poem
seems Biblical, perhaps echoing "The Song of Songs" (in which the
bride is comely "as the tents of Kedar") and Psalm 92 (in which the
godly "grow like a cedar in Lebanon"). Not only does the "central
cedar pole" signify the woman's spiritual rectitude, it points
toward heaven.
   In teaching this poem, one can quote Frost's remark to Louis
Untermeyer, "I prefer the synecdoche in poetry, that figure of
speech in which we use a part for a whole." In 1931 Frost recalled
that he had called himself a Synecdochist back when other poets

were calling themselves Imagists: "Always, always a larger
significance. A little thing touches a larger thing" (qtd. in
Elizabeth Shepley Sergeant, Robert Frost: The Trial by Existence
[New York: Holt, 1960] 325).

JAMES C. KILGORE, The White Man Presses the Locks, page 98

White body (the suburbs) holds black body (the inner city) in
a tight grip, as if squeezing the life out of it. Students may be
asked to spell out the connotations of certain well-loaded words
and phrases. Why is the body in line 3 darkening? (Because more
and more blacks are gathering in the inner city?) And blighted
suggests both disease and the familiar phrase "urban blight." In
the bloodstream, white corpuscles act as aggressive devourers.
Possibly the hugging white arms suggest the commuter's wife and
children, to whom he speeds home--but from the black poet's point
of view in the poem, they appear sinister.

OGDEN NASH, Very Like a Whale, page 98

Nash's meandering lines and forced rimes may have been
inspired by the work of Mrs. Julia A. Moore, the self-styled "Sweet
Singer of Michigan" (1847-1920); but any number of quasi-literate
poets could have shown him the way. Compare these lines (running
on for as long as necessary, then riming like a screech of trampled
brakes) by the Bard of Dundee, William McGonagall (1830-1902) on
"The Tay Bridge Disaster":

Oh! ill-fated Bridge of the Silv'ry Tay,
I must now conclude my lay
By telling the world fearlessly without the least dismay,
That your central girders would not have given way,
At least many sensible men do say,
Had they been supported on each side with buttresses,
At least many sensible men confesses,
For the stronger we our houses do build,
The less chance we have of being killed.

Exercise: Figure Spotting, page 100

RICHARD WILBUR, Sleepless at Crown Point, page 100

In Wilbur's implied metaphor, promontory and wind are to each
other as bull is to matador.

ANONYMOUS, The fortunes of war, I tell you plain, page 100

There are two instances of metonymy: <u>wooden leg</u> (being wounded) and <u>golden chain</u> (being decorated). This couplet was current in England at the time of the Crimean War.

ROBERT FROST, The Secret Sits, page 100

Besides its personification of the sitting Secret, Frost's poem contains an implied metaphor. To dance round in a ring is to make futile efforts to penetrate a secret--merely going around in circles.

MARGARET ATWOOD, You fit into me, page 100

The first two lines state a simile. In the second couplet, <u>hook</u> and <u>eye</u> turn out (to our surprise) to be puns.

JOHN TAGLIABUE, Maine vastly covered with much snow, page 100

This poem starts with a comparison that keeps expanding. First, we get a simile ("as busy as monks"), then a metaphor (the seeds are capsules containing the Dead Sea scrolls, or something), then another simile (theology like the flourish), and finally an implied metaphor (continuing the idea that the squirrels are scholarly monks).
The poet, who teaches at Bates College in Maine, has traveled extensively in the Orient.

JOHN ASHBERRY, The Cathedral Is, page 101

<u>Slated</u> is a pun.

ETHERIDGE KNIGHT, For Black Poets Who Think of Suicide, page 101

To search in "sweet dark caves" and "hunt for snipe / Down psychic trails" seem metaphors (for "indulging in sentimental thoughts of death" and "looking for Freudian symbols," maybe?). Lines 9-12 introduce four more metaphors. The poem ends in synecdoche: "marching feet" suggest an advancing army.
In lines 1-2 perhaps Knight recalls a white poet who took his own life: Hart Crane, who leaped to his death from a steamship, wrote <u>The Bridge</u>.

47

101-102 (text pages)

W. S. MERWIN, Song of Man Chipping an Arrowhead, page 101

The poem contains an apostrophe to the chips of flint or stone. That the chips are "little children" is also a metaphor; so is "the one you are hiding"--the emerging arrowhead.

ROBERT BURNS, Oh, my love is like a red, red rose, page 101

Figures of speech abound in this famous lyric: similes (lines 1-2, 3-4), a metaphor (sands o' life, 12), overstatements (8 and 9, 10), and possibly another overstatement in the last line.

See other professions of love couched in hyperbole, among them Waller's "On a Girdle" (page 95), Roethke's "I Knew a Woman" (page 96), Marvell's "To His Coy Mistress" (page 8), and Auden's "As I Walked Out One Evening" (page 277). Are the speakers in these poems mere throwers of blarney, whom no woman ought to trust?

For a discussion of this poem that finds more in it than figures of speech, see Richard Wilbur, "Explaining the Obvious," in Responses (New York: Harcourt, 1976). Burns's poem, says Wilbur, "forsakes the lady to glory in Love itself, and does not really return. We are dealing, in other words, with romantic love, in which the beloved is a means to high emotion, and physical separation can serve as a stimulant to ideal passion." The emotion of the poem is "self-enchanted," the presence or absence of the lady isn't important, and the very idea of parting is mainly an opportunity for the poet to turn his feelings loose. Absurd as this posture may be, however, we ought to forgive a great songwriter almost anything.

GIBBONS RUARK, The rose growing into the house, page 102

The whole poem develops one metaphor. There is also a simile: "like a thief."

This contemporary lyric invites comparison with Burns's poem, immediately preceding it. But the subjects are not identical: by love Burns means the loved one; Ruark's speaker, his own loving. Burns's poem is a series of figures; Ruark's all one metaphor. Both poets see the rose as active and energetic: Burns makes it spring, Ruark makes it an invader. This juxtaposition puts Ruark's poem in high company, but we think it can stand comparison.

7

SONG

SINGING AND SAYING

Most students who wrote comments about this book in its last edition said that this chapter was the one that most appealed to them. "It shows that poetry isn't all found in books," was a typical comment; and many were glad to see song lyrics that they knew.

Even if there is not time for a whole unit on song, the instructor who wishes to build upon this interest can use at least some of this chapter to introduce the more demanding matters of sound, rhythm, and form (treated in Chapters 8, 9, and 10). Some instructors take the tack that lyric poetry begins with song, and so begin their courses with this chapter, supplemented by folk ballads elsewhere in the text.

Besides Ben Jonson's classic nondrinking song, many other famous poems invite singers. The tradition of poems set to music by fine composers is old and honorable. For a list of such poems with musical settings (and recordings), see Douglas Murray, "The English Teacher and English Song: An Annotated Bibliography," College English (Feb. 1985): 176-80. If a class seems in grave need of livening, it can be fun to sing poems to unsuitable tunes: Robert Frost's "Stopping by Woods on a Snowy Evening" to the tune of "Hernando's Hideaway" (a combination originally discovered by waiters at the Bread Loaf Writers Conference, who sang it to Frost); or Wordsworth's "She Dwelt Among the Untrodden Ways" to the tune of Yankee Doodle" (which tune supplies a beautifully flip ending: "But she is in her grave, and oh, / The difference to me!").

BEN JONSON, To Celia, page 104

Students may not know that in line 2 I will pledge means "I will drink a toast." Also, I would not change for thine (line 8) in modern English becomes "I would not take it in exchange for yours."

To demonstrate that "To Celia" is a living song, why not ask the class to sing it? Unfortunately, you can no longer assume that the tune is one that everyone knows, so you may need to start them off.

105-108 (text pages)

ANONYMOUS, The Cruel Mother, page 105

    Some versions of this ballad start the narrative at an earlier
point in time, with a woman discovering that she is pregnant by the
wrong man when she is about to marry another. See Alan Lomax's
notes to The Child Ballads, vol. 1, Caedmon, TC 1145, which record
contains an Irish version.
    If the instructor cares to discuss the bottomless but student-
spellbinding topic of archetypes, this ballad will serve to illustrate an archetype also visible in the stepmother figure of many
fairy stories.

EDWIN ARLINGTON ROBINSON, Richard Cory, page 108

PAUL SIMON, Richard Cory, page 108

    This pair sometimes provokes lively class discussion,
especially if someone in the class maintains that Simon converts
Robinson into fresh, modern terms. Further discussion may be
necessary to show that Robinson's poem has a starkly different
theme.
    Robinson's truth, of course, is that we envy others their
wealth and prestige and polished manners, but if we could see into
their hearts we might not envy them at all. Simon's glib song does
not begin to deal with this. The singer wishes that he too could
have orgies on a yacht, but even after he learns that Cory died a
suicide, his refrain goes right on, "I wish that I could be Richard
Cory." (Live rich, die young, and make a handsome corpse!)
    Some questions to prompt discussion might include:

    1. In making his song, Simon admittedly took liberties with
Robinson's poem. Which of these changes seem necessary to make the
story singable? What suggestions in the original has Simon picked
up and amplified?
    2. How has Simon altered the character of Richard Cory? Is
his Cory a "gentleman" in Robinson's sense of the word? What is
the tone of Simon's line, "He had the common touch"? Compare this
with Robinson: "he was always human when he talked." Does
Robinson's Cory have anything more than "Power, grace and style"?
    3. In the song, what further meaning does the refrain take on
with its third hearing, in the end, after the news of Cory's
suicide?
    4. What truth about life does Robinson's poem help us see?
Is it merely "Money can't make you happy" or "If you're poor you're
really better off than rich people"? Does Simon's narrator affirm
this truth, deny it, or ignore it?

BALLADS

ANONYMOUS, Bonny Barbara Allan, page 110

Despite the numerous versions of this, the most widespread of
all traditional ballads in English, most keep the main elements of
the story with remarkable consistency. American versions tend to
be longer, with much attention to the lovers' eventual side-by-side
burial, and sometimes have Barbara's mother die of remorse, too!
Commentators since the coming of Freud have sometimes seen Barbara
as sexually frigid, and Robert Graves once suggested that Barbara,
a witch, is killing Sir John by sorcery. An Irish version makes
Barbara laugh hideously on beholding her lover's corpse.
    To show how traditional ballads change and vary in being sung,
a useful recording is The Child Ballads, vol. 1, Caedmon, TC 1145,
containing performances collected in the field by Alan Lomax and
Peter Kennedy. Six nonprofessional singers are heard in sharply
different versions of "Barbara Allan," in dialects of England,
Scotland, Ireland, and Wales.

JOHN LENNON and PAUL McCARTNEY, Eleanor Rigby, page 113

    "Eleanor Rigby," we think, is a poem. Although swayed by the
superstition that priests are necessarily lonely because celibate,
Lennon's portrait of Father McKenzie and of Eleanor have details
that reflect life. Both music and words contain an obvious beat,
and if students pick out those syllables in long lines 4 and 7, 14
and 17, and 24 and 27, they will be getting into the subject of
meter. (Each of the lines contains a stressed syllable followed by
four anapests.)

FOR REVIEW AND FURTHER STUDY

ADRIENNE RICH, Song, page 115

    Loneliness is a favorite theme of recent popular songwriters
("Eleanor Rigby"), so Rich's poem seems right in a familiar vein.
The language of "Song" seems relatively simpler than that in most
other poems by this poet, and can be understood from a single
hearing, like that of most songs. Each stanza begins with a kind
of incremental refrain.
    Is there a musician in the class who might be persuaded to try
setting "Song" to music?

Exercise: Songs or Poems or Both? page 116

ANONYMOUS, Fa, mi, fa, re, la, mi, page 116

ANONYMOUS, The silver swan, who living had no note, page 116

51

116-117 (text pages)

WILLIE NELSON, Heaven and Hell, page 116

BRUCE SPRINGSTEEN, Born to Run, page 117

Of these four song lyrics, only "Fa, mi," seems completely
unreadable: its words do little more than fill up a tune.

Comparing the two madrigals, the instructor can raise the
question, Why is "The silver swan" a memorable poem while "Fa, mi"
isn't? With luck and a little prompting, students may see that
poetry isn't mere musical noise: poems say something. They also
tend to contain figurative language, such as the metaphor "unlocked
her silent throat" and the apostrophe to death; and interesting
sounds--the subtle silver / living and other alliterations. What,
by the way, is a "swan song"? Some students may need an
explanation.

Willie Nelson's "Heaven and Hell" is surprisingly metaphysical! What sense do students make out of "front tracks" and
"back tracks"? Does the singer feel like a moving train leaving a
freezing wasteland and headed for refreshing waters? Nelson has a
fine ear, and his lyric gains richness from internal rime (back
track), alliteration, and sonorous repetition. A Texas-born
country-and-western singer and composer, Nelson hit the big time in
1975 with his album Red Headed Stranger. He starred in the 1980
movie Honeysuckle Rose.

Springsteen's early lyric, which helped make him famous, seems
to us better when heard than when read on the page. Still, it has
elements of poetry: strong feeling; metaphors in "Baby this town
rips the bones from your back" (also hyperbole there) and in lines
12-13 (those sexual innuendoes), 16 (the lovers compared to
high-wire walkers), and 36 ("we'll walk in the sun"); some vivid
imagery, most realistic in stanza 3: girls combing their hair in
rearview mirrors, kids huddled on the beach in a mist; rime,
rhythm, internal rime in lines 7, 24, and 33.

8

SOUND

SOUND AS MEANING

ALEXANDER POPE, True Ease in Writing comes from Art, not Chance, page 120.

Nowadays, looking at the pages of an eighteenth-century book of poetry, we might think the liberal capitalization and use of italics merely decorative. But perhaps Pope wished to leave his readers little choice in how to sound his lines. Most of his typo-graphical indications seem to us to make sense--like a modern stage or television script with things underlined or capitalized, lest the actors ignore a nuance.
   Line 12 is deliberately long: an alexandrine or twelve-syl-lable line that must be spoken quickly in order to get it said within the time interval established by the other shorter, pentameter lines.

WILLIAM BUTLER YEATS, Who Goes with Fergus? page 122

Originally a song in Yeats's play The Countess Cathleen, this famous lyric overflows with euphony. Take just the opening question (lines 1-3): the assonance of the various o-sounds; the initial alliteration of w, d, and sh; the internal alliteration of the r in Fergus, pierce, and shore--musical devices that seem especially meaningful for an invitation to a dance. The harsh phrase brazen cars seems introduced to jar the brooding lovers out of their reveries. Unless you come right out and ask what brazen cars are, a few students probably will not realize that they are brass chariots. In ancient Ulster, such chariots were sometimes used for hunting deer--though how you would drive one of them through the deep woods beats us.
   If you discuss meter, what better illustration of the power of spondees than "And the WHITE BREAST of the DIM SEA"?
   The last line of the poem, while pleasingly mysterious, is also exact. The personification "dishevelled wandering stars" makes us think of beautiful, insane, or distracted women with their hair down: Ophelia in Olivier's film Hamlet. That they are wandering recalls the derivation of the word planet: Greek for "wanderer." In what literal sense might stars look disheveled? Perhaps in that their light, coming through the atmosphere (and being seen through ocean spray) appears to spread out like wild

53

122-124 (text pages)

long hair. For comparable figures of speech, see Melville's "The Portent" (page 44), in which John Brown's beard is a meteor; and Blake's "Tyger," (page 282), in which the personified stars weep and throw spears.

Exercise: Listening to Meaning, page 123

JOHN UPDIKE, Winter Ocean, page 123

FRANCES CORNFORD, The Watch, page 123

WILLIAM WORDSWORTH, A Slumber Did My Spirit Seal, page 123

EMANUEL di PASQUALE, Rain, page 124

Onomatopoeia is heard in Updike's scud-thumper and pusher (echoing the boom and rush of the waves), and is heard even more obviously in Cornford's watch-ticks. In di Pasquale's lines, the s-sounds fit well with our conception of rain, and hushes is an especially beautiful bit of onomatopoeia. By the way, di Pasquale's poem is especially remarkable in view of the fact that the poet, born in Sicily, did not learn English until he was sixteen.

In Wordsworth's Lucy poem, sound effects are particularly noticeable in the first line (the soporific s's) and in the last two lines (the droning r's and n's). If students go beyond the sound effects and read the poem more closely, they might find problems in the first stanza. Is the poet's slumber a literal sleep or a figurative one? That is: is Wordsworth recalling some pleasant dream of Lucy (whether the living Lucy he used to know, or the dead Lucy in Eternity), or is he saying that when she was alive he was like a dreamer in his view of her? If so, he was deluded in thinking that she would always remain a child; he had none of the usual human fears of death or of growing old. However we read the poem, there is evidently an ironic contrast between the poet's seeing Lucy (in stanza 1) as invulnerable to earthly years, and his later view that she is affected, being helplessly rolled around the sun once a year with the other inanimate objects. And simple though it looks, the poem contains a paradox. The speaker's earlier dream or vision of Lucy has proved to be no illusion but an accurate foreshadowing. Now she is a "thing," like rocks and stones and trees; and she cannot feel and cannot suffer any more from time's ravages.

ALLITERATION AND ASSONANCE

A. E. HOUSMAN, Eight O'Clock, page 125

The final struck is a serious pun, to which patterns of alliteration begun in the opening line (st . . . st, r), and continued through the poem, have led up. The ticking effect of the clock is, of course, most evident in the clock collected.

Compare Housman's strapped and noosed lad with the one in Hugh Kingsmill's parody of Housman (page 235); and this lad's cursing his luck with what Terence has to say about luck in "Terence, this is stupid stuff" (page 321).

ROBERT HERRICK, Upon Julia's Voice, page 126

Julia, apparently, is singing; for the lutes provide accompaniment. At the beginning and end, this brief poem is particularly rich in music: the sibilance of so smooth, so sweet, so silv'ry; and the alliteration (both initial and internal) of the m- and l-sounds in the last line.
The second line seems a colossal hyperbole, meaning, "Julia, your singing is sweet enough to make the damned in Hell forget to wail." In Herrick's poems, such flattery is never out of place. This is the quality of Herrick's work--a lovely deliberate absurdity--XJK has tried to echo (feebly) in a two-line parody:

When Vestalina's thin white hand cuts cheese,
The very mice go down upon their knees.

JANET LEWIS, Girl Help, page 126

A sensitive comment on this poem is that of the poet's husband, Yvor Winters:

There is almost nothing to it, really, except the rich characterization of a young girl with her life before her and the description of a scene which implies an entire way of life. The meter is curious; one is tempted to call it irregular three-beat accentual, but it seems to be irregular iambic trimeter. On the second basis, the first line starts with a monosyllabic foot, and the fourth line has two feet, both iambic. But wide and broom are almost evenly accented, and both are long; if one is moved by this to choose the accentual theory, her is too lightly accented to count, although it would count as the accented syllable of an iambic foot. There are a few other such problems later in the poem. But there is no problem with the rhythm; the fourth line virtually gives us the movement of the broom, and the seventh and eighth give us the movement of the girl; the movement of the poem is that of indolent summer in a time and place now gone; the diction, like the rhythm, is infallible.

Winters (1900-1968)--see his own poem on page 377--wrote this analysis in Forms of Discovery (Denver: Swallow, 1967), page 332.
The poet reads "Girl Help" on her recording Janet Lewis Reading at Stanford, News & Publications Service of Stanford University, 1975; available from Serendipity Books, 1970 Shattuck Ave., Berkeley CA 94709.

"Domestic poetry" is her province, remarks Kenneth Fields in the notes on that record album's sleeve. He cites (in order to disagree with) a review of Lewis's work by Theodore Roethke: "The nursery, the quiet study, the garden, the graveyard do not provide enough material for talent of such a high order."

Janet Lewis, known for The Wife of Martin Guerre, The Trial of Soren Qvist and other novels, has brought out her Poems Old and New: 1918-1978 (Athens: Swallow-Ohio UP, 1981). The volume includes recent work.

Exercise: Hearing How Sound Helps, page 127

Wyatt's version surpasses Surrey's for us, especially in Wyatt's opening line, with its remarkable use of assonance--a good instance of the way long vowel-sounds can slow our reading of a line and make us linger over it. The initial alliteration and internal alliteration in these first two lines help besides. In its rhythm, Surrey's version sounds a bit singsong by comparison. The inverted word order in the last line seems awkward.

ALFRED, LORD TENNYSON, The splendor falls on castle walls, page 127

If read aloud rapidly, this famous lyric from Tennyson's The Princess will become gibberish; and the phrase Blow, bugle, blow, a tongue twister. But if it is read with any attention to its meaning, its long vowels and frequent pauses will compel the reader to slow down. Students may want to regard the poem as mellifluous nonsense, but may be assured that the poem means something. In fact, it is based on a personal experience of the poet's. Visiting the lakes of Killarney in 1848, Tennyson heard the bugle of a boatman sound across the still water, and counted eight distinct echoes. "The splendor falls" is the poet's attempt to convey his experience in accurate words.

RIME

BRAD LEITHAUSER, Trauma, page 131

Brilliant riming here, we think. What does this terse poem mean? Students ought to know what a trauma is (from the Greek: "wound"), and a suture. Is this trauma physical or psychic? We aren't told. The suture (surgical thread) suggests a physical wound or incision; but in a metaphoric sense a psychic wound, too, can be closed and made to heal. That the amassed past becomes the future is a classic idea, perhaps "ne'er so well expressed."

Leithauser is a new writer to watch. His first book of poems, Hundreds of Fireflies (New York: Knopf, 1982), and a first novel, Equal Distance (Knopf, 1984), about Americans in Japan, have both been warmly received.

JAMES HAYFORD, Mason's Trick, page 132

This brief poem exhibits what it affirms. Hayford, student and disciple of Robert Frost (but his own man), surely must be among the finest living metrical poets in English. Too few know of him, for his major collections, published by small presses in New England, may be hard to find elsewhere. His poems (all tending to be, like "Mason's Trick," laconic and well crafted) embody life in a Northeast Kingdom village, and in the universe. They add up, we think, to an unexplored green mountain of American poetry. For books available and prices, the curious might inquire of James Hayford himself, at 5 Cliff St., Orleans, VT 05860.

ROBERT FROST, Desert Places, page 132

Some possible answers:

1. Terrible pockets of loneliness.
2. The word snow, occurring three times. Other o-sounds occur in oh, going, showing, no, so, and home. The l of lonely is echoed by alliteration in looked, last, and lairs.
3. It makes us feel a psychic chill! Yet the feminine rime lightens the grim effect of what is said and gives it a kind of ironic smirk.

WILLIAM BUTLER YEATS, Leda and the Swan, page 133

The deliberately awful off-rime up / drop ends the sonnet with an appropriately jarring plop as the God-swan discards the used Leda and sinks into his postejaculatory stupor.
Other questions that can be raised:

1. What knowledge and power does Yeats refer to in line 14?
2. Do the words staggering (line 2) and loosening (line 6) keep to the basic meter of the poem or depart from it? How does rhythm express meaning in these lines? (It staggers on staggering and loosens on loosening.)
3. Compare this poem to Donne's sonnet "Batter my heart" (page 40). Is the tone of Yeats's sonnet--the poet's attitude toward this ravishing--similar or dissimilar?

For an early draft of the poem, see Yeats's Memoirs, ed. Denis Donoghue (New York: Macmillan, 1973) 272-74.

GERARD MANLEY HOPKINS, God's Grandeur, page 133

Students who think Hopkins goes too far in his insistence on rimes and other similar sounds will have good company, including Robert Bridges, William Butler Yeats, and Yvor Winters. Still, it is hard not to admire the euphony of the famous closing lines--that

ingenious alternation of <u>br</u> and <u>w</u>, with a pause for breath at that
magical <u>ah</u>!-- and the cacophony of lines 6-8, with their jangling
internal rimes and the alliteration that adds more weight to
<u>smeared</u>, <u>smudge</u>, and <u>smell</u>. For Hopkins, of course, sound is one
with meaning; and the cacophonous lines just mentioned are also, as
John Pick has pointed out, "a summary of the particular sins of the
nineteenth century." For a brilliant demonstration that sound
effects in Hopkins's poetry have theological meaning, see J. Hillis
Miller, <u>The Disappearance of God</u> (Cambridge: Harvard UP, 1963) 276-
317. Miller finds the poet's theory revealed in his sermons and
journals: "Any two things however unlike are in something like";
therefore, "all beauty may by a metaphor be called rhyme."
    In the text, it seemed best not to bury the poem under
glosses, but to let the instructor decide how thoroughly to expli-
cate it. Here are a few more glosses in case they seem necessary:

    1. <u>charged</u>: as though with electricity. 3-4: <u>It gathers</u>
. . . <u>ooze of oil / Crushed</u>: God's grandeur will rise and be
manifested from the world that man has abused, even as oil rises
and collects from crushed olives. 4. <u>reck his rod</u>: obey his law.
7. <u>man's smudge</u>: the blight of smoke and ugliness cast over the
countryside by factories and mines. As a student for the priest-
hood in North Wales and as a parish priest in London and Liverpool,
Hopkins had known the blight intimately. Another suggestion in the
phrase: nature is fallen and needs to be redeemed, like man, who
wears the smudge of original sin. 10. <u>deep down things</u>: Hopkins
omits the preposition <u>in</u> before <u>things</u>. Tightly packing a poem, he
sometimes drops small words like a man composing a telegram against
a word limit. 11. <u>last lights off the black West went</u>: when the
English church broke from Rome at the reformation? 12. <u>morning</u>
. . . <u>springs</u>: The risen Christ is like the sun at dawn. Eastward
is the direction of Jerusalem, also of Rome. (Hopkins cherished
the hope that the Church of England and the Pope would one day be
reconciled.) 13-14: <u>bent / World</u>: Perhaps because of its curva-
ture the earth looks bent at the horizon; or perhaps the phrase is
a transferred epithet, attributing to the earth the dove's
bent-over solicitude. (And as the world seems to break off at the
horizon, line 13 breaks at the word <u>bent</u>.) 14. <u>broods</u>: like a
dove, traditional representation of the Holy Ghost.
    For still more suggestions, see Pick, <u>Gerard Manley Hopkins</u>,
<u>Priest and Poet</u>, 2nd ed. (Oxford: Oxford UP, 1966) 62-4; Paul L.
Mariani, <u>Commentary on the Complete Poems of Gerard Manley Hopkins</u>
(Ithaca: Cornell UP, 1970); and (not least) the poet's "Pied
Beauty."
    A sonnet by Wordsworth (page 217) also begins "The world is,"
and Hopkins no doubt knew of it. In their parallel (though different) complaints against trade and commerce, the two deserve to
be compared. Both poets find humanity artificially removed from
nature: this seems the point of Hopkins's observation in lines 7-8
that once soil was covered (with grass and trees) and feet were
bare; now soil is bare and feet are covered. Clearly we have lost
the barefoot bliss of Eden; but in answer to Wordsworth, one almost

expects Hopkins to cry, "Great God! I'd rather be a Christian."
(Wordsworth by world means "worldliness.")

EMILY DICKINSON, The Soul selects her own Society, page 134

   Door / more is the one exact rime in the poem. Gate / Mat and
One / Stone are slant rimes--at the end, the latter provides a particularly hollow and reverberating off-note. Other couplings
(Society / Majority, nation / attention) sound roughly like
feminine rimes, but seem too far out to be called slant rimes.
(Quasi rimes, perhaps?) Although falling where we expect rimes,
pausing and kneeling seem not to rime at all.
   In general, when a poet follows a line with another line mark-
edly shorter, the shorter line receives the larger share of our
attention--it is as though it had been underlined. (See, for
instance, Eliot's "Prufrock" [page 303], lines 8-9 and 118-19.)
Dickinson's poem is built entirely of such long-and-short pairs.
In the last stanza, wherein the shorter, even-numbered lines have
dwindled to two syllables, both syllables taking full stresses, the
effect is powerful. Colossal emphasis is placed upon Like Stone,
which shuts the door of the poem.
   Two interpretations of this cryptic poem seem likely; and students might be asked whether, like the Soul, they care to Choose
One, or perhaps to come up with another:

   1. The chosen One is poetry. The Soul has selected it as the
sole object of her attention, and decisively spurns other society.
Biographical conjecture tends to support this view: by 1862, about
when the poem was written, Dickinson had given up trying to publish
her work. Feeling her creative powers at their height, she more
frequently shunned society, apparently in order to devote her con-
centrated energies to her poetry. This poem "can be taken as a
motto for her own guidance" in her now-decided way of life. (This
is the opinion of Thomas H. Johnson in Emily Dickinson: An Inter-
pretive Biography [Cambridge: Harvard UP, 1955].)
   2. The One is God, whose society the Soul has selected over
that of men. Her "low Gate" is her tombstone; "her Mat," the grass
on her grave. The "Valves of her attention" are the avenues of her
senses, now closed in death and become (like stone) impenetrable.

READING AND HEARING POEMS ALOUD

   Here is a fresh comment by William Stafford on why certain
poets read their poems with apparent carelessness. Poets spend
their energies in writing poems and are not effective public
speakers. Unlike the Russian poet Andrei Voznesensky, a great
performer, Stafford remarks,

   most of the poets I know would feel a little guilty about
   doing an effective job of reading their poems. They throw
   them away. And I speak as one who does that. It feels fakey

enough to be up there reading something as though you were reading it for the first time. And to say it well is just too fakey. So you throw it away.

(Interview in The Literary Monitor 3, no 3/4, [1980]).

This comment raises provocative questions for discussion. What is the nature of a poetry reading? Should it be regarded as a performance, or as a friendly get-together?

For a symposium on poetry readings, with comments by Allen Ginsberg, James Dickey, Denise Levertov, and twenty-nine other poets, see Poets on Stage (New York: Some/Release, 1978).

A rich and convenient source of recorded poetry, no doubt the best in the country, is the Poets' Audio Center, a nonprofit service to the literary community and academe operated by the Watershed Foundation. The center can supply on cassette more than 700 readings by great and minor poets living and dead, both commercial and noncommercial productions. They issue a free list of 200 of their most popular recordings, also a complete catalog. (This last costs $3, but is free to acquisitions librarians who write on a letterhead.) Among the cassette offerings are their own Watershed Tapes, an extremely well produced and interesting series of readings by contemporaries. Address: Poets' Audio Center, P.O. Box 50145, Washington, DC 20004.

Exercise: Reading for Sound and Meaning, page 136

MICHAEL STILLMAN, In Memoriam John Coltrane, page 137

WILLIAM SHAKESPEARE, Full fathom five thy father lies, page 137

A. E. HOUSMAN, With rue my heart is laden, page 137

T. S. ELIOT, Virginia, page 138

GALWAY KINNELL, Blackberry Eating, page 138

In Michael Stillman's tribute to the great jazz saxophonist, coal train is not only a rich pun on Coltrane's name, it also becomes the poem's central image. The poet has supplied this comment:

One thing about that poem which has always pleased me--beyond its elegiac strain--is the way the technique of the lines and phrases corresponds to a musical effect on Coltrane's playing. He was known for his ability to begin with a certain configuration of notes, then play pattern after pattern of variations. The repetition of "Listen to the coal . . . listen to the . . . listen to . . . listen" was one way to capture a feature of his playing. The image of the coal train disappearing into the night comes, particularly,

from a place on the James River, west of Richmond, where I
happened to be when I heard of Coltrane's death. Like all
jazz musicians, I felt the loss very deeply.

Shakespeare's song contains an obvious illustration of onomatopoeia (the bell's sound), obvious alliteration in the f-full
first line, and (less obviously) internal alliteration (note the r
and n sounds), and assonance galore. Like a drowned man's bones,
ordinary language becomes something "rich and strange" in this
song.

Housman's lyric will reward the same sort of scrutiny, not
that a class will sit still for much scrutiny of this sort!

Eliot's "Virginia" is an experiment in quantitative verse,
according to George Williamson (A Reader's Guide to T. S. Eliot
[New York: Noonday, 1957]). You might read aloud "Virginia" and
Campion's quantitative "Rose-cheeked Laura" (page 152), and ask the
class to detect any similarity. Ted Hughes has written of "Virginia" with admiration. How is it, he wonders, that Eliot can
create so vivid a landscape without specific images? "What the
poem does describe is a feeling of slowness, with a prevailing
stillness, of suspended time, of heat and dryness, and fatigue,
with an undertone of oppressive danger, like a hot afternoon that
will turn to thunder and lightning" (Poetry Is [New York: Doubleday, 1967]).

Kinnell, reading his poems at Bentley College on 17 March
1981, read "Blackberry Eating" vigorously, with special attention
to the two long one-syllable words strengths and squinched.
"They're the longest one-syllable words I could find," he remarked.
"Nine letters long. If I had known any one-syllable words of ten
or eleven letters, I would have put them in instead."

140-145 (text pages)

9

RHYTHM

STRESSES AND PAUSES

In the first section of this chapter, rhythm is discussed with
as few technicalities as possible. For the instructor wishing to
go on to the technicalities, the second part of the chapter,
"Meter," will give the principles of scansion and the names of the
metrical feet.

Except for one teacher at the University of Michigan, James
Downer, who would illustrate the rhythms of Old English poetry by
banging on his desk for a drum, we have never known anyone able to
spend whole classes on meter without etherizing patients. Meter,
it would seem, is best dealt with in discussing particular poems.

Exercise: Appropriate and Inappropriate Rhythms, page 141

The rollicking anapests of Poe and Cook seem inappropriate,
ill-suited to the poets' macabre subject matter. Cook, by the way,
is the author of another wretched specimen, "The Old Arm-Chair"
(page 248).

Tennyson's monosyllabic words, further slowed by pauses, convey not only the force of the tide, but its repetitiveness.

The rhythms of these lines by Keeler and Shakespeare seem
suitably rollicking.

GWENDOLYN BROOKS, We Real Cool, page 144

The poet might have ended every line with a rime, as poets who
rime usually do:

We real cool.
We left school.

The effect, then, would have been like a series of hammer blows,
because of so many short end-stopped lines and so many rimes in
such quick succession. But evidently Brooks is after a different
rhythm. What is it? How to read the poem aloud? Let members of
the class take turns trying and compare their various oral
interpretations. If you stress each final We, then every syllable
in the poem takes a stress; and if, besides, you make even a split-
second pause at every line break, then you give those final We's

still more emphasis. What if you don't stress the We's, but read
them lightly? Then the result is a skipping rhythm, rather like
that of some cool cat slapping his thighs.

   After the class has mulled this problem, read them Brooks's
own note on the poem (from her autobiography Report from Part One
[Detroit: Broadside, 1972] 185):

>   The ending WEs in "We Real Cool" are tiny, wispy,
>   weakly argumentative "Kilroy-is-here" announcements. The
>   boys have no accented sense of themselves, yet they are
>   aware of a semi-defined personal importance. Say the "We"
>   softly.

   Kilroy, as students may need to know, was a fictitious--even
mythical--character commemorated in graffiti chalked or penciled by
U.S. soldiers wherever they traveled in World War II. KILROY WAS
HERE was even scrawled in the sands of Anzio. A small testimonial
that the graffitist is a person.

   As a student remarked about the tone and theme of this poem,
"She doesn't think they're real cool, she thinks they're real
fool--to die so young like that."

   Brooks has recorded her own reading of the poem for The Spoken
Arts Treasury of 100 Modern American Poets, vol. 13, SA 1052.

ROBERT FROST, Never Again Would Birds' Song Be the Same, page 144

   He is Adam. In line 9, you say "as MAY be," because the
iambic rhythm wants you to. The effect of Frost's closing string
of sixteen monosyllables is quietly powerful, in keeping with his
final understatement. Much of our pleasure in those lines comes
from hearing ordinary, speakable phrases so beautifully
accommodated.

   Sometimes teachers and critics try to account for the unique
flavor of Frost's language by claiming that it is all a matter of
his vocabulary. But what rural words are there in this poem, a
poem as Yankee-sounding as they come, despite some highly literate
diction ("Admittedly an eloquence")? No, what makes the lines
memorable is that they embody what Frost called the "sound of
sense." He was convinced that certain phrases, customarily spoken
with feeling, have a pattern of intonation so distinctive that we
can recognize them and catch their meaning even if we hear only the
drone of them from behind a closed door. (See Frost's explanations
and illustrations in Selected Letters, ed. Lawrance Thompson [New
York: Holt, 1964] 79-81 and 111-13.)

   Reading this poem to an audience in Ann Arbor in March 1962
when he was 88, Frost delivered its closing line with the air of a
slowball pitcher hurling a flawless third strike into the catcher's
glove to retire the side. The audience caught it and burst out
clapping.

   Pope's line of monosyllables, by the way, doesn't seem dull
either.

145-147 (text pages)

BEN JONSON, Slow, slow fresh fount, keep time with my salt tears, page 145

O sounds slow the opening line, whose every word is a mono-syllable. Further slowing the line, eight of the ten monosyllables take heavy beats. "Drop, drop, drop" obviously racks up still more stresses, as do the spondees that begin lines 4, 5, and 6. The entire effect is that we are practically obliged to read or sing the poem slowly and deliberately--as befits a lamentation.

ALEXANDER POPE, Atticus, page 145

Generosity, kindness, courage, wholeheartedness, and humility seem mainly what Atticus/Addison lacks. As this famous dissection shows, Pope's custom is to break each line after a word that completes not only the line but also a syntactical unit. And so the argument advances in couplets like locked boxes, each box neatly packed with phrases, dependent clauses, things in series, antitheses. Only line 3 is a run-on line, if you go by the book's simple advice that a run-on line doesn't end in a punctuation mark. A sensitive reader, reading the passage aloud, would probably pause slightly after fires anyway, for these couplets enforce a rhythm hard to ignore.

For a definition of the heroic couplet and a brief discussion of it, students may be directed to pages 159-60.

Exercise: Two Kinds of Rhythm, page 146

SIR THOMAS WYATT, With serving still, page 146

DOROTHY PARKER, Résumé, page 147

These two poems differ in rhythm: Wyatt compels a heavy pause only at the end of every quatrain, while Parker end-stops every line. Students may be shown that pauses and meanings go together. Both poems are cast in two sentences, but Wyatt develops one uninterrupted statement throughout the entire poem (in sonnet fashion: first the summary of the speaker's problem in the opening three stanzas, then the conclusion beginning with "Wherefore all ye"). "Résumé," as its punctuation indicates, makes a new self-contained statement in every line.

A question on meaning: Must light verse necessarily be trivial in its theme? State Parker's theme in "Résumé." Surely, it isn't trivial. At least in theme, the poem seems comparable to Hamlet's soliloquy, "To be or not to be. . . ."

After Not So Deep as a Well, her collected poems of 1936, Parker brought out no more poetry collections. "My verses," she insisted to an interviewer. "I cannot say poems. Like everybody was then, I was following in the exquisite footsteps of Miss Millay, unhappily in my own horrible sneakers" (Writers at Work: The Paris Review Interviews, 1st ser. [New York: Viking, 1959]). Parker's wit, acerbic and sometimes macabre, is as clear from

"Résumé" as it is from her celebrated remark on being informed that Calvin Coolidge had just died: "How do they know?"

METER

XJK used to think of a meter as a platonic ideal norm from which actual lines diverge, but J. V. Cunningham's essay "How Shall the Poem be Written?" changed his mind. Metrical patterns (in the abstract) do not exist; there are only lines that poets have written, in which meters may be recognized. "Meter," declares Cunningham, "is perceived in the actual stress-contour, or the line is perceived as unmetrical, or the perceiver doesn't perceive meter at all" (The Collected Essays of J. V. Cunningham [Chicago: Swallow, 1976] 262).

MAX BEERBOHM, On the imprint of the first English edition of The Works of Max Beerbohm, page 147

John Updike has paid tribute to this brilliant bit of fluff:

The effortless a-b-a-b rhyming, the balance of "plain" and "nicely," the need for nicety in pronouncing "iambically" to scan--this is quintessential light verse, a twitting of the starkest prose into perfect form, a marriage of earth with light, and quite magical. Indeed, were I a high priest of literature, I would have this quatrain made into an amulet and wear it about my neck, for luck.

> ("Rhyming Max," a review of Beerbohm's collected verse reprinted in Assorted Prose [New York: Knopf, 1965].)

THOMAS CAMPION, Rose-cheeked Laura, come, page 152

Campion included this famous lyric in his polemic Observations on the Art of English Poesie (1602), in which he argued that English poets ought to adopt the quantitative meters of Greek and Latin. "This cannot be done in English," says John Hollander, "with its prominent word stress, save by assigning Latin vowel lengths to the written English, and simply patterning what amounts to a typographical code which cannot be heard as verse. . . . 'Rose-cheekt Lawra' is therefore merely an unrhymed English trochaic poem, perfectly plain to the ear" (introduction to Selected Songs of Thomas Campion, selected by W. H. Auden [Boston: Godine, 1973]).

WALTER SAVAGE LANDOR, On Seeing a Hair of Lucretia Borgia, page 153

In first printing Landor's poem in 1825 in the New Monthly, Leigh Hunt explained, "A solitary hair of the famous Lucretia

Borgia . . . was given me by a wild acquaintance who stole it from
a lock of her hair preserved in the Ambrosian Library at Milan."
(Lord Byron could very well have been the wild acquaintance.)
According to Hunt, when he and Landor had met in Florence, they had
struck up a conversation over the Borgia hair "as other acquain-
tances commence over a bottle."

Exercise: Meaningful Variation, page 153

    Aside from minor variations from metrical norm (such as the
substitution of a trochee for an iamb), the most meaningful
departures in these passages seem to occur in these words or
phrases:

    1. Dryden: deviates. (Now there's a meaningful deviation!)
    2. Pope: the spondees snake, drags, and slow length.
    3. King: like a soft drum.
    4. Longfellow: autumnal, and the last line, which we would
scan, "The CAT a ract of DEATH FAR THUN der ing from the HEIGHTS."
Wonderful arrangement of unstressed syllables in that line! Its
rhythm is like that of an avalanche bumbling around for a while
before rumbling down.
    5. Stevens: spontaneous, casual, ambiguous.

Exercise: Recognizing Rhythms, page 154

EDNA ST. VINCENT MILLAY, Counting-out Rhyme, page 154

A. E. HOUSMAN, When I was one-and-twenty, page 154

WILLIAM CARLOS WILLIAMS, The Descent of Winter (section 10/30),
page 155

WALT WHITMAN, Beat! Beat! Drums! page 155

    Probably it is more important that students be able to recog-
nize a metrical poem than that they name its meter. The Millay and
Housman poems are thoroughly metrical; the Williams and Whitman are
not, but include metrical lines when the poets are describing or
imitating the sound of something with a regular rhythm: the clank
of freight car wheels, the whistle's wha, wha, the beating of
drums. In Whitman's poem, besides the refrain (lines 1, 8, and 15)
there are the primarily iambic lines that end each stanza.

10

CLOSED FORM, OPEN FORM

      Beginning students of poetry often have a hard time appreci-
ating either a sonnet or a poem in open verse because they have yet
to distinguish one variety of poetry from the other. On first
meeting an unfamiliar poem, the <u>experienced</u> reader probably recognizes it as metrical or nonmetrical from its opening lines--perhaps
even can tell at first glance from its looks on the page (compact
sonnet or spaced-out open verse). Such a reader then settles down
to read with appropriate expectations, aware of the rules of the
poem, looking forward to seeing how well the poet can play by them.
But the inexperienced reader reads mainly for plain prose sense,
unaware of the rhythms of a Whitmanic long line or the rewards of a
sonnet artfully fulfilling its fourteenth line. Asked to write
about poetry, the novice reader may even blame the sonnet for being
"too rigid," or blame William Carlos Williams for "lacking music"
(that is, lacking a rime scheme), or for "running wild." Such
readers may have a right to their preferences, but they say nothing
about a poem, nor about the poet's accomplishment.
      That is why this chapter seems essential. To put across to
students the differences between the two formal varieties, it isn't
necessary to deal with every last fixed form, either. One can do
much by comparing two poems (closed and open) on the theme of
sorrow--Elizabeth Barrett Browning's fine sonnet "Grief" and
Stephen Crane's astonishing "The Heart"; possibly the two brief
elegies, Robert Herrick's "Upon a Child That Died" and Saint
Geraud's "Poem." Before taking up closed form, you might care to
teach some song lyrics--those in Chapter 7, or a couple of traditional folk ballads. That way the student isn't likely to regard
fixed forms as arbitrary constructions invented by English
teachers. A stanza, you can point out, is the form that words
naturally take when sung to a tune. That is how stanzas began.
Sing a second round of a song, and you find yourself repeating the
pattern of it.

CLOSED FORM: BLANK VERSE, STANZA, SONNET

JOHN KEATS, This living hand, now warm and capable, page 159

      After Keats's death, these grim lines were discovered in the
margin of one of his manuscripts. Robert Gittings has pointed out
that the burden of the poem is much like that of two letters Keats
wrote late in life to Fanny Brawne, charging her conscience with

159-165 (text pages)

his approaching death and blaming her for enjoying good health.
"This," says Gittings, "marks the lowest depths of his disease-
ridden repudiation of both love and poetry" (John Keats [Boston:
Atlantic-Little, 1968] 403). To discuss: can a repudiation of
poetry nevertheless be a good poem?

JOHN DONNE, Song ("Go and catch a falling star"), page 161

Maybe it is worth pointing out that, in bringing together
short stanzas to make one longer one, Donne hasn't simply joined
quatrain, couplet, and tercet like a man making up a freight train
by coupling boxcars. In sense and syntax, each long stanza is all
one; its units would be incomplete if they were separated.

RONALD GROSS, Yield, page 163

Fitting together drab and prosaic materials, Gross leaves them
practically unaltered. What he lends them are patterns that seem
meaningful. By combining traffic-sign messages in "Yield," he implies that the signs insistently pressure us with their yips and
barks. "Yield" states its theme implicitly: we are continually
being ordered to conform, to give in, to go along with laws laid
down for us. We must heed the signs in order to drive a car, but
perhaps it is chilling to find their commands so starkly
abstracted. Students might wish to discuss whether it is reading
too much into the poem to suspect that this theme applies to other
areas of our lives, not only to driving.
A discussion of Gross's work may be one of those rare sessions
that end with the students' realization that to remove speech from
its workaday contexts and to place it into lines is, after all,
what most poets do. Many poems, not only found poems, reveal
meanings by arranging familiar things into fresh orders.

Experiment: Finding a Poem, page 165

Timothy F. Walsh, of Otero Junior College in Colorado,
discovered another found poem in this book's previous edition:

"The sonnet,"
in the view of Robert Bly,
"is where old professors
go to die."

"It was fun," he writes, "to discuss found poems following my
students' reading about them on page 168, then point to one I found
just two pages later."

MICHAEL DRAYTON, Since there's no help, come let us kiss and part, page 166

Nay, yea, wouldst, and mightst are the only words that couldn't equally well come out of the mouth of a lover in the twentieth century.

There seems to be an allegorical drama taking place, as Laurence Perrine has pointed out in "A Drayton Sonnet," CEA Critic 25 (June 1963): 8. Love is also called Passion; and apparently his death is being urged along by the woman's infernal Innocence.

ELIZABETH BARRETT BROWNING, Grief, page 166

The octave may be forgettable, but the sestet is perhaps one of the eight or ten high moments in English sonnetry. "Grief" antedates the more famous Sonnets from the Portuguese (mostly composed in 1845 and 1846). In 1842, when working on "Grief" and some sonnet exercises, Mrs. Browning wrote to her friend Mary Mitford, "The Sonnet structure is a very fine one, however imperious, and I never would believe that our language is unqualified for the very strictest Italian form." But as Alethea Hayter has noticed, "Grief" isn't at all in the strictest Italian form; the shift in its argument comes in the middle of line 8. In her early sonnets, says Hayter, the poet seems to be "arranging roses now in a tall vase, now in a flat bowl, but always in something either too tall or just too shallow" (Mrs. Browning [New York: Barnes, 1963]). Still, in gratitude for the sestet of "Grief," we can accept many awkward roses.

See also "How do I love thee? Let me count the ways," page 286.

ARCHIBALD MacLEISH, The End of the World, page 167

What is the tone of this sonnet? Not at all grim, though the poet speaks of the most horrific event imaginable. Our pleasure in the poem comes from many elements besides its subject: its sounds (including rimes), its rhythm (metrical lines of even length), its portrait of a circus frozen in a split second, and its colossal pun in the top blew off (top meaning the "big top" or circus tent, perhaps also the lid of the enormous pot of all Creation). Whose are the "vast wings"? Nothingness's.

The octave, with its casual description of routine merriment, stands in contrast to the sestet, which strikes a note of awe. Perhaps the pale faces and dazed eyes of the circus spectators reflect the attitude of stunned wonder that the poet feels--or would have us feel. Obviously, to rearrange MacLeish's lines would be to weaken his poem. For one thing, the closing rimed couplet in the original throws great emphasis in the final nothing at all. In both sound and sense, "the black pall / Of nothing, nothing, nothing--nothing at all" seems more powerful than "canceled skies /

167-171 (text pages)

Of nothing. . . ." In this sonnet, as in Shakespeare's sonnets, the concluding couplet firmly concludes.

ALEXANDER POPE, MARTIAL, SIR JOHN HARRINGTON, WILLIAM BLAKE, E. E. CUMMINGS, J. V. CUNNINGHAM, JOHN FREDERICK NIMS, ROBERT CRAWFORD, PAUL RAMSEY, BRUCE BENNETT, a selection of epigrams, pages 168-170.

Not all epigrams come in rimed couplets, as Bennett's shows. Whether the form of an epigram is closed or open, brevity is of its essence; so is an arch tone and a final dash of wit.

Besides writing "Of Treason," called the best epigram in English, Harrington has another claim to immortality: he invented the water closet.

Cunningham, American master of the verse epigram in our time, has had few recent rivals. Instructors who wish further examples of this fixed form will find many to quote in his Collected Poems and Epigrams (Chicago: Swallow, 1971).

Nims, closest rival to Cunningham, has collected his epigrams, including "Contemplation," in Of Flesh and Bone (New Brunswick: Rutgers UP, 1967). When first printed, in The New Yorker, this poem was called "A Thought for Tristram"--suggesting that you means Isolde, betrothed of King Mark, with whom Tristan/Tristram shares a love potion.

If the haikulike brevity of epigrams tempts you to ask your class to write a few, resist the temptation. Even from a bright class the results are likely to depress you. A successful epigrammatist needs, besides the ability to condense, the ability to deliver that final rapier thrust of nastiness. A talented creative writing class, after tackling poems in a few of the less demanding forms (ballads, villanelles, sestinas) might try epigrams, either rimed or rimeless.

MARK TWAIN, A Limerick, page 171

A student or two will puzzle over Twain's abbreviations. Why not have a volunteer read this item aloud in class?

DYLAN THOMAS, Do not go gentle into that good night, page 171

No mere trivial exercise (as a villanelle tends to be), Thomas's poem voices his distress at the decline and approaching death of his father. At the time, the elder Thomas was a semi-invalid, going blind, suffering from the effects of tongue cancer. As a teacher of English at Swansea Grammar School, the poet's father had ruled his class with authority; but those who knew him only in his last years knew a different, humbled man. (See Constantine FitzGibbon, The Life of Dylan Thomas [Boston: Atlantic-Little, 1965] 294-95.)

Like many other Thomas poems, this one contains serious puns: good night, grave. "Another assumption in this poem," says Amy

Mulvahill (in a student paper written at Tufts), "may be Thomas's own self-destructive drive that led him to drink himself to death. It's possible that he preferred to taunt death with his boisterous life--to go down unrepentant and brawling."

Repetitious as a villanelle is, the form suits this poem, making its refrains sound like prayers said over and over. If you have any student poets, they might be challenged to write villanelles of their own. The hard part is to make the repeated lines occur naturally, to make them happen in places where there is something to be said. But the repetitious form is helpful. Write the two refrain lines and already your labors are eight nineteenths over.

For another instance of Thomas's fondness for demanding, arbitrary forms, see the poem "Prologue," at the beginning of Daniel Jones's edition of The Poems of Dylan Thomas (New York: New Directions, 1971). A poem of 102 lines, its first and last lines rime with each other, as do lines 2 and 101, 3 and 100, 4 and 99, and so on, until two riming lines collide in the poem's exact center. Except for that inmost pair of lines, no reader is likely to notice the elaborate rime scheme since rimes so far apart can't be heard; but apparently it supplied the poet with obstacles to overcome and with a gamelike pleasure.

OPEN FORM

WALT WHITMAN, Coffin that passes through lanes and streets, page 174

In this quotation from "When Lilacs Last in the Dooryard Bloom'd," the device of the word repeated at the beginning of each line is echoed by Allen Ginsberg in Howl. "I depended," Ginsberg has said, "on the word 'who' to keep the beat, a base to keep measure, return to and take off from again onto another streak of invention." (The New American Poetry, ed. Donald M. Allen [New York: Grove, 1960] 415.) Such a repetition is a kind of meter.

For further use of this device see Psalms 29:3-9 and 109 in the Bible, King James Version.

Roger Mitchell has discussed the stress pattern of this passage in "A Prosody for Whitman?" (PMLA 84 [Oct. 1969]: 1606-12.)

Late in life, Whitman made a revealing comment to W. R. Thayer: "Of course my poetry isn't formless. Nobody could write in my way unless he had the melody singing in his ears. I don't often contrive to catch the best musical combination nowadays; but in the older pieces I always had a tune before I began to write" ("Personal Recollections of Walt Whitman," Scribner's 65 [June 1919] 682).

E. E. CUMMINGS, Buffalo Bill's, page 176

Cleanth Brooks and Robert Penn Warren have taken this poem to be an admiring tribute to William Cody (Understanding Poetry, 3rd ed. [New York: Holt, 1960]). But Louis J. Budd, in an interesting dissent, thinks Cummings is satirizing the theatricality of the old sideshow straight shooter and finds Mister Death "a cosmic corporal gathering up defunct tin-gods and stuffed effigies" (The Explicator 11, [June 1953]: item 55).

EMILY DICKINSON, Victory comes late, page 177

     Of all Dickinson's poems, this is the most formally open, and as a result it sounds almost contemporary. Clearly the poet is in charge of her open form, for each line-break comes after a word that (being essential to meaning) easily stands for the special emphasis. We could imagine a few other possible locations for line-breaks. (After Love in the last line?--or would that make the poem seem to end in a riming couplet?) But no doubt the poet knew her own mind.
     Dickinson's outsized hyphens (or delicate minidashes) usually seem to indicate pauses, little hesitations, as if to give a word or phrase (whether following the dash or preceding it) special emphasis.
     If there is time to work further with this splendid poem, both language and meaning deserve a deeper look. Note the pun in line 3: rapt for "wrapped." In the next-to-last-line, keep seems a subjunctive verb: the statement may be a prayer. What sort of "Victory" does the poet mean? Thomas H. Johnson thought she referred to a Civil War battle, but we think this is one of her several poems concerned with reputation and fame. Perhaps the sparrows are minor poets, like Dickinson, unprinted and unacclaimed. Perhaps the Eagle is a famous bard glutted with renown: Ralph Waldo Emerson, maybe. The conclusion seems a bitter acceptance, as if to say: "God is wise not to feed me too generously." (Compare Kafka's story "A Hunger Artist"--certainly an analogy.) Ironically, the poem today seems literally true: Dickinson's victory has indeed come, although she cannot taste it.

ROBERT HERRICK, Upon a Child That Died, page 177
SAINT GERAUD (BILL KNOTT), Poem ("The only response"), page 178

     Herrick's metrically regular lines make his poem a kind of small, carefully crafted funeral urn of words. Its steady rhythms almost have the effect of a posthumous lullaby for the child. Knott's poem seems one in which freedom from artifice helps what is said: a direct, seemingly casual (and yet playful) statement of grief.

WILLIAM CARLOS WILLIAMS, The Dance, page 178

     Scanned, the poem is seen to abound in pairs of unstressed syllables. The result is a bouncing rhythm--anapestic or dactylic, depending on where one wishes to slice the lines into feet. This rhythm seems appropriate to a description of frolicking dancers and helps establish the tone of the poem, which is light, however serious.

Williams severs his units of sense again and again in midphrase: placing his line-breaks after and, the, about, thick-, those, such. In this poem run-on lines predominate, and this is not only a technical device but a way of underlining the poem's meaning. Williams conveys a sense of continuous movement in a syntax that keeps overflowing line units.

By repeating its opening line, the poem, like Breughel's dancers, comes round in a circle to where it began. Another metaphor is possible: like a painting enclosed in a frame, the poem encloses its central scene in a frame of words.

Williams first saw Breughel's painting in Vienna in 1924, but wrote this poem in 1942, some eighteen years later. A French critic, Jacqueline Saunier-Ollier, has speculated on the curious fact that the poem, in describing a vividly colorful tableau, omits all color images. Her work on Williams's Breughel poems is summed up in William Carlos Williams: Man and Poet, ed. Carroll F. Terrell (Orono: National Poetry Foundation, 1983) 528-29.

STEPHEN CRANE, The Heart, page 179

WALT WHITMAN, Cavalry Crossing a Ford, page 180

Two nineteenth-century American poems, the pair seem comparable mainly in brevity and use of narration. The assonance and internal alliteration in Whitman's phrase silvery river are echoed in the poem's very opening line: the assonance of the i-sound in line, wind, islands; the internal alliteration of the r in array, where, green. But any line of this short poem will repay such inspection. Crane's "The Heart" is obviously less heavy on verbal music, although Held his heart in his hands is heavily alliterative; and the second stanza favors the letter b. There is rime, too: it / bitter, bitter / heart.

Whitman seems to lambaste his poem with sound-effects in his enthusiasm for his grand military spectacle. Crane cares for music, too, and yet his is a subtler, harsher one. Although longer in words, Whitman's "Cavalry" contains fewer pauses than "The Heart" (fifteen compared to Crane's seventeen, if every comma and line-end counts as a pause). The result is, in Crane's poem, a much more hesitant, start-and-stop movement--appropriate, perhaps, to a study of self-immolation. Whitman apparently wants an expansive, continuous progress in his syntax, as in his cavalry.

WALLACE STEVENS, Thirteen Ways of Looking at a Blackbird, page 180

Suggestive as blackbirds may be, the theme of the poem is, "Pay attention to physical reality." Stevens chides the thin, ascetic men of Haddam who would ignore good blackbirds and actual women for golden phantasms. He also chides that asinine aristocrat who rides about Connecticut (of all places) in a glass coach as if thinking himself Prince Charming. The poem ends in a section whose tone is matter-of-fact flatness, rather as though Stevens were saying, "Well, here's the way the world is; if you don't like it, go read newspapers." Taken as a series of notes for an argument for literalism, this much-discussed poem seems to have unity and to lead to a definite conclusion. For another (and more complicated) view of it, see Helen Hennessy Vendler, On Extended Wings (Cambridge: Harvard UP, 1969).

Way-of-looking number 5 recalls Keats's "Grecian Urn": "Heard melodies are sweet. . . ."

Way number 10 eludes final paraphrase. Are the "bawds of euphony" supposed to be, perhaps, crass ex-poets who have sold out their Muses, who utter music to please the box office instead of truth? But blackbirds flying in a green light are so strikingly beautiful that even those dull bawds would be moved to exclaim at the sight of them.

GARY GILDNER, First Practice, page 182

Some possible answers to the questions:

1. Hill is a sadist. He is determined to render defenseless boys as bitter as he is.
2. The speaker doesn't want to identify himself with such a world-view; apparently, he wishes to remove it from himself by thrusting the hideous Hill away off in the third person.
3. The broken line indicates a pause--while the boy athletes suck in their breaths and don't dare answer.
4. Closure.
5. The rewrite would make Gildner's appalling poem seem neat, swingy, and jingly.
6. Poems don't have to traffic in moonlight and roses. Nothing in human experience need be alien to them--not even Hill.

In a recent comment on "First Practice," Gildner recalls that the poem came straight from his boyhood in the 1950s. When his parochial school (Holy Redeemer, grades one through eight) started a football team, an ex-Marine who had played ball in service volunteered to coach it. Practice was held in The Bomb Shelter, a thick-walled basement with a low ceiling. "Some of us later felt slimy and ashamed at hitting out like that--at being moved by Cliff's speech. And I know that many of us were more afraid to lose a game than to break a bone. . . . For years I tried to write a short story about this experience, but the attempts always sounded wrong, false. One day I decided to simply 'list' the story's important elements. Except for one unnecessary word, the poem 'First Practice" appeared" (comment in Poetspeak: In their work, about their work, ed. Paul B. Janeczko [Scarsdale: Bradbury, 1983] 39-41).

LEONARD COHEN, All There Is to Know about Adolph Eichmann, page 184

Like a "found poem," Cohen's list of the mass murderer's characteristics seems to take a preexisting structure (in this case, an application blank or a police blotter form); the poet has gone on to complete it. Read aloud, the lines ending in Medium and Ten sound as though rimed; and None / Ten is an off-rime. One way to state Cohen's theme: even a mass murderer is human, like you, like me. He does not walk around with fangs like a movie vampire. And by implication, perhaps, there is an element of evil in every human being. Let us not wax smug, or dismiss genocide as the invention of Hollywood.

BRUCE GUERNSEY, Louis B. Russell, page 184

Like a sonnet, a formally open poem may have a clear-cut structure, as "Louis B. Russell" demonstrates. Each stanza is a sentence in itself, closely similar in length. In the first two, Russell recalls his past; in the third, he takes in the present moment and looks forward to the day to come. In the second stanza, besides, he identifies himself with the seventeen-year-old whose heart he has received. Guernsey, incidentally, professed surprise when it was pointed out that his poem falls into three parts! But a poet does not need to select a structure consciously in order to fulfill it.

Having a new heart makes Russell feel like a young sprinter. In the metaphor-laden last stanza, heartbeat is juxtaposed with the clock's ticking and (more startlingly) with the beat of tightly held hammers. The tone of this poem is richly complicated. What does the central character feel? An elation mingled with wistful loneliness and perhaps, in the middle stanza, a certain guilty dread.

In question 3, the opinion seems too literal-minded and too rigidly bound by rules. The movement of this poem seems already strong; a regular heartbeat would seem unlikely to improve it.

"Louis B. Russell" is from Guernsey's collection January Thaw (U of Pittsburgh P, 1982).

CHRISTOPHER BURSK, First Aid at 4 a.m., page 185

A powerful short narrative poem, whose lines are broken meaningfully. Words and phrases that take emphasis (because line-breaks follow them) include choking; throat; around him; astonishingly strong; sobs; weakening body; Breathe, damn you; and breathe, daddy; half-saving his father; half-hanging on to him-- the most vital terms of the story and of its theme. Breaks also follow (and underscore) the cats' ironic meowing and waiting to be fed (while the protagonist chokes), and the ironic remarks "To die on the way to Pinocchio" and "To choke to death on aspirin."

185-187 (text pages)

The point of view is the father's, until in the last two lines
we seem to get the poet's insight--a realization larger and deeper
than might occur at the moment to a choking man.
    Among Bursk's collections are Standing Watch (Boston:
Houghton, 1978) and Little Harbor (Princeton: Quarterly Review of
Literature Contemporary Poetry Series 4, 1982). He teaches English
at Bucks County Community College in Pennsylvania.

FOR REVIEW AND FURTHER STUDY

LEIGH HUNT, Rondeau, page 186

    Jenny (so the story goes) was Jane (Mrs. Thomas) Carlyle, who
gave Hunt a buss when he brought word that one of Carlyle's books
had been accepted by a publisher.
    A true French rondeau has fifteen lines, and follows rules
more ingenious than those Hunt set for himself. For specifica-
tions, see Lewis Turco, The Book of Forms (New York: Dutton, 1968).

STEVIE SMITH, I Remember, page 187

    This poem keeps pulling rugs out from under us. From its
opening, we might expect some rollicking, roughly metrical ballad
or song, but then the short fourth line draws us up with a jolt.
Any reader still hoping for a conventional ballad might say line 4
rimes at least. However, the passage introducing the bombers
(lines 5-8) shatters any such anticipation. Far from songlike,
these prosaic lines sprawl, end in far-out feminine rimes (over-
head and Hampstead, perversely and Germany), and bring to mind the
artful outrages of Ogden Nash. With the Bride's question, the poem
unexpectedly returns to medium-length lines, and the rime that
clicks it shut (collide, bride) is masculine and exact once more.
Though full of surprises, this poem has less anarchy than order in
it.
    As its playful form indicates, "I Remember" is supposed to be
fun, yet at the same time it seems awful and ominous. John Simon
has made some provocative remarks about it in "The poems of Stevie
Smith," Canto 1 (Spring 1977): 197-98:

    This, you might well say, is poetry of low intensity or,
    simply, minor poetry. And yet, and yet! Why should a
    young girl marry an old man of 73? Because she is dying of
    consumption, and because it is wartime. The younger men
    are off to war, and may never come back. Even the old
    bridegroom and the tubercular bride may not live out their
    short remaining terms: the bombs may kill them first. The
    two of them may even desire such an ending; they have
    refused the relative safety of an air-raid shelter. . . .
    Are there perversely preposterous collisions in the sky?
    Can there be between our own so unalike selves so unlikely a
    collision, explosion, orgasm? . . . "I do not think it has

even happened," he said. Still, he must have hoped that it
might.

Smith's quiet, semireclusive life with her elderly aunt in
Palmers Green, North London, is the subject of a fine, sensitive
(but uneventful) film, Stevie, with Glenda Jackson playing the
poet, generally released in the United States in 1981. The
Collected Poems of Stevie Smith (New York: Oxford UP, 1976) is the
best edition. Many of the poems are illustrated with Smith's
sophisticatedly crude, somewhat macabre cartoons.

KEITH WALDROP, Proposition II, page 187

Like an epigram, this poem is concise, and the whole poem
leads up to a conclusive word: wind. Unlike an epigram, its
subject isn't human folly, and its apparent purpose may be to
express an insight, not to deliver a witty blow.

ELIZABETH BISHOP, Sestina, page 188

We would answer the questions like this.

1. That some terrible loss--a death in the family?--causes
the grandmother to weep seems a guess that fits the poem. The old
woman tries to hide her grief from the child (lines 6, 10, 31-32);
she thinks it was somehow foretold (9).
2. We have no authority to read this poem as autobiography,
but the figure of the grandmother--the most important person in
Bishop's early life--and the stormy setting (such as we might find
in a village on the Nova Scotia coast) invite us to do so. The
source of grief may have been the death of the poet's father
(hence, an irony that the child draws a man with tear-shaped
buttons) or it may have been the illness of her mother, hospital-
ized several times for a mental disorder. When Bishop was eight
months old her father died, and according to Robert Giroux, "The
first real home Elizabeth knew was in the coastal town of Great
Village, Nova Scotia, where her widowed mother returned in order to
be with her parents" (introduction to Bishop's Collected Prose [New
York: Farrar, 1984]). When the poet was five, her mother had a
final breakdown, leaving the girl in the care of her grandmother.
Apparently Bishop looked back on her days in Nova Scotia with
affectionate yearning. When she was six, her father's wealthy
parents moved her to Worcester, Massachusetts, for a less happy
stay.
3. Small round pieces of paper. Almanacs (such as The Old
Farmer's) come with punched holes to make them easy to string and
hang on a hook or a nail.
4. The playful ingenuity of the sestina, like that of the
villanelle, tempts a poet to wax clever; yet Bishop is writing a
deeply felt, moving poem in it. The tone is lightly serious,
compassionate--yet with touches of gentle humor: the Little Marvel

Stove, the child's drawings. Irony, too, informs the poem: a contrast between the grandmother's sorrow and the child's innocent ignorance.

5. Nims's comment seems an apt description of "Sestina." In the six repeated words, we are given the setting (house), the characters (grandmother, child), and key symbols (stove, almanac, tears). "Sestina" weaves all six into a subtle relationship. This poem is full of things that suggest magic: the prophetic almanac, the teacup (with which fortune-tellers divine), the "marvellous stove." It also is full of secret-keepers: the grandmother, the almanac with its powers of prophecy, the concluding reference to the "inscrutable house." The repetitions are worth tracing: tears, in particular, accumulates an effect. In stanza 2 the tears arrive like an equinoctial storm; in 3, the kettle also weeps; in 4, tea is tears; in 5, the man in the child's drawing wears tears; in 6, the almanac weeps paper tears; and finally, in the envoy, tears are flowers. "Time to plant tears" may be a literal quotation from the almanac, tears being (if memory serves) the name of a small white flower favored by rock gardeners.

Bishop's Complete Poems contains another intriguing sestina: "A Miracle for Breakfast." At the time it was written Bishop remarked (in a 1937 letter to Marianne Moore):

> It seems to me that there are two ways possible for a sestina--one is to use unusual words as terminations, in which case they would have to be used differently as often as possible--as you say, 'change, of scale.' That would make a very highly seasoned kind of poem. And the other way is to use as colorless words as possible--like Sidney, so that it becomes less of a trick and more of a natural theme and variations. I guess I have tried to do both at once. (Quoted by Nims in his essay, cited in question 5)

In the later "Sestina," the terminal words seem deliberately usual ones.

Experiment: Urgent Repetition, page 189

This experiment just might leave you surprised at the quality of some of its results. Whoever writes a sestina has a powerful ally--the form--on his or her side.

In a tour de force, a student I knew in a poetry workshop at Tufts once wrote a fairly successful sestina taking one, two, three, four, five, and six for its repeated words. The result seemed only mildly boring and mechanical!

GEOFFREY CHAUCER, Your yen two wol slee me sodenly, page 189

It can be great fun for students to learn (well, more or less) how to pronounce Chaucer's English, provided one has the time and

strength to help them make the attempt. One does much better by
Chaucer's lines if one puts on an Irish brogue. (A couple of
Guinness stouts before class usually help.)

Some scholars doubt that Chaucer himself wrote this poem; but
if he did not, someone who thoroughly knew Chaucer's work probably
did.

"Since I escaped from love, I've grown so fat . . ." is, of
course, a crude modernization of another poem from the "Merciles
Beaute" series. Carlos Baker offers another modern American
version of it in his book of poems, A Year and a Day (Nashville:
Vanderbilt UP, 1963).

Three dozen students who used the last edition responded to
our invitation to send in roundels beginning, "Your eyes present a
pin to my balloon. . . ." Some of the strongest entries came from
San Jose State University, Brevard Community College (Melbourne,
Florida), the University of Scranton, and Saint Lawrence University
(where Robert M. DeGraaff collected and passed along roundels in
great quantity). One of the least expected rimes came from Michael
Behan of Scranton: "Your smile's a drug from which there's no
withdrawal." At Brevard, Communications II section 3M collaborated
on an erotic version ("My ship was deep-sixed in your calm
lagoon"). Lin Mackenzie at Saint Lawrence followed the line "One
pointed look and I start growing small" with, "The way you glare
could tumble down a wall." Many others showed flashes of
inspiration.

Exercise: Seeing the Logic of Open Form Verse, page 190

E. E. CUMMINGS, in Just-, page 190

LINDA PASTAN, Jump Cabling, page 191

DONALD FINKEL, Gesture, page 191

CHARLES OLSON, La Chute, page 192

Cummings's poem is one of his "Chansons Innocentes," little
songs for children. In it, however, we meet a poet who is familiar
with the classics and who naturally associates spring with goat-
footed Pan. In Greek mythology, the god's pipes heralded the
return of Persephone, and caused birds and beasts to start up at
his call. In Cummings's view, he seems a kind of Pied Piper who
brings children running.

Line-breaks and capital letters in the poem seem designed to
emphasize particulars. Just-spring, capitalized, is the name of a
holiday: the moment when spring begins. Dividing its name with a
line-break gives it more importance, perhaps; and mud- / luscious
similarly takes emphasis. Why are the children's names telescoped
(eddieandbill, bettyandisbel)? So that these names will be spoken
rapidly, pell-mell, the way their owners run and the way children
speak about their friends. And when the lame balloonman completes
his transformation into Pan, the word goat-footed is framed with

white space on a line by itself. Except by putting it in capitals, the poet could hardly have thrown more weight on it.

Pastan, in telling us of two cars, divides each line and builds separate columns of words. The last line, all one, fits the proposed action (that the two merge) to the words. Jump cabling we take to be a metaphor for coitus. (For a similar comparison, see E. E. Cummings's well-known "she being Brand / -new," in his Complete Poems.) The playful "Jump Cabling" is starkly different in tone from Pastan's "Ethics" (page 6); it was first published in an anthology of light verse, Robert Wallace's Light Year '85 (Cleveland: Bits, 1984).

Finkel's "Gesture" arranges lines so that the reader's following eyes make movements like those described. The poem centers on a witty metaphor: a poet presenting a poem to a reader is like someone cracking a whip. Indentations in lines 6-9 roughly depict the path of the whip in uncoiling. Then the eye-arresting block of type--

snaps
softly

--brings the reader's eyes to a momentary halt, suggesting the crack of the whip. There's a small pause before the whip straightens and the poem goes on to end. Obviously, to be appreciated, this poem needs to be seen in print.

Charles Olson's "La Chute," like "in Just-," can be effective even if merely heard aloud. So many times repeated, the words drum and lute acquire impressive emphasis; and by repeating phrases and hesitating (who / will bring it up, my lute / who will bring it up where it fell), Olson makes his poem sound unrehearsed and conversational. White space seems used somewhat cryptically and arbitrarily, but it does throw great weight on my lute (line 7) and They (line 10), essential words that can take the emphasis. What is the poem saying? We take it to be (like "Gesture") a poem about poetry, with lute and drum representing the poet's talents. Well aware that he was the forefather of a poetic school (the Black Mountain poets), Olson may have foreseen his death and wondered who would carry on his work for him.

11

POEMS FOR THE EYE

For more examples of graphic poetry, consult the anthologies
edited by Klonsky and Kostelanetz (cited in footnotes to this
chapter). Other useful anthologies include Emmett Williams's
Anthology of Concrete Poetry (New York: Something Else, 1967),
Eugene Wildman's Chicago Review Anthology of Concretism (Chicago:
Chicago Review, 1967), Mary Ellen Solt's Concrete Poetry: A World
View (Bloomington: Indiana UP, 1969), and Emmett Williams's selec-
tion of "Language Happenings" in Open Poetry: Four Anthologies of
Expanded Poems, ed. Ronald Gross and George Quasha (New York:
Simon, 1973).

GEORGE HERBERT, Easter Wings, page 193

JOHN HOLLANDER, Swan and Shadow, page 194

     The tradition of the shaped poem, or Carmen figuratum, seems
to have begun in Renaissance Italy, and the form flourished
throughout Western Europe in the seventeenth century. English
practitioners of the form, besides Herbert, included Robert Herrick
(in "The Pillar of Fame") and George Puttenham.
     On "Easter Wings," Joan Bennett has remarked, "The shape of
the wings on the page may have nothing but ingenuity to recommend
it, but the diminuendo and crescendo that bring it about are
expressive both of the rise and fall of the lark's song and flight
(Herbert's image) and also of the fall of man and his resurrection
in Christ (the subject that the image represents)" (qtd. by F. E.
Hutchinson in his edition of Herbert's Works [Oxford: Oxford UP,
1941]). Visual shape and verbal meaning coincide strikingly when
the second stanza dwindles to Most thin.
     Like Herbert, Hollander clearly assumes that a word-shape has
to have a meaningful relation to what is said in it. His reflected
swan is one of twenty-five shaped poems collected in Types of Shape
(New York: Atheneum, 1969). Other graphic poems in the book
include a car key, a goblet, a beach umbrella, an Eskimo Pie, and
the outline of New York State. Paul Fussell, Jr., discussing
"Easter Wings" and Hollander's shaped poems, expresses reservations
about this kind of poetry. Most shaped poems, he finds, are
directed more to eyes than ears--"or better, we feel that the two
dimensions are not married: one is simply in command of the
other." But the greatest limitation in the genre is that there are
few objects that shaped poems can effectively represent: "their

81

shapes can reflect the silhouettes of wings, bottles, hourglasses, and altars, but where do we go from there?" (Poetic Meter and Poetic Form [New York: Random, 1965] 185-87). Students might be told of Fussell's view and asked to comment. A further disadvantage of most shaped poetry is that it cannot be heard aloud without loss.

WILLIAM BLAKE, A Poison Tree, page 196

Reproduced in approximately the same size as the original, Blake's engraving first appeared in his Songs of Experience (1794). According to the poet, he had long sought the best method for presenting his poems. At last it was revealed to him by his dead brother Robert in a dream. He was to engrave both poem and design on a copper plate and, when the pages were printed, outlines would be filled in with watercolors. Each copy would be a bit different from every other. Many editions of Blake's poems and drawings show this method. An inexpensive color facsimile of the first edition of Songs of Innocence has been issued by Dover (New York, 1971).

"A Poison Tree" seems one of Blake's more fortunate marriages of visual art with poetry. His illustration for his celebrated "Tyger" (page 282), also from the Songs of Experience, shows a beast much less formidable than the one we imagine from the words alone. A topic for discussion or writing: Should poetry be illustrated? or should a poem be left to the eye of the mind?

EDWIN MORGAN, Siesta of a Hungarian Snake, page 198

While too much can be made of this work, evidently it has sound values as well as eye appeal. Some brave volunteer might read it aloud. The initial sz sounds like the word Siesta. Perhaps the artist reverses the letters S and Z to make his line sound more like a snore (inhale: SZ--exhale: ZS). SZ looks and sounds like the end of an Eastern European name; perhaps that is why the snake is Hungarian.

Why the alternation of large and small letters? To look like stripes in the middle of the snake at his fattest part.

If a poem by definition is made of words, it may be questioned whether this concrete poem may be called a poem.

RICHARD KOSTELANETZ, Disintegration, page 199

The method of Kostelanetz is apparently to regard a word as a thing and to have its meaning befall it. Let students suggest a different word that might be turned into a similar one-word concrete poem.

Alternate suggestion: try making a concrete poem (perhaps drawing it on the blackboard) out of any one of the following words: explosion, revolution, interruption, repetition, diminution, exaggeration, conglomeration.

DORTHI CHARLES, Concrete Cat, page 200

This trifle first appeared in the second edition of An Introduction to Poetry and has been retained out of loyalty to the past.
While hunting for an illustration of the sillier kind of concrete
poem that simply and unfeelingly arranges words like so many
Lincoln Logs, XJK found the very thing in one of William Cole's
anthologies of humorous poetry: "Concrete Poem" by the British wit
Anthony Mundy. Mundy's work repeats miniskirt several times in the
form of a miniskirt, and tacks on a couple of legleglegleglegs. No
doubt he was parodying concrete poetry, too. But the cheapskate in
XJK rebelled at the thought of paying for permission to reprint
such a simple doodad, so decided to cut and paste together a homemade specimen. While constructing the cat, he started having some
fun with it, making the tongue a U, and so on. As far as we know,
however, the pun in the cat's middle stripe (tripes) is the only
place where language aspires toward poetry and becomes figurative.

12

SYMBOL

T. S. ELIOT, The <u>Boston Evening Transcript</u>, page 202

To help a class see the humor of Eliot's poem, try reading it aloud and pronouncing the name of the newspaper slowly and deliberately, in the dullest tones you can muster. This small gem can serve effectively to introduce an early, longer Eliot poem of spiritual desolation, "The Love Song of J. Alfred Prufrock" (page 303).

EMILY DICKINSON, The Lightning is a yellow Fork, page 203

Perhaps the poet would have added more punctuation to this poem had she worked longer on it; a rough penciled draft is its only surviving manuscript. Students may ask, Isn't the fork a symbol? No, it is the other half of a metaphor: what the lightning is like. The lightning (like most literary symbols) is a physical thing or event, reportedly seen. The Apparatus of the Dark (neither fork nor lightning) is whatever dimly glimpsed furniture this cosmic house may hold. The fork seems too simple an instrument to deserve the name of Apparatus. The lightning is doing the revealing, not itself being revealed.

THOMAS HARDY, Neutral Tones, page 205

Students usually like to sort out the poem's white, gray, washed-out, and ashy things. Can anyone think of a more awful description of a smile than that in lines 9-10? The God in line 2 seems angry and awe-inspiring. He has chided or reproved the sun, and caused it to turn pale in fear (like a schoolboy before a stern headmaster).
Line 8 is a stickler. In Hardy's first draft it read, "On which was more wrecked by our love." Both versions of the line seem awkward, and the present version is obscure, but probably the sense of this and the previous line goes: we exchanged a few words about the question, Which one of us had lost (suffered) the more by our love affair? (That is, after <u>which</u> we should mentally insert "of the two of us.")
For speculation about the facts behind "Neutral Tones," see Robert Gittings's fine biography, <u>Young Thomas Hardy</u> (Boston: Little, 1975) 86-93. Much has been guessed about the possible love

affair between young Hardy and his cousin Tryphena Sparks; but if
the woman in "Neutral Tones" was indeed real, no one has identified
her for sure.

Similar in imagery to "Neutral Tones" is this horrific line
from Hardy's novel The Woodlanders, chapter 4, when a poverty-
stricken woman, Marty South, sees her last hopes expire: "The
bleared white visage of a sunless winter day emerged like a dead-
born child" (cited by F. B. Pinion in A Commentary on the Poems of
Thomas Hardy [New York: Barnes, 1977]).

GEORGE HERBERT, Redemption, page 207

The old burdensome lease that the speaker longs to cancel is
original sin, which Christ, by his sacrifice (lines 12-14) allows
humankind to throw off. Who is the speaker? Humanity--or perhaps
(like Bunyan's Pilgrim) an individual soul in search of salvation.

What figure of speech is "a ragged noise"? (It's like the
"Blue - uncertain stumbling buzz" of the Emily Dickinson poem
discussed below.)

SIR PHILIP SIDNEY, You that with allegory's curious frame, page 208

This sonnet seems a classic expression of a poet's resentment
toward readers and critics who read needlessly profound meanings
into his lines--a valuable warning for students to heed when studying symbolism.

The second line may refer to a traditional folk belief. Like
an evil fairy, the hunter after allegory spirits away a natural
child and leaves a changeling--an odd, ill-favored, supernatural
brat--in its place.

EMILY DICKINSON, I heard a Fly buzz - when I died, page 208

Plump with suggestions, this celebrated fly well demonstrates
a symbol's indefiniteness. The fly appears in the room--on time,
like the Angel of Death--and yet it is decidedly ordinary. A final
visitor from the natural world, it brings to mind an assortment of
suggestions, some offensive (filth, stenches, rotting meat, offal,
and so forth). But a natural fly is a minor annoyance; and so is
death, if one is certain of Eternity. Unsure and hesitant in its
flight, the fly buzzes as though faltering. It is another failing
thing, like the light that comes through the windows and through
the eyes (which are, as a trite phrase calls them, "the windows of
the soul"). For other transferred epithets (like "Blue - uncertain
stumbling Buzz"), see pages 92-93 of the text, in the chapter on
figures of speech.

Most students will easily identify "Eyes around" as those of
surrounding friends or relatives, and "that last Onset" as death
throes. Is "the King" Death or Jesus? It seems more likely that
the friends and relatives will behold death. What is the speaker's

assignable portion? Physical things: keepsakes bequeathed to
friends and relatives; body, to the earth.

Discussion will probably focus on the final line. It may help
students to remember that the speaker is, at the present moment of
the poem, in Eternity. The scene she describes is therefore a
vision within a vision. Perhaps all the last line means is (as
John Ciardi has argued), "And then there was no more of me, and
nothing to see with." But to me the last line suddenly thrusts the
speaker to Heaven. For one terrible moment she finds herself, with
immortal eyes, looking back through her mortal eyes at a blackness
where there used to be light.

GJERTRUD SCHNACKENBERG, Signs, page 209

Signs, in the poet's sense of the word, seem plain indicators
of approaching doom, hardship, or loss. In the opening stanza,
lines in a hand await a palm-reader's interpretation. Students
should have little trouble seeing what the other signs foretell.

We wouldn't call these items symbols: their meanings seem too
specific and obvious. Dickinson's fly carries a larger cargo of
suggestions. (This comparison is not meant to put down "Signs," a
poem with a different purpose.)

To date, Schnackenberg has published two fine collections,
Portraits and Elegies (Boston: Godine, 1982) and The Lamplit Answer
(New York: Farrar, 1985). "Signs" comes from the more recent.

LOUIS SIMPSON, The Boarder, page 209

The most apparent symbols occur in the last stanza: the pale
stranger, paper roses, cracking ceilings. Like all good central
symbols, they point toward the poem's expressed theme: what a
mediocre, unimaginative life! The boarder, this mysterious
stranger, isn't part of a happy, mindless life (the But in line 9
cuts him off from it). Roses made of paper seem clearly inferior
to the real thing. Cracked ceilings, flawed, may well collapse.

In stanza 2, the full moon, that omen of romance, is reduced
to the level of a glass of Budweiser. Similarly, love is reduced
to trivial, conventional exclamations.

Both Simpson in "The Boarder" and Eliot in "The Boston Evening
Transcript" satirize a dull backwater of American life. Eliot
chides Boston Brahmins; Simpson, a small-town middle class. Still
another comparable poem is Wallace Stevens's "Disillusionment of
Ten O'Clock" (page 64).

CHRISTINA ROSSETTI, Uphill, page 210

This allegorical poem develops a conventional simile: life is
like a journey (shades of Pilgrim's Progress!). The road is the
path of life; the day, a lifespan; the inn at the end of the road,
the grave; other wayfarers, the dead; the door, the mouth of the

grave (or perhaps the gate of Heaven); the beds, cold clay (or perhaps Heavenly rest). The title suggests another familiar notion: that life is a struggle all the way.

One possible way to paraphrase line 14: "You'll find the end result of your lifelong strivings: namely, death, and the comfort of extinction." A more happily Christian paraphrase is possible, for Rossetti professed herself a believer: "Your labor shall bring you to your goal, the sight of the Lord." Without admitting the possibility of such a faith, the poem will seem grimmer and more cynical than it is.

Do these two characters seem individuals? Not in the least. This is a straight question-and answer poem, a dialogue between two stick figures.

"Oh No" (page 22) seems another poem about where you arrive when you die. Creeley, we suspect, kids a conventional notion of Heaven: he makes it a smug, artificial place where the saved sit around smirking at one another.

PHILIP DOW, Drunk Last Night with Friends, I Go to Work Anyway, page 210

Dow's bottled snail seems a hintful symbol. Surrounded not only by its shell but also by dreams (and its wine bottle), this particular mollusk is well insulated. Lazily vegetating, it reminds us of the speaker himself: helpless and stationary among the weeds, relieved of his duties, feeling unreal, and wrapped in his half-painful, half-comfortable hangover. He too feels small, sleepy, slimy, and stuck fast. Moreover, snail and bottle seem one. Discarded and empty, the bottle has come to hold something little and exquisite. That it is old recalls the boss who apparently still dreams of "strange dolls" from his hard-drinking past. Some may read this richly imaged poem by the light of experience: remembering the sensations of waking up with a throat like the throat of a wine bottle with a snail in it. In Dow's poem, the snail would appear to be a vision, an epiphany. Incidentally, the poet has mentioned snails in a note on himself written for an anthology: "Although I burn to know how the artist does it, poems remain miraculous to me as snails, ineluctable as the iron flute. . . . I write to celebrate" (Quickly Aging Here, ed. Geof Hewitt [New York: Anchor, 1969]).

"Drunk Last Night with Friends" appears in Dow's extremely good collection Paying Back the Sea (Pittsburgh: Carnegie-Mellon UP, 1979).

Exercise: Symbol Hunting, page 211

WILLIAM CARLOS WILLIAMS, Poem, page 211

THEODORE ROETHKE, Night Crow, page 211

JOHN DONNE, A Burnt Ship, page 212

211-212 (text pages)

WALLACE STEVENS, Anecdote of the Jar, page 212

"Night Crow" and "Anecdote of the Jar" contain central symbols; "Poem" and "A Burnt Ship" are to be taken literally.
(Apparently Donne is just delighting in the three paradoxes in his
last two lines.)

Students familiar with Stevens sometimes reason, "The jar is a
thing of the imagination, that's why it's superior to the wilderness—it makes order out of formless nature, the way Stevens thinks
art is supposed to do." But Stevens is constantly warning us of
the dangers of mind divorced from the physical world, and we think
he means this gray, bare, dominion-taking jar to be ominous. Who
could think a wilderness slovenly before it came along? Some
critics take the phrase of a port in air to mean a portal, "an
evanescent entry . . . to order in a scene of disorder" (Ronald
Sukenick, Wallace Stevens: Musing the Obscure [New York: New York
UP, 1967]). We read it differently: portly, imposing, pompous.
Although it is true that Stevens frequently raises the same philosophic or aesthetic questions, from poem to poem he keeps supplying
very different answers. See the brilliant essay on Stevens by J.
Hillis Miller in Poets of Reality (Cambridge: Harvard UP, 1965).

13

MYTH

Besides the poems in this chapter, other poems in the text
will readily lend themselves to the study of myth and its perva-
siveness in poetry.
Personal myths may be found in the poems of Blake; in Hardy's
"Convergence of the Twain" (page 311); and in certain poems of
Yeats outside this chapter, such as "Leda and the Swan" (page 133)
and "Sailing to Byzantium" (page 250).
Poems containing central references to familiar classical
myths are Cummings's "in Just-" (page 190), with its reincarnation
of the Great God Pan; Mark Alexander Boyd's "Cupid and Venus" (page
283); and Allen Ginsberg's "A Supermarket in California" (page
309). Christian mythos is of course inseparable from the
devotional poems of Donne and Herbert; from Hopkins's poems and
G. K. Chesterton's "The Donkey" (page 291); from Eliot's "Journey
of the Magi" (page 302) and Yeats's "The Magi" (page 382); from
Paul Zimmer's "The Day Zimmer Lost Religion" (page 20); from
Milton's sonnets; from the hymn by Cowper (page 294); and from many
more.
In this chapter, Thomas Hardy (in "The Oxen") and William
Wordsworth (in "The World Is Too Much with Us") sadly contemplate
myths in decline--a theme found also in William Stafford's "At the
Klamath Berry Festival" (page 363).

D. H. LAWRENCE, Bavarian Gentians, page 215

Written in 1929 when Lawrence was ill and nearing death, this
splendid poem has been read as a kind of testament. As Keith Sagar
has paraphrased it, "the poet's soul has been invited to the nup-
tials and accepts with joy." Dissolution offers not mere oblivion
but the promise of renewed life, the cyclical rebirth of both the
gentians and Persephone. (The Art of D. H. Lawrence [Cambridge:
Cambridge UP, 1966], 244-45.) Another famous poem of Lawrence's
last months, "The Ship of Death," may be read as a companion to
this.
Why is "Bavarian Gentians" a better title for the poem than
Lawrence's first thought, "Glory of Darkness"?

89

216-217 (text pages)

THOMAS HARDY, The Oxen, page 216

The legend that farm animals kneel on Christmas Eve is widespread in Western Europe. Hardy takes it to suggest the entire
Christian mythos, which "in these years" (since Darwin) few embrace
as did the "flock" of children and old people remembered in the
opening stanza. The gloom in line 15 may resemble the gloom of the
unbeliever, and its doleful sound is enforced by its riming with
coomb--like barton, a word from older rural speech.
     The tone of "The Oxen" is not hostility toward faith, but
wistfulness. Not exactly the village atheist Chesterton said he
was, Hardy in late life kept going to church and hoping for a
reconciliation between the Church of England and science-minded
rationalists.

WILLIAM WORDSWORTH, The World Is Too Much with Us, page 217

     As its sense and its iambic meter indicate, the opening line
calls for a full stress on the with.
     Wordsworth isn't arguing, of course, for a return to pagan
nature worship. Rather like Gerard Manley Hopkins blasting trade
in "God's Grandeur" (page 133), he is dismayed that Christians,
given to business and banking, have lost sight of sea and vernal
woods. They should pay less heed to the world, more to the earth.
What "powers" have they laid waste? The ability to open themselves
to nature's benevolent inspirations. Modestly, the poet includes
himself in the us who deserve reproof. The impatient outburst
("Great God!") is startlingly unbookish and locates the break in
sense between octave and sestet in an unconventional place.
     Compare Wordsworth's "Composed upon Westminster Bridge" (page
378) for a somewhat similar theme. For another comment on the
decline of certain traditional myths, see William Stafford's "At
the Klamath Berry Festival" (page 362).

WILLIAM BUTLER YEATS, The Second Coming, page 217

     The brief discussion in the book leaves several points
untouched. Students may be asked to explain Yeats's opening image
of the falcon and the falconer; to discuss the meaning of the
Blood-dimmed tide and the ceremony of innocence; to explain how the
rocking cradle at Bethlehem can be said to "vex" twenty centuries
to nightmare; and to recall what they know about the sphinx.
     In A Vision, Yeats sets forth his notion of the two eras of
history (old and new) as two intertwined conelike gyres, revolving
inside each other in opposing directions. He puts it succinctly in
a note for a limited edition of his poem Michael Robartes and the
Dancer (1921):

          The end of an age, which always receives the revelation
     of the character of the next age, is represented by the coming
     of one gyre to its place of greatest expansion and of the

90

other to that of its greatest contraction. At the present
moment the life gyre is sweeping outward, unlike that before
the birth of Christ which was narrowing, and has almost
reached its greatest expansion. The revelation which approaches will however take its character from the contrary
movement of the interior gyre.

Students can be asked to apply this explanation to "The Second
Coming." (In fact, this might be a writing assignment.)
   For other evidence of Yeats's personal mythology, direct stu-
dents to "Leda and the Swan" (page 133) and "Sailing to Byzantium"
(page 250). For alternative versions of "The Second Coming," see
Yeats's worksheets for the poem as transcribed by Jon Stallworthy
in Between the Lines: Yeats's Poetry in the Making (Oxford:
Oxford UP, 1963).

JOHN MILTON, Lycidas, page 219

   "Lycidas," for many students is formidable, and before teaching the poem, at least a half hour of class time will probably be
needed for preparation. Marlowe's "Passionate Shepherd" (page 335)
can be read first, to introduce a few pastoral conventions. At
least a smattering of information on the time and place of Milton's
elegy is helpful, if students are to see that their own lives (and
friendships) and Milton's life at Cambridge are not completely
remote from each other. A book useful for background is Lois
Potter's A Preface to Milton (New York: Scribner's, 1971),
especially 122-25. Many students are intrigued by mythology and
find that to read up on a flock of classical myths reveals much to
them, besides making them able to follow Milton's allusions. You
may wish to allow two class hours to the poem itself, enough time
to deal with only a few passages. Milton's powerful condemnation
of the false shepherds (lines 119-31) is usually a high point of
the poem for students, and students generally end with at least
some respect for Milton as a mythmaker.
   Michael Fixler has seen the poem's multifold allusions to myth
as one with its "unheard" or "unexpressive" music. "In myth
Orpheus sings even as his severed head, resting on his silent lyre,
races down the swift Hebrus. But in 'Lycidas' that song is
'unexpressive' in yet a further sense, being implicit, a part of
the allusion" ("'Unexpressive Song': Form and Enigma Variations in
Lycidas, a New Reading," Milton Studies 15 [1981]: 213-55).
   For the instructor who wishes further aid in reading the poem,
the amount of available criticism is, of course, vast. Modern
studies we have found valuable include Rosemond Tuve's "Theme,
Pattern, and Imagery in Lycidas," in Images and Themes in Five
Poems of Milton (Cambridge: Harvard UP, 1957); Jon S. Lawry's
"'Eager Thought': Dialectic in Lycidas," in Milton: Modern Essays
in Criticism, ed. Arthur E. Barker (Oxford: Oxford UP, 1965); and
Michael Fixler's discussion in Milton and the Kingdoms of God
(Evanston: Northwestern UP, 1964) 56-60.

14

ALTERNATIVES

THE POET'S REVISIONS

WILLIAM BUTLER YEATS, The Old Pensioner, page 226

WILLIAM BUTLER YEATS, The Lamentation of the Old Pensioner,
page 226

The first pensioner is a lackluster old coot; the later one,
strong-willed and defiant. In the "Lamentation" the speaker sees
his own ruin clearly and coldly: in line 14, he himself becomes
the broken tree. In context, <u>transfigured</u> is a splendid word; it
helps to transfigure the original feeble refrain, and in the new
refrain Time becomes a flesh-and-blood enemy. The 1890 version is
full of end-stopped lines; in the final poem, syntax tends to be
seamless: stanzas are whole sentences. About all that Yeats kept
from the 1890 version is the chair by the fire and one tree, the
dominant rime-sound and the stanza pattern. Perhaps by aging (and
by learning more of love and politics), Yeats came to know at first
hand how an old man feels.
     Another early poem Yeats completely recast is "The Sorrow of
Love." See The <u>Variorum Edition of the Poems of W. B. Yeats</u> (New
York: Macmillan, 1957).

WALT WHITMAN, A Noiseless Patient Spider, page 229

WALT WHITMAN, The Soul, reaching, throwing out for love, page 229

     In revising "The Soul, reaching," Whitman scrapped all but the
first two lines; then extended their metaphor into a whole poem.
In doing so, he slightly changed his original conception and in its
finished form, "A Noiseless Patient Spider" isn't a poem about
human beings reaching out in love to other human beings, but about
the soul trying to form contact with higher reality.
     "A Noiseless Patient Spider" may be used effectively in dis-
cussing symbolism in poetry, as well as figures of speech.
Whitman's poem is open in form, and yet certain lines fall into
traditional measures (almost into rime, too), as would be indicated
by rearranging them:

     Till the bridge you will need be form'd
     Till the ductile anchor hold,

Till the gossamer thread you fling
Catch somewhere, O my soul.

TRANSLATIONS

FEDERICO GARCÍA LORCA, La guitarra (Guitar), page 230

The translator's liberty with Lorca's lines 23-24 seems well
taken: "on the branch" would be weaker as a line by itself than
"and the first dead bird on the branch."
Lorca's poem comes from his Poema del cante jondo (1921), an
early sequence of brief lyrics based on traditional folk music.
The cante jondo ("deep song") was an Andalusian form related to
flamenco; and in 1922 Lorca and composer Manuel de Falla organized
a festival of the cante jondo, offering prizes for new songs in the
old tradition.
Carl W. Cobb has suggested that the "Heart heavily wounded /
by five sharp swords" is the guitar itself, struck by the player's
five fingers (Federico García Lorca [New York: Twayne, 1967]).

Exercise: Comparing Translations, page 231

HORACE, Odes I (38), page 231

WILLIAM COWPER, Simplicity, page 231

HARTLEY COLERIDGE, Fie on Eastern Luxury! page 232

EUGENE FIELD, The Preference Declared, page 232

Cowper's neoclassical translation seems fair both to the tone
of Horace's poem and to its sense. Cowper rearranges ideas to make
his rimes come out right (ringing in "Thus outstretched beneath my
vine" rather early) and to emphasize the boy rather than the
drinker. He does not adorn, however, and he preserves the
simplicity of style of the original.
The work of Hartley Coleridge (the son of Samuel Taylor
Coleridge) had moments of felicity, but this translation is not one
of them. He expands the original eight lines to twelve, falls into
awkward syntax in the entire second stanza, and chooses a diction
that exhibits the "studious pomp" Horace would avoid (toilsome
pain, mis-seems).
Vigorous and direct, Field's irreverent version is a small
masterpiece of speaking colloquially inside tight metrical verse.
Obviously, however, Field shatters the tone of the original. That
the author of such sentimental mawkishness as the famous "Little
Boy Blue" often could write this well is also evident in Field's
other translations from Horace, published with his brother Roswell
Martin Field in Echoes from the Sabine Farm (New York: Scribner's,
1896). (XJK offers some gratitude for this neglected book in The
Carleton Miscellany, Fall 1963.)

232-234 (text pages)

    Interesting translations of this famous ode are plentiful:
the Poems of Gerard Manley Hopkins contains a bookish one ("Ah
child, no Persian--perfect art! / Crowns composite and braided bast
. . .). Cowper made another version of the poem, apparently, like
Campion's "Rose-cheeked Laura," an attempt to write English
Sapphics (the Greek measures that Horace was imitating):

        Boy! I detest all Persian fopperies,
        Fillet-bound garlands are to me disgusting,
        Task not thyself with any search, I charge thee,
            Where latest roses linger;
        Bring me along (for thou wilt find that readily)
        Plain myrtle. Myrtle neither will disparage
        Thee occupied to serve me, or me drinking
            Beneath my vine's cool shelter.

            (from Cowper's Poems of 1815, ed. John Johnson)

CHARLES BAUDELAIRE, Recueillement (Meditation), page 232

LORD ALFRED DOUGLAS, Peace, be at peace, O thou my heaviness, page
233

ROBERT BLY, Inward Conversation, page 233

ROBERT LOWELL, Meditation, page 233

RICHARD HOWARD, Meditation, page 234

    These four translations from Baudelaire exhibit divergent
fashions. Douglas keeps the music while high-handedly changing the
sequence of ideas; his version has a most Swinburnean fin-de-siècle
tinge ("To pluck the fruits of sick remorse and fear").
Personally, we like Douglas's version the best of the
four--considered as English poetry. The opening line does not say
what Baudelaire says, but it is splendid in music and sense. The
ending, too, seems an inspired distortion, worthy of Edward
FitzGerald.
    Bly's translation is a combination of invention and fidelity.
The opening line seems wordy, gauche, and inaccurate. Bly's rotten
herds are far cruder than Baudelaire's multitude vile, and we
confess ourselves unable to understand what a lyncher without touch
is. Bly's version improves as it goes along, both as a translation
and as an English poem. The sense of loss in line 11 is a fine way
to render Regret, and the last three lines, lovely in English, seem
to come closer to the tone of Baudelaire's original than either
Douglas or Lowell does. On general principle, Bly refuses to
translate rimed metrical verse into rimed metrical verse. At the
end he is able to keep the sense of Baudelaire's poem though the
music is drastically altered.
    Lowell's version is from his collection of Imitations, where
it is offered not as a faithful translation but as a free

adaptation. It is very close in sense, however, to the original. Here and there, Lowell adds a characteristic stroke of his own: the addition of the metaphor in <u>coffined</u> (line 3), the blunt rendering of <u>robes surrannés</u> as <u>old clothes</u> (line 10). Though a close cognate of <u>marche</u>, the last word, <u>march</u>, with its military connotations, seems an unfortunate choice. But Lowell's translation occupies the middle ground between fidelity and free improvisation and manages to convey some sense of the music of the original.

Richard Howard's new rendering of <u>Les Fleurs du Mal</u> (Boston: Godine, 1982) has proved a surprise best-seller for its publisher and has won generous praise. A professional translator of Gide, Camus, Genet, de Beauvoir, Perse, Barthes--about 150 French books altogether--Howard has given us what may be the most finely accurate translation of the nasty <u>Fleurs</u> to date, not counting prose paraphrases. Beautifully, Howard communicates the sense of the poems, that is, their silliest part, while conveying little sense of the most impressive part: Baudelaire's music. By and large, Howard ignores the rime and meter of the original, on occasion letting a rime occur but usually going out of his way to avoid any. The product is a Baudelaire who sounds like most current contributors to <u>American Poetry Review</u>, a helpful and sensitive crib for readers who know some French.

These general reservations aside, Howard's "Meditation" seems among his more satisfying versions, done with something of the rhythm of the original. The opening lines are brisk and colloquial; the ending is lovely--how much better to make the night arrive than, as Lowell does, to make it march! And "dear departed dowdy years" is an inspired touch--one of the few places where Howard adds something, and makes up for some of what, in any translation, must inevitably be lost.

PARODY

Ezra Pound, in his <u>ABC of Readings</u>, urges students of poetry to write parodies of any poems they find ridiculous, then submit their parodies to other students to be judged. "The gauging pupil should be asked to recognize what author is parodied. And whether the joke is on the parodied or the parodist. Whether the parody exposes a real defect, or merely makes use of an author's mechanism to expose a more trivial content."

T. E. BROWN, My Garden, page 235

J. A. LINDON, <u>My</u> Garden, page 235

With a few thrusts of his rake, Lindon punctures Brown's high-falutin language (<u>wot</u> and <u>grot</u> are the most flagrantly "poetic"), his overwrought reliance on exclamation points, and the shaky logic he uses to prove the existence of God. Of the two, the parody is unquestionably the better poem.

95

235-236 (text pages)

HUGH KINGSMILL, What, still alive at twenty-two?, page 235

   Kingsmill's insistence on dying young suggests "To an Athlete
Dying Young" (page 323), but the parodist grossly exaggerates
Housman's hint of nihilism. Like bacon, Kingsmill's lad will be
"cured"--of the disease of life. (And how often Housman himself
says lad, by the way.) In his tetrameter couplets, Kingsmill
echoes "Terence, this is stupid stuff" (page 321). His
metaphysical conceit of ink and blotting pad coarsens Housman's
usual view of night and day. (Some comparable Housman lines, from
"Reveille": "Wake: the silver dusk returning / Up the beach of
darkness brims, / And the ship of sunrise burning / Strands upon
the eastern rims."

KENNETH KOCH, Mending Sump, page 236

   Perhaps it would be well to read aloud Frost's "Mending Wall"
before having students read Koch's hatchet job. To appreciate
Koch's allusions to Frost, students also might hear a little of
"The Death of a Hired Man." It is often included in high-school
textbooks but may not be familiar to all students.

GEORGE STARBUCK, Margaret Are You Drug, page 236

   "Margaret Are You Drug" is a deliberately crass, lowbrow,
American version of Hopkins's "Spring and Fall" (page 319).

15

EVALUATING A POEM

TELLING GOOD FROM BAD

Ezra Pound long argued for the value of bad poetry in peda-
gogy. In his ABC of Reading, Pound declared that literary
education needs to concentrate on revealing what is sham, so that
the student may be led to discover what is valid. It is a healthy
gesture to let the student see that we don't believe everything
contained in a textbook to be admirable. Begin with a poem or two
so outrageously awful that the least sophisticated student hardly
can take it seriously--some sentimental claptrap such as Cook's
"The Old Arm-Chair." From these, you can proceed to subtler
examples. It is a mistake to be too snide or too self-righteous
toward bad poems, and it is well to quickly turn to some excellent
poetry if the classroom starts smelling like a mortuary. There is
a certain sadness inherent in much bad poetry; one can readily
choke on it. As Allen Tate has said, the best attack upon the bad
is the loving understanding of the good. The aim in teaching bad
poetry has to be the admiration of good poetry, not the diffusion
of mockery.

One further suggestion on bad poetry: a program of really
execrable verse orated with straight faces by a few students and
members of the faculty can be, with any luck, a fine occasion. For
bad poems to work on besides those offered in this chapter, see the
dustier stacks in a library or the following anthologies: Heart
Throbs and More Heart Throbs, ed. Joe Mitchell Chapple (New York:
Grosset, 1905 and 1911 respectively; many later editions); The
Stuffed Owl: An Anthology of Bad Verse, ed. D. B. Wyndham Lewis
and Charles Lee (London: Dent, 1930; reprinted in the United States
by Capricorn paperbacks); Nematodes in My Garden of Verse, ed.
Richard Walser (Winston-Salem: Blair, 1959); Worst English Poets,
ed. Christopher Adams (London: Wingate, 1958); and Pegasus
Descending: A Book of the Best Bad Verse,ed. James Camp, X. J.
Kennedy, and Keith Waldrop (New York: Macmillan, 1971).

ANONYMOUS, O Moon, when I gaze on thy beautiful face, page 240

Glorious behind seems inexact, and so does boundaries for
"boundlessness."

97

241-242 (text pages)

GRACE TREASONE, Life, page 241

    Treasone's poem develops a central metaphor, but its language
is wildly imprecise. Is the tooth "that cuts into your heart"
one's own or somebody else's? (It is probable that the poet means
not tooth but "toothache.") Anatomically, the image seems on a par
with the "heart's leg" of the tradesman poet quoted by Coleridge
(page 243). Through the murk of her expression, however, the poet
makes clear her theme: the familiar and sentimental notion that
life is really all right if you see it through (or have a competent
dentist).
    Treasone's item first adorned a Dover, New Jersey, newspaper
column of local poets called "This Way to Parnassus."

M. KRISHNAMURTI, The Spirit's Odyssey, page 241

    Rimes can hardly be more rudely forced than these, especially
sudden-truth'd, slumber-sooth'd--as reading the poem aloud will
reveal. Question 2 is probably unanswerable, even by those well
learned in Eastern religions.
    "The Spirit's Odyssey" is a self-contained part of a
book-length sequence, The Cloth of Gold, a "mystical dance-drama"
(Rutland: Tuttle, 1950).

STEPHEN TROPP, My Wife Is My Shirt, page 241

    To give this item the benefit of doubt, its metaphor is elabo-
rated consistently; but is hard to see anatomically. To compare
the shirt-sleeves to the wife's armpits and the shirt's neck to her
mouth, rather than to other parts of her, seems arbitrary. In a
personification an inanimate object is seen as human. In "My Wife
Is My Shirt" a person is seen as an inanimate object.
    If this paraphrase of his idea is a fair one, Tropp does not
get it across at all. The buttoning of the blood--a thoughty and
ingenious figure--seems merely horrible. Tenderness is lost.
    This poem appears in Beat Coast East: An Anthology of
Rebellion (New York: Excelsior, 1960) and may be a relic of a kind
of work once fashionable, in which the poet tries to turn off his
feelings and to "play it cool." Whatever the poet's intentions,
the result is bathetic. All we know about Tropp comes from a note
in a poetry magazine that said he lived in New York City and had a
little boy named Tree.

EMILY DICKINSON, A Dying Tiger - moaned for Drink, page 242

    This is not, by any stretch of critical imagination, a good
poem. Besides the poet's innocent lack of perception that His
Mighty Balls can suggest not eyeballs but testicles, the concluding
statement (that the fact that the tiger was dead is to blame) seems
an unDickinsonian failure of invention. Perhaps the poet intended

a religious allegory (Christ the Tiger). Her capitalization of <u>He</u> in the last line doesn't seem sufficient proof of such intent, for her habits of capitalization cannot be trusted for consistency.

The failures of splendid poets are fascinating. As in this case, they often seem to result from some tremendous leap that sails over and beyond its object, causing the poet to crash to earth on the other side.

<u>Exercise</u>: Seeing What Went Wrong, page 242

1. "I'm Glad" takes a crassly mechanistic view of the universe: sky and earth are slapped with coats of paint, air is a sandwich. Trite, padded diction: <u>nice fresh air</u>.

2. Mills forces his rime, shaving the <u>s</u> from <u>always</u>.

3. The image of a heart with a leg is <u>ludicrous</u>.

4. Apparently the poet says <u>dashes</u> only because it rimes with <u>ashes</u>, even though it completely disrupts the tone of a stately elegy.

5. Maynell's second line is redundant: what else besides sheep would a shepherdess tend?

6. Dryden's lines suffer from excessive ingenuity, in imitation of the metaphysical poetry of Cleveland and others current in his youth. The image of the tearful pimple sentimentalizes this little pustule.

7. Sappy, simpleminded sentiment. The rimes seem hairy, except for <u>fan</u> / <u>Diane</u>. This is verse devoid of practically any element of poetry.

8. Guest falls into a wildly inappropriate hippety-hop rhythm, and the unfortunate connotations of <u>scum</u> louse up the lofty tone of his platitude.

9. Johnson deliberately gives us a simpleminded, stupid, narrative in a monotonous rhythm. Fond of Latinate diction, he may have been trying to illustrate the perils of writing in words of one syllable.

10. Chivers, a friend and imitator of Poe, weaves a language so ornate that it often turns incomprehensible. Who can define a <u>Cydonian sucket</u>? Who has seen a glowing <u>chrysoprase</u>? The rime <u>suckets</u> / <u>buckets</u> seems unintentionally comic; and the image of the "wild emerald cucumber tree" reduces the poem to nonsense by suggesting the poet's terrible distance from the real world of cucumber vines. The model, of course, is Poe's "Annabel Lee."

11. The rime <u>leave her</u> / <u>Scarlet Fever</u> is unintentionally funny, and the poet repeats with enormous emphasis dull words with dismal connotations.

ROBERT BURNS, John Anderson my jo, John, page 245

Strange to tell, Burns's genuinely touching poem is a polite revision of a bawdy folk song he had found in an old songbook. It goes in part: "John Anderson, my jo, John / When first that ye began, / Ye had as good a tail-tree, / As any ither man." For the

245-249 (text pages)

whole of the original see Burns's <u>The Merry Muses of Caledonia</u>, ed.
James Barke and Sydney Goodsir Smith (New York: Capricorn, 1965)
147-48.

ROD McKUEN, Thoughts on Capital Punishment, page 246

WILLIAM STAFFORD, Traveling Through the Dark, page 246

    McKuen is still popular with some students, and any dogmatic
attempt to blast him may be held against you. There may be value
in such a confrontation, of course; or you can leave evaluation of
these two works up to the class. Just work through McKuen's
effusion and Stafford's fine poem, detail by detail, in a
noncommittal way, and chances are good that Stafford will win the
contest.
    It may not be apparent that Stafford's poem is ordered by a
rime scheme from beginning to end: <u>abcb</u> stanzas and a final
couplet. Stafford avoids obvious rimes in favor of the off-rimes
<u>road</u> / <u>dead</u> and <u>engine</u> / <u>listen</u> and the cutoff rimes <u>killing</u> /
<u>belly</u>, <u>waiting</u> / <u>hesitated</u>, and <u>swerving</u> / <u>river</u>--this last a
device found in some folk ballads. McKuen's poem announces an
obvious rime scheme but fails to complete it. Unlike Stafford, he
throws rime out the window in the end, with the effect that his
poem stops with a painful inconclusiveness.
    Stafford contributes a long comment on his poem to <u>Reading</u>
<u>Modern Poetry: A Critical Introduction</u>, ed. Paul Engle and Warren
Carrier (Glenview: Scott, 1968).

<u>Exercise</u>: Fine or Shoddy Tenderness, page 247

HART CRANE, My Grandmother's Love Letters, page 247

ELIZA COOK, The Old Arm-Chair, page 248

D. H. LAWRENCE, Piano, page 249

ALFRED, LORD TENNYSON, Tears, Idle Tears, page 249

    Like a mother's old arm-chair, Crane's subject might well
invite mawkishness. Starting work on the poem, Crane knew that he
risked sentimentality. "I don't want to make the dear old lady too
sweet or too naughty," he wrote to a friend, "and balancing on the
fine line between these two qualities is going to be fun" (<u>Letters</u>,
ed. Brom Weber [New York: Hermitage, 1952] 22). Unlike a sentimen-
talist, he observes the very paper these letters are written on:
"brown and soft / And liable to melt as snow." Nor does Crane give
us a tear-jerking portrait of dear old Grandma herself. As John
Unterecker has pointed out, this poem evokes the grandmother
without describing her, "assigning her qualities to remembered
stars, to soft rain, to insubstantial snow, to gentle laughter, to
music thought about--not played" (<u>Voyager: A Life of Hart Crane</u>

[New York, Farrar, 1969] 153). Sentimentality is avoided, too, by the final image of the rain on the roof: a slightly mocking, gently ironic commentary.

Cook's "The Old Arm-Chair" seems flagrantly sentimental. Unless one is prone to weep spontaneously at the mere mention of the word mother, it is hard to take part in this teary bath. The mother is sainted, hallowed (we are told), but we do not see her clearly as a person. Like D. H. Lawrence in "Piano," Cook describes the way a mother looks to a child, but she does so without Lawrence's awareness that a mature mind could find a discrepancy between child's and adult's point of view. Though Cook evidently realizes that others may find her devotion to the armchair foolish, she is not about to give it up: "who shall dare / To chide me . . .?" she asks, with chip on shoulder. Far from communicating a sense of reality, she employs distracting hyperboles: "'Tis bound by a thousand bands to my heart"; tears are "a lava tide." Sentimental poets like Cook tend to care more about their own grief than about what inspired it. Here, the poet glorifies her own sighs that embalmed the chair (surely a word chosen with little awareness of its connotations of undertaking).

Who was Eliza Cook? An English poet (1818-89) once popular. "The Old Arm-Chair" won such high acclaim in its time that the poet followed it with "The Old Farm-Gate," "I Miss Thee, My Mother," and others of the ilk. Lewis and Lee have an irreverent account of her and her work in their anthology of bad verse, The Stuffed Owl (London: Dent, 1930).

"Piano" is not a flawless poem. Lawrence was seldom at ease in rime, and the strained rime clamor / glamor indicates his discomfort. (However, glamor is in its context an accurate word: it implies that the mature man knows that the child's eyes cast an illusory beauty upon the past, as does memory.) In general, the superiority of Lawrence's poem to Cook's may be seen in the specificity of his descriptions: "the boom of the tingling strings," "the small, poised feet." Lawrence enters into the child's perspective. Moreover, the speaker is resisting his urge to cry-- as the connotations of his words indicate (the song is insidious; it betrays). But at last, he is unable to prevent his tears and, sensibly, yields to them. Cook's speaker coaxes them forth and goes wading in them.

How does Lawrence's poem escape bathos? Lately, Robert Pinsky has offered a detailed explanation in his essay "Poetry and Pleasure," worth looking up in Threepenny Review for Fall 1983. The subject of "Piano," Pinsky finds, is a stock source for poems, "as mothers-in-law or airplanes with ethnically various passengers are stock sources for jokes." Yet the poem pierces us with "something fresh, not stock." Its language is vivid, nonconventional ("tingling strings . . . small, poised feet"); its words insidious and betrays add a "steely spring"; it sets up an energetic tension between present and past. In the same issue of Threepenny Review, D. L. Emblen comments further on "Piano," and discusses an earlier version of the poem that Lawrence left in manuscript.

247-249 (text pages)

Tennyson's famous song from The Princess differs from
sentimental poetry in that the tears start from adequate cause:
the passage of time, the loss of "days that are no more." Far from
sentimental, too, are the poem's host of concrete, specific images:
the "first beam glittering on a sail" of a ship from the underworld, the "earliest pipe of half-awakened birds," the "glimmering
square" of a casement seen through dying eyes.

A classic study of this poem, revealing of its depths, is
Cleanth Brooks's "The Motivation of Tennyson's Weeper" in The Well
Wrought Urn (New York: Harcourt, 1947). That the tears are
"idle," Brooks reasons, indicates that they spring from no
immediate specific grief, but from a deeper cause that the poem
goes on to discover. The poem would have failed, thinks Brooks, if
for the weeper the past had remained (as, we might suppose, it
remains for the weeper in "The Old Arm Chair") "melancholy but
dimmed, sad but worn and familiar." But the experiences recorded
in the poem are those of shock, of the vivid realization of
ever-fresh loss, of intense regret for something ended (or
missed?): wild, passionate life.

Perhaps the idea in Tennyson's last line is similar to that in
Brad Leithauser's "Trauma": the sorrowful past never passes, it
just amasses, becoming Death in Life.

KNOWING EXCELLENCE

WILLIAM BUTLER YEATS, Sailing to Byzantium, page 250

Has XJK implied that this poem is a masterpiece so far beyond
reproach that no one in his right mind can find fault with it?
That is, of course, not the truth. If the instructor wishes to
provoke students to argument, he might read them the withering
attack on Yeats's poem by Yvor Winters (Forms of Discovery
[Chicago: Swallow, 1967] 215-16). This attack really needs to be
read in its entirety. Winters is wrong, we believe, but no one can
begin to answer his hard-headed objections to the poem without
being challenged and illuminated.

Other discussions of the poem, different from XJK's and also
short, include Richard Ellmann's in Yeats: The Man and the Masks
(New York: Macmillan, 1949) and John Unterecker's in A Reader's
Guide to William Butler Yeats (New York: Noonday, 1959). Those
who wish to go deeper still and to read a searching examination
(informed by study of Yeats's manuscripts) can be directed to
Curtis Bradford, "Yeats's Byzantium Poems," PMLA 75 (Mar. 1960):
100-25. For those interested in alternatives, Jon Stallworthy
reprints nearly all the legible manuscript versions in Between the
Lines: Yeats's Poetry in the Making (Oxford: Clarendon, 1963)
87-112.

A deconstructionist reading of "Sailing to Byzantium," sub-
jecting the poem to relentless questioning, showing where it fails
to make sense and how it doesn't work, is offered by Lawrence I.
Lipking in "The Practice of Theory" (in Profession 83: selected
articles from the Bulletins of the Association of Departments of

English and the Association of Departments of Foreign Languages,
MLA, 1983). But in his role as a poststructuralist, Lipking
confesses himself "a sheep commissioned to say something
sympathetic about wolves." He finds deconstructionist tactics
offending his students, especially bright idealistic ones who
expect their teachers to show them why certain works are great, and
who wish poems to 'make sense' and to relate to their own lives.

Exercise: Two Poems to Compare, page 253

ARTHUR GUITERMAN, On the Vanity of Earthly Greatness, page 253

PERCY BYSSHE SHELLEY, Ozymandias, page 253

    The title of Guiterman's bagatelle playfully echoes that of a
longer, more ambitious poem: Samuel Johnson's "The Vanity of Human
Wishes." If Guiterman's achievement seems smaller than Shelley's
in "Ozymandias," still, it is flawless. "Ozymandias," although one
of the monuments of English poetry, has a few cracks in it. Many
readers find line 8 incomplete in sense: the hand that fed what,
or fed on what? From its rime scheme, we might think the poem a
would-be Italian sonnet that refused to work out.
    Nevertheless, Shelley's vision stretches farther than Guiter-
man's. Ozymandias and his works are placed at an incredibly
distant remove from us. The structure of the poem helps establish this remoteness: Ozymandias's words were dictated to the
sculptor, then carved in stone, then read by a traveler, then told
to the first-person speaker, then relayed to us. Ironies abound,
more subtle than Guiterman's. A single work of art has outlasted
Ozymandias's whole empire. Does that mean that works of art endure
(as in "Not marble nor the gilded monuments")? No, this work of
art itself has seen better days, and soon (we infer) the sands will
finish covering it. Obviously, the king's proud boast has been
deflated, and yet, in another sense, Ozymandias is right. The
Mighty (or any travelers) may well despair for themselves and their
own works, as they gaze on the wreckage of his one surviving
project and realize that, cruel as Ozymandias may have been, time
is even more remorseless.
    What are the facts behind Shelley's poem? According to the
Greek historian Diodorus Siculus, Ozymandias was apparently a
grand, poeticized name claimed for himself by the Egyptian pharaoh
Rameses II. Diodorus Siculus saw the king's ninety-foot-tall
statue of himself, carved by the sculptor Memnon, in the first
century B.C. when it was still standing at the Ramesseum in Thebes,
a mortuary temple. Shelley and his friend Horatio Smith had read a
description of the shattered statue in Richard Pococke's
Description of the East (1742). Smith and Shelley wrote sonnets
expressing their imagined views of the wreckage, both of which
Leigh Hunt printed in his periodical The Examiner in 1818. This is
Smith's effort, and students might care to compare it with
Shelley's in quality:

253-254 (text pages)

On a Stupendous Leg of Granite, Discovered
Standing by Itself in the Deserts of Egypt

In Egypt's sandy silence, all alone,
    Stands a gigantic leg, which far off throws
    The only shadow that the desert knows.
'I am great Ozymandias,' saith the stone,
    'The king of kings: this mighty city shows
The wonders of my hand.' The city's gone!--
    Nought but the leg remaining to disclose
The site of that forgotten Babylon.

We wonder, and some hunter may express
Wonder like ours, when through the wilderness,
    Where London stood, holding the wolf in chace,
He meets some fragment huge, and stops to guess
    What powerful but unrecorded race
    Once dwelt in that annihilated place.

For more background to the poem, see H. M. Richmond, "Ozymandias
and the Travelers," Keats-Shelley Journal 11 (1962): 65-71.

WILLIAM SHAKESPEARE, My mistress' eyes are nothing like the sun,
page 254

    Have students state positively each simile that Shakespeare
states negatively, and they will make a fair catalog of trite
Petrarchan imagery. Poking fun at such excessive flattery is a
source of humor even today, as in an old wheeze: "Your teeth are
like the stars--they come out at night."

THOMAS CAMPION, There is a garden in her face, page 254

    In tone, Campion's lyric is admiring and tender, and yet there
are ironies in it. The street vendor's cry, as Walter R. Davis has
pointed out, "undercuts, with its earthy commercialism, the high
Petrarchan style of the rest of the song." In Campion's society, a
girl of marriageable age was, in a sense, on sale to the highest
bidder.
    For Campion's music to his song--incorporating the set melody
of the street cry "Cherry ripe, ripe, ripe!"--see Davis's edition
of Campion's Works (New York: Doubleday, 1967). Campion has been
called (by W. H. Auden) "the only man in English cultural history
who was both a poet and a composer."
    Some students, taking the figures of speech literally, may
find the last stanza absurd or meaningless. They can be led to see
that Campion's angels with bended bows enact his theme that the
young girl's beauties are defended. Who defends them? She
herself, by her nay-saying frowns and by her immaturity.
Throughout the poem run hints of Eden. The garden, that heav'nly
paradise, holds sacred cherries--forbidden fruit--and so the

guardian angels seem traditional. John Hollander thinks the
Petrarchan cliché of bowlike eyebrows "redeemed" by its new asso-
ciations. "The courtly compliment now turns out to be found in
beautiful sexual attainment, in the plucking of cherries that are
not forbidden apples, and just for that reason, such attainment
isn't always easy" (introduction to Selected Songs of Thomas
Campion [Boston: Godine, 1973]).

WALT WHITMAN, O Captain! My Captain! page 255

    This formerly overrated poem is uncharacteristic of Whitman in
its neatly shaped riming stanzas and in its monotonously swinging
observation of iambic meter, so inappropriate to a somber elegy.
The one indication that an excellent poet wrote it is the sudden
shift of rhythm in the short lines that end each stanza--
particularly in line 5, with the unexpected turning-on of heavy
stresses: "O heart! heart! heart!"

THOMAS GRAY, Elegy Written in a Country Churchyard, page 257

    Students, like other critics, may disagree widely in their
statements of Gray's theme. Roger Lonsdale (cited below) sees the
main preoccupation of the poem to be "the desire to be remembered
after death, a concern which draws together both rich and poor,
making the splendid monuments and the 'frail memorials' equally
pathetic." Concern with being remembered after death informs the
Epitaph as well, making it seem intrinsic to the poem (despite
Landor's objections). But Gray also seems to suggest that there is
positive virtue in remaining little known.
    About question 10: most students will readily see that Gray,
Shelley, and Guiterman all state (however variously) a common
theme--the paths of glory lead but to the grave. In ranking the
three poems in order of excellence, however, they risk getting into
a futile debate unless they can agree that (1) Guiterman's
excellent comic poem need not be damned for not trying to be an
elegy; and (2) Gray's poem is more deep-going, moving, musical, and
ultimately more interesting in what it says than Guiterman's.
    Of three stanzas found in the earliest surviving version of
the poem (the Eton manuscript) and deleted from the published
version of 1753, one has been much admired. It followed line 116,
coming right before the Epitaph:

        There scatter'd oft, the earliest of the year,
        By hands unseen, are showers of violets found:
        The Red-breast loves to build, and warble there,
        And little footsteps lightly print the ground.

Topic for discussion: Should Gray have kept the stanza?
    Topic for a paper of moderate (600- to 1,000-word) length:
'Two Views of Anonymity: Gray's 'Elegy' and Auden's 'Unknown
Citizen.'"

257-261 (text pages)

Twentieth Century Interpretations of Gray's Elegy, ed. H. W.
Starr (Englewood Cliffs: Prentice, 1968), is a convenient gathering
of modern criticism. A good deal of earlier criticism is
summarized by Roger Lonsdale in his edition of The Poems of Gray,
Collins, and Goldsmith (New York: Norton, 1969), which provides
extensive notes on texts and sources. For a recent poem at least
partly inspired by the "Elegy," see Richard Wilbur's "In a
Churchyard" in Walking to Sleep (New York: Harcourt, 1969). Among
the countless parodies, there is an anonymous "Allergy in a Country
Churchyard" that begins, "The kerchoo tolls, Nell's 'kerchief swats
away."

DAVID BOTTOMS, Smoking in an Open Grave, page 261

Some tentative answers to the questions:

1. There is an irony (also a paradox) in the opening line.
The past, which the speaker and his fellow smokers cheerfully dese-
crate, is hinted at by the old spirituals, by dead soldiers
interred in Confederate Row. Getting high is a form of departure,
like taking a journey. The language of the poem suggests that this
trip is somehow mechanized--the trainlike industrial river that
whispers on its track; the smokers are geared.
    2. This critical opinion seems a pompous bit of cant. What
does it say that isn't obvious?
    3. Gray's "Elegy" is a difficult act for any contemporary
poet to follow, but whether or not Bottoms's graveyard poem invites
comparison, it is, we'd argue, a good poem. In brief compass
Bottoms draws his scene of this half-gloomy pot party with great
exactness, even to the location of the bag and the fact that the
brick is half-fallen. The poem ends in a powerful mixture of
feelings: strangeness, joy, nostalgia, and dread. Perhaps this
poem pretends to greater significance than it actually contains.
But it captures something hard to forget, and students are probably
going to respond to it.

    "Smoking in an Empty Grave" is reprinted from Bottoms's first
collection, Shooting Rats at the Bibb County Dump (New York:
Morrow, 1980), which received the Walt Whitman Award of the Academy
of American Poets. As his poem suggests, he is a fan of folk and
country music; in fact, he has played guitar and banjo in several
bluegrass and country-and-western bands.

MARIA LOWELL, An Opium Fantasy, page 262

    Various sense-images inform this good, goofy poem--sounds,
vibrations, coolness ("freshening winds"), the vision of red
poppies. Surely those silver balls that ring into golden bowls (a
synesthetic blend of sight and sound) are most memorable. The
ball-dropper is identified in lines 31-32: someone under a spell,
a prince in owl's clothing.

Like David Bottoms in "Smoking in an Open Grave" (and
Coleridge in his own pipe-dream, "Kubla Khan" [page 292]), Lowell
reports the experience of getting stoned. (Her high, unlike that
of pot-smokers in a open grave, must have been legal.) Bottoms and
Lowell both mention an owl--a mere coincidence? Lowell's vision
seems the wilder and loopier. It includes the experience of
feeling transformed into a weed in a poppy bed. By comparison,
Bottoms's contemporary poem seems almost rational. Formally,
Lowell's poem is the more constrained: most of it is cast in the
stanza of a literary ballad (riming abab--a rime scheme more
tightly knit than the usual abcb of folk balladry).

Any revival of interest in the poems of Lowell should take in
at least one other good forgotten poem, "Africa," which S. Foster
Damon calls "the only Abolitionist poem I know of which rises above
oratory and propaganda into pure literature." He sums it up: "The
African continent becomes a titanic mother brooding over the fate
of the two races she has brought forth: the Egyptians who perished
and the negroes who are enslaved. . . . The poem is a symbol
sculptured from black marble" (introduction to Hope Vernon's
edition of Lowell's Poems).

264-267 (text pages)

16

WHAT IS POETRY?

ARCHIBALD MacLEISH, Ars Poetica, page 264

     MacLeish plays upon a number of verbal paradoxes, which stu-
dents sometimes like to point out. He says a poem ought to be
mute, dumb, and wordless; and yet obviously he is writing a poem in
speakable, audible words.
     The poem contains a larger paradox, a possible topic for class
argument. "A poem should not mean / But be," declares the poet.
But is his poem pure being? Is it not heavy on meaning--a tendency
that an ars poetica, a poem that tells us how poetry should be
written, can hardly be expected to avoid?

POEMS IN THE ANTHOLOGY SECTION,
ARRANGED BY ELEMENTS

Many instructors tell us that they use the poems in the back-
of-the-book Anthology as an extra reservoir or second fuel tank of
illustrations. Others, to be sure, think the book already offers
too many examples. If that is your feeling, don't bother with
this.

If, however, you would like a few more poems (or some
different poems) to illustrate matters taken up in the body of the
book, then the following list can help you put your finger on them.
It classifies only poems in the Anthology section, and it works
through the book chapter by chapter.

Obviously, poems, like any living creatures, are made up of
many elements. Far from being exclusive, this list merely points
to a few poems in which we think a certain element is prominent,
visible to students, and in some instances even likely to spark
discussion in class. (Are the poems classified under "Irony" to be
taken ironically, or straight? Are the poems listed under "Literal
Meaning" all that simple? Can the Child ballads still be sung?
Does "The Convergence of the Twain" have bad spots?)

For Writing Topics. After your students have studied a
chapter of the book, you can direct them to certain poems in the
Anthology. Assign a poem or two and a short paper that springs
from their reading. (An essay of two or three paragraphs might be
enough: at this stage, overlong papers on topics such as figures
of speech, rime and meter, stanza form, and so on, might be
debilitating.) Topics will occur: The Character of the
Soliloquist in Robert Browning's "Spanish Cloister" (after studying
The Person in the Poem); The Effectiveness of the Repeated Booms
and Two-steps in Stafford's "At the Klamath Berry Festival" (after
studying Sound and Rhythm), The Attitude of the Daughter in Plath's
"Daddy" (Tone), The Sex Symbolism of Dickinson's Dog-walk (Symbol,
referring to "I started Early - Took my Dog"), and more.

For suggesting that this manual could use such a classifi-
cation of the Anthology poems, and for starting to make one of his
own, thanks to Professor Harvey Birenbaum of San Jose State
University.

2   Listening to a Voice

Tone

Some poems in which the poet's attitude is especially clear:

E. B. Browning   How do I love thee? Let me count the ways
Momaday   The Delight Song of Tsoai-talee
Owen   Anthem for Doomed Youth

269-270 (text pages)

Plath	Daddy
Tennyson	Dark house, by which once more I stand
Wordsworth	Composed upon Westminster Bridge
Yeats	To a Friend Whose Work Has Come to Nothing

Some poems that express, as Auden says, "mixed feelings":

Bishop	Filling Station
Eliot	The Love Song of J. Alfred Prufrock
Hopkins	Thou art indeed just, Lord, if I contend
R. Lowell	Skunk Hour

The Person in the Poem

Some poems in which the identity of the speaker is interestingly different from the poet's "I":

R. Browning	My Last Duchess
R. Browning	Soliloquy of the Spanish Cloister
Chesterton	The Donkey
Larkin	A Study of Reading Habits
Pound	The River-Merchant's Wife: a Letter

Irony (other kinds besides ironic point of view, as in the five poems just listed):

Anonymous	Sir Patrick Spence (sarcasm toward the Scots nobles; possibly irony of Fate)
Chappell	Skin Flick (a discrepancy between X-movie customers and pioneers; verbal irony)
Dickinson	Because I could not stop for Death (a discrepancy between dying and being taken out driving; verbal ironies: "kindly," "Civility," etc.)
Hardy	The Convergence of the Twain (irony of Fate)
Hardy	Five Satires of Circumstance (ironies galore!)
Merrill	Laboratory Poem (a discrepancy between the clinical setting and the tender feelings of the characters)
Reed	Naming of Parts (a discrepancy between the study of a gun and the study of nature, between the voice of the instructor and the view of the soldier; verbal irony in the pun easing the spring)
Stafford	At the Klamath Berry Festival (a discrepancy between traditional dances and ways of life today)
Wilbur	Museum Piece (ironic contrast between art and dancers and art's guardians; verbal irony)

3   Words

Literal Meaning: What a Poem Says First

Poems that can be taken at face value, without looking for
symbols, endless suggestions, huge significance (not that they
won't repay thought and close reading):

Anonymous	Sumer is icumen in
Brooks	Sadie and Maud
Gioia	California Hills in August
Hall	Names of Horses
Hongo	The Hongo Store
Marlowe	The Passionate Shepherd to His Love
Raleigh	The Nymph's Reply to the Shepherd
Shakespeare	When daisies pied and violets blue
Shakespeare	When icicles hang by the wall
Updike	Ex-Basketball Player
Yeats	The Lake Isle of Innisfree
Yeats	To a Friend Whose Work Has Come to Nothing

The Value of a Dictionary

Poems containing two or more brief allusions:

Dryden	To the Memory of Mr. Oldham
Eliot	The Love Song of J. Alfred Prufrock
Hecht	The Vow
Moore	The Mind is an Enchanting Thing
Snodgrass	The Operation

Poems with central allusions:

Auden	Musée des Beaux Arts
Broumas	Cinderella
Chesterton	The Donkey
Eliot	Journey of the Magi
Keats	On First Looking into Chapman's Homer (the celebrated blooper in the allusion to Cortez)
Kinnell	Saint Francis and the Sow
Milton	When I consider how my light is spent
Randall	Ballad of Birmingham
Sexton	To a Friend Whose Work Has Come to Triumph
Stevens	Peter Quince at the Clavier (allusions to Shakespeare and to the story of Susanna and the Elders)
Tennyson	Ulysses
Yeats	The Magi

Word Choice and Word Order

Poems in dialect:

Anonymous	Edward
Anonymous	Sir Patrick Spence
Anonymous	The Twa Corbies
Boyd	Cupid and Venus
Lawrence	A Youth Mowing

Poems in Middle English:

Anonymous	Sumer is icumen in
Anonymous	I sing of a maiden

Poems whose diction and syntax depart from those of speech:

Blake	The Tyger
Clampitt	The Cormorant in His Element
Coleridge	Kubla Khan
Hardy	The Convergence of the Twain
Hopkins	Spring and Fall
Hopkins	Thou art indeed just, Lord, if I contend
Hopkins	The Windhover
Keats	Ode to Melancholy
Keats	On First Looking into Chapman's Homer (inverted syntax: "Much have I . . . ," "Yet did I never breathe," "Then felt I," etc.
Keats	To Autumn
Moore	The Mind is an Enchanting Thing

Poems containing technical words:

Merrill	Laboratory Poem
Reed	Naming of Parts

Poems in colloquial diction:

Brooks	Sadie and Maud
Frost	Stopping by Woods on a Snowy Evening
Frost	The Wood-Pile
Hughes	Dream Deferred
Ignatow	Get the Gasworks
Larkin	A Study of Reading Habits (also vulgate: "a load of crap")
Levine	To a Child Trapped in a Barber Shop
Olds	The One Girl at the Boys Party
Updike	Ex-Basketball Player

Poems containing an interesting mix of formal and colloquial diction:

Bishop	Filling Station
Winters	At the San Francisco Airport

4   Saying and Suggesting

Some poems full of words rich in connotations:

Anonymous	The Three Ravens
Anonymous	The Twa Corbies
Coleridge	Kubla Khan
Eliot	The Love Song of J. Alfred Prufrock
Keats	Ode on Melancholy

5   Imagery

Bishop	Filling Station
Clampitt	The Cormorant in His Element
Keats	To Autumn
Kizer	The Intruder
Marlowe	The Passionate Shepherd to His Love
Moore	The Mind is an Enchanting Thing
Shakespeare	When daisies pied and violets blue
Shakespeare	When icicles hang by the wall
Swift	A Description of the Morning
Tennyson	Dark house, by which once more I stand
Thomas	Fern Hill
W. C. Williams	Spring and All
W. C. Williams	To Waken an Old Lady
Yeats	The Lake Isle of Innisfree

6   Figures of Speech

   Metaphor and Simile

   Poems with central metaphors:

Chappell	Skin Flick
Dickinson	My Life had stood - a Loaded Gun
Donne	The Bait
Hopkins	The Windhover
Nemerov	Storm Windows
Phillips	Running on Empty
Rich	Diving into the Wreck
Sexton	To a Friend Whose Work Has Come to Triumph
W. Whitman	I Saw in Louisiana a Live-Oak Growing
W. C. Williams	To Waken an Old Lady
Wordsworth	Composed upon Westminster Bridge

Poems containing extended similes:

Brontë	Love and Friendship
Keats	On First Looking into Chapman's Homer ("Then felt I like . . .")

Other poems with prominent metaphors:

Shakespeare	That time of year thou mayst in me behold
Shapiro	The Dirty Word
Simic	Butcher
J. Wright	A Blessing

Other Figures

Blake	The Sick Rose (apostrophe)
Carew	Ask me no more where Jove bestows (hyperbole)
Chappell	Skin Flick (pun)
Chesterton	The Donkey (personification)
Clifton	to the unborn and waiting children (apostrophe)
Dickinson	Because I could not stop for Death (personification)
Dickinson	I started Early - Took my Dog (personification)
Donne	Death be not proud (apostrophe, personification)
Donne	A Valediction: Forbidding Mourning (paradox)
Herrick	Delight in Disorder (synecdoche)
Keats	To Autumn (apostrophe, personification)
Plath	Daddy (hyperbole)
Reed	Naming of Parts (pun)
Swenson	Question (apostrophe, personification)
Waller	Go, Lovely Rose (apostrophe, personification)
W. C. Williams	Spring and All (personification)

7 Song

Singing and Saying

Some poems originally sung (see also Ballads):

Anonymous	I sing of a maiden
Anonymous	Western Wind
Cowper	Praise for the Fountain Opened
Shakespeare	When daisies pied and violets blue
Shakespeare	When icicles hang by the wall

Ballads

Anonymous	Edward
Anonymous	Sir Patrick Spence
Anonymous	The Three Ravens
Anonymous	The Twa Corbies

| Auden | As I Walked Out One Evening (not a ballad, but balladlike) |
| Randall | Ballad of Birmingham |

8   Sound

Sound as Meaning

Poems containing onomatopoeia:

Shakespeare	When daisies pied and violets blue
Shakespeare	When icicles hang by the wall
Stafford	At the Klamath Berry Festival
Stevens	Peter Quince at the Clavier

Alliteration and Assonance

Blake	The Tyger
Carew	Ask me no more where Jove bestows
Coleridge	Kubla Khan
Hopkins	The Windhover
Levertov	The Ache of Marriage
Ransom	Bells for John Whiteside's Daughter ("primly propped"!)
Roethke	The Waking
Thomas	Fern Hill
Waller	Go, Lovely Rose

Rime

Poems whose rimes may well repay study:

Blake	The Sick Rose
Clampitt	The Cormorant in His Element
Dickinson	[all poems: masterworks of off-rime]
Eliot	The Love Song of J. Alfred Prufrock
Larkin	A Study of Reading Habits
R. Lowell	Skunk Hour
Plath	Daddy
Stevens	Peter Quince at the Clavier

9   Rhythm

Stresses and Pauses

In any good metrical poem, rhythms matter, of course, and can't be disentangled from meanings. Here are some poems in open or syllabic forms in which rhythms play strong parts:

Dugan	Love Song: I and Thou
Hall	Names of Horses
Heaney	Sunlight
Momaday	The Delight Song of Tsoai-talee

115

269-270 (text pages)

Reed   Naming of Parts
Smart   For I will consider my cat Jeoffrey
Stafford   At the Klamath Berry Festival (consider the
                          effect of "he took two steps," repeated
                          four times)

Meter

Wyatt   They flee from me that sometime did me seke (an
                          exercise is suggested in the note after the
                          poem)
Yeats   The Magi (worth scanning: irregularities
                          battle with regularity for supremacy)

10   Closed Form, Open Form

Closed Form: Blank Verse, Stanza, Sonnet

Poems in blank verse:

Frost   The Wood-Pile
Tennyson   Ulysses
Updike   Ex-Basketball Player

Poems in closed (heroic) couplets:

Dryden   To the Memory of Mr. Oldham
Johnson   On My First Son
Rich   Aunt Jennifer's Tigers
Swift   A Description of the Morning

Poem in open couplets:

R. Browning   My Last Duchess

Poem in tercets:

Hardy   The Convergence of the Twain

Poems in tightly structured riming stanzas:

Donne   The Flea
Hecht   The Vow
Herbert   Love
Keats   Ode on Melancholy
Keats   To Autumn
Moore   The Mind is an Enchanting Thing

Poems in syllabic stanzas:

Moore   The Mind is an Enchanting Thing
Thomas   Fern Hill

Sonnets:

Boyd	Cupid and Venus
Brooks	The Rites for Cousin Vit
E. B. Browning	How do I love thee? Let me count the ways
Clampitt	The Cormorant in His Element
Donne	Death be not proud
Hopkins	Thou art indeed just, Lord, If I contend
Hopkins	The Windhover
Keats	On First Looking into Chapman's Homer
Meredith	Lucifer in Starlight
Milton	When I consider how my light is spent
Owen	Anthem for Doomed Youth
Sexton	To a Friend Whose Work Has Come to Triumph
Shakespeare	That time of year thou mayst in me behold
Shakespeare	When, in disgrace with Fortune and men's eyes
Wordsworth	Composed upon Westminster Bridge

A villanelle:

Roethke	The Waking

Open Form

A few classics of open-form poetry:

Eliot	Journey of the Magi
Ginsberg	A Supermarket in California
Levertov	The Ache of Marriage
Plath	Morning Song
Pound	The River-Merchant's Wife: a Letter
Roethke	Elegy for Jane
W. Whitman	I Saw in Louisiana a Live-Oak Growing
W. C. Williams	Spring and All
W. C. Williams	To Waken an Old Lady
J. Wright	A Blessing

A prose poem:

Shapiro	The Dirty Word

11 Poems for the Eye

No graphic poems in the Anthology section, but if you care to
work further with the looks of poems, you might compare the
appearances on the page of the open-form poems and the tightly
structured stanzaic poems listed above. These appearances
mean something; at the very least, they announce the name of
the game, and the reader knows whether or not to expect rime
and meter.

12   Symbol

Blake   The Sick Rose
Eliot   The Love Song of J. Alfred Prufrock
Lowell   Skunk Hour
Rich   Aunt Jennifer's Tigers

13   Myth

Carew   Ask me no more where Jove bestows
Keats   Ode on Melancholy
Sexton   To a Friend Whose Work Has Come to Triumph
Snodgrass   The Operation
Stafford   At the Klamath Berry Festival

14   Alternatives

     Translations

Anonymous   Sumer is icumen in (original and modern
                      version)

     Parody

Donne   The Bait

15   Evaluating a Poem

     Telling Good from Bad

Hardy   The Convergence of the Twain (a poem surely bad
                   in parts--e.g., stanza 5--but good in its
                   entirety!)

     Knowing Excellence

[Your choice.]

ANTHOLOGY: POETRY

ANONYMOUS, Edward, page 271

ANONYMOUS, Sir Patrick Spence, page 272

Two Scottish ballads of men sent to death or exile at
another's bidding, both "Edward" and "Sir Patrick Spence" are told
with a wonderful economy. "Edward," with its surprise ending in
the last line, is so neatly built that it is sometimes accused of
not being a popular ballad at all, but the creation of a sophisticated poet, perhaps working from a popular story. Students might
be asked to read the information about ballads in Chapter Seven,
"Song," either before or after reading these ballads.

Questions for discussion:

1. In "Edward," why is the first line so effective as an
opening? What expectations does it set up in the hearer's mind?
How does the last line also display the skill of a master storyteller?

2. Reading a ballad such as "Edward" on the printed page, we
notice that its refrains take up much room. Do you find this repetitiousness a hindrance to your enjoying the poem? Is there anything to be said in favor of the repetitiousness?

3. What is the value to the poem of the question-and-answer
method of storytelling? ("Edward" proceeds like a courtroom cross-
examination in which the mother, by pointed questioning, breaks
down her son's story. Dramatically, the method is powerful; and it
holds off until the very end the grimmest revelation.)

4. What else could the author of "Edward" conceivably have
told us about this unhappy family? Do you find it troublesome that
Edward and his mother behave without our quite knowing why? Might
the story have suffered if told by a storyteller who more deeply
explored the characters' motivations?

5. What do the dramatic situations of "Edward" and "Sir
Patrick Spence" have in common? What is similar in the image of
the blood-dripping sword in "Edward" and, in "Sir Patrick Spence,"
the image of the "blude-reid wine"? (Both images are introduced
early in their ballads and foreshadow grim events or revelations.)

6. Does Sir Patrick emerge as a fully understandable character? What do you make of his abrupt transition from laughter to
tears?

7. Coleridge and other critics have greatly admired the stanza in "Spence" about the new moon and the old (lines 25-28). Why is it memorable?

8. Is the author of "Sir Patrick Spence" making (or hinting at) any adverse comment on lords and ladies who lead a comfortable life at court?

For instructors who like to begin with narrative poetry, here are a few suggestions. Other traditional English and Scottish ballads in the book, which might be taken together with these two, are "Bonny Barbara Allan" (page 110), "The Cruel Mother" (page 105), and (immediately following "Sir Patrick Spence") "The Three Ravens" and "The Twa Corbies." There is also the anonymous American popular ballad "Scottsboro" (page 58). These can be supplemented by the Beatles' "Eleanor Rigby" (page 113) and Dudley Randall's "Ballad of Birmingham" (page 347). "Richard Cory" resembles a ballad, too, in both its Edwin Arlington Robinson and its Paul Simon versions (page 108).

ANONYMOUS, The Three Ravens, page 273

ANONYMOUS, The Twa Corbies, page 274

Questions for discussion:

1. In "The Three Ravens," what is suggestive in the ravens and their conversation? How are the ravens opposed in the poem by the hawks and the hounds? (The ravens are selfish eaters of carrion, but the hawks and hounds are loyally standing guard over their dead master's body. Their faithfulness also suggests that of the fallow doe.)

2. Are you persuaded by Friedman's suggestion (quoted in the note under "The Three Ravens") that the doe is a woman who is under some enchantment? What other familiar fairy tales or stories of lovers transformed into animals do you recall?

3. Do you agree that "The Twa Corbies" is "a cynical variation of 'The Three Ravens,'" as it has been called? Compare the two poems in their comments on love and faithfulness.

4. For all the fantasy of "The Three Ravens," what details in the ballad seem realistic reflections of the natural world?

ANONYMOUS, Sumer is icumen in, page 275

If you are not an expert in Middle English pronunciation, ask a colleague who is to give you a briefing and take a stab at reading "Sumer is icumen in" aloud to the class. Even the experts are only guessing (educatedly) how thirteenth-century English sounded, and your reading need do no more than suggest that the language has not always stood still.

This slight, exquisite, earthy song may be compared with Shakespeare's "When daisies pied," in which the song of the cuckoo suggests cuckoldry (as it doesn't in this innocent, humorless lyric).

For a parody, see Ezra Pound's "Ancient Music," beginning "Winter is icummen in," in his collection Personae (New York: New Directions, 1949), and in Selected Poems (from the same publisher, 1957).

ANONYMOUS, I sing of a maiden, page 275

How could Christ be conceived and Mary remain a virgin? This medieval lyric appears to reply to the question: as easily and naturally as the dew falls.

The cesura in each line shows that English poetry, as late as the fifteenth century, had not quite broken away from the Old English two-part line.

"I sing of a maiden" can be used to remind students of the value to poetry of figures of speech. In line 1, makeless (meaning both "matchless" and "without a mate") is a serious pun. Each of the poem's three middle couplets contains a simile.

ANONYMOUS, Western Wind, page 276

Originally a song for tenor voices, "Western Wind" probably was the work of some courtier in the reign of Henry VIII. Untouched by modernization, it reads (in its one surviving manuscript):

Westron wynde when wyll thow blow
the smalle rayne douune can rayne
Chryst yf my love wer in my armys
and I yn my bed agayne

Questions for discussion:

1. In reading the poem, how does it help to know that the moist, warm west wind of England brings rain and is a sign of spring?
2. What do the first pair of lines and the last pair have to do with each other?
3. Do you agree with a critic who suggested that the speaker is invoking Christ, asking for help in obtaining sex? "By a blasphemous implication Christ is in effect assigned the role of a fertility spirit" (F. W. Bateson, English Poetry: A Critical Introduction [London: Longmans, 1966]).
4. Consider another critic's view: the unhappy speaker is stressing his (or her) longing to go to bed with his (or her) loved one, and so the word Christ is an exclamation. (We prefer this view; see Arthur O. Lewis, Jr., writing in The Explicator 15 Feb. 1957: item 28.)

276-277 (text pages)

MATTHEW ARNOLD, Dover Beach, page 276

Arnold and his family did such an efficient job of expunging the facts of his early romances that the genesis of "Dover Beach" is hard to know. Arnold may (or may not) have been in love with a French girl whom he called Marguerite, whose egotistic gaiety made her difficult. See Lionel Trilling's discussion of the poem and of Arnold's Marguerite poems in his biography Matthew Arnold (New York: Columbia UP, 1949). Marguerite, Trilling suspects, viewed the world as much more various, beautiful, and new than young Arnold did.

A sympathetic reading of "Dover Beach" might include some attention to the music of its assonance and alliterations, especially the s-sounds in the description of the tide (lines 12-14). Line 21 introduces the central metaphor, the Sea of Faith. Students will probably be helped by a few minutes of discussion of the historical background of the poem. Why, when the poem appeared in 1867, was religious faith under attack? Darwin, Herbert Spencer, and Victorian industrialism may be worth mention. Ignorant armies (line 37) are still with us. Arnold probably had in mind those involved in the Crimean War of 1853-56, perhaps also those in the American Civil War. For sources of the poem, see C. B. Tinker and H. F. Lowry, The Poetry of Matthew Arnold (New York: Oxford UP, 1940) 173-78.

A dour view of the poem is taken by Donald Hall in "Ah, Love, Let Us Be True" (American Scholar Summer 1959). Hall finds "love invoked as a compensation for the losses that history has forced us to sustain," and adds, "I hope there are better reasons for fidelity than disillusion. . . . Like so many Victorian poems, its negation is beautiful and its affirmation repulsive." This comment can be used to provoke discussion. A useful counterfoil to "Dover Beach" is Anthony Hecht's satiric poem "The Dover Bitch," in his collection The Hard Hours (New York: Atheneum, 1960) and in many anthologies. For other critical comment, see William E. Cadbury, "Coming to Terms with 'Dover Beach,'" Criticism 8 (Spring 1966): 126-38; James Dickey, Babel to Byzantium (New York: Farrar, 1968) 235-38 (a good concise general essay); and A. Dwight Culler, Imaginative Reason: The Poetry of Matthew Arnold (New Haven: Yale UP, 1966).

Compare Hardy's attitude in "The Oxen" (page 216) with Arnold's wistful view of the Sea of Faith.

JOHN ASHBERY, City Afternoon, page 277

At first we thought this subtle poem was the poet's contribution to the American bicentennial celebration: If one could seize America. And it was no accident, we guessed, that the collection in which it appears, Self-Portrait in a Convex Mirror, came out in 1975. After further thought, we feel certain only that Ashbery's poem resists attempts to pin a subject on it. Ashbery's recent work (which is his best) seems immune to the accusation that Wallace Stevens once leveled at Robert Frost: "Your trouble,

Robert, is that you write poems about--things." Ashbery's
strategy, instead, is to relate suggestive things by means of
ambiguous words. Sometimes he calls upon rime to join things in
relationships: something fine does define, air lifts hair. Although not strictly "about" a city afternoon, neither is the poem
an infinite series of reflecting mirrors. After one has read it a
few times, one knows what to think and how to feel--at least until
the next reading.

In the opening lines (we now believe), the poet regards an old
and perhaps yellowed photograph of a city street, whose veil of
haze keeps its scene preserved. The haze, because of the age of
the photograph or because of the weather on the day of the photograph, suggests the "fine forgetfulness" of line 6. And it seems
that the people in the picture have entered what John Crowe Ransom
called "the forgetful kingdom of death." The tone shifts startlingly from the quiet opening words to a sudden outcry of sympathy.
The force of the poet's dread of the passage of time is indicated
by violent imagery and heavy stresses: "SUCKED SCREAMing through
OLD AGE and DEATH."

"Fine forgetfulness," then, suggests haze and the absent-
mindedness of old people, and the permanently absent minds of the
dead. But there is another, more central suggestion. In a sense,
art too is forgetful. A work of art (whether a photograph or a
poem) reflects the living, who die and forget; and eventually the
work dies and "forgets" in its turn. Poets' collections (our
volumes) collect the patina of time until they disintegrate. For
all a poet's attempts to capture life in an outline, time flows
until the outline blurs and disappears.

Three persons in the photograph wear "gray garlands." Is it
gray hair, or hair that looks gray because limned and defined by
hazy light? We are reminded of a poet's garlands of laurel. And
in the delicate final image, one person is seen reflected upside
down--like an image of actual life momentarily captured in a work
of art. The phrase reflecting pool suggests the camera's lens, or
film; and, on reflection, may suggest the mind of a poet as well.

Any paraphrase will be crude. Still, "City Afternoon" has one
or two unmistakable themes. If "fine forgetfulness" is a quality
we expect of art, then Ashbery is wishing that he were able to
seize actual life and hold it fast in poetry--at least temporarily.
A poem, he affirms, is not useless, despite its stain of common
mortality. It does define. It commemorates, that is, it overcomes
forgetfulness and awakens memory.

W. H. AUDEN, As I Walked Out One Evening, page 277

This literary ballad, with its stark contrast between the
innocent song of the lover and the more knowing song of the clocks,
affords opportunities to pay close attention to the poet's choice
of words. Auden selects words rich in connotations: the brimming
of the river (which suggests also the lover's feelings), the
crooked neighbor (with its hint of dishonesty and corruption as
well as the denotation of being warped or bent by Time, like the

"diver's brilliant bow"). Figures of speech abound: the opening
metaphor of the crowds like wheat (ripe and ready to be scythed by
Time the Reaper), the lover's extended use of hyperbole in lines
9-20, the personifications of Time and Justice, the serious pun on
appalling in line 34 (both awe-inspiring and like a pall or shroud,
as in Blake's "London," page 62), the final reconciliation in
metaphor between the original "brimming river" and the flow of
passing Time. Auden's theme appears to be that as young lovers
grow old, their innocent vision is smudged and begrimed by contact
with realities--and yet "Life remains a blessing" after all.

The lover's huge promises in stanzas 3 and 4 ("I'll love you /
Till China and Africa meet . . .") have reminded Richard Wilbur of
the hyperbolic boasts of the speaker in Burns's "Oh, my love is
like a red, red rose" (page 101). Burns speaks for the romantic
lover, wrapped in his own emotions, but Auden's view of romantic
love is skeptical. "The poem then proceeds to rebut [the lover's]
lines, saying that the human heart is too selfish and perverse to
make such promises" (Responses [New York: Harcourt, 1976] 144).

This poem may appear to have too little action in it to resemble folk ballads in more than a few touches. Auden himself, according to Monroe K. Spears, did not call this a ballad but
referred to it as "a pastiche of folk-song."

"As I Walked Out One Evening" is one of the "Five Lyrics"
included on W. H. Auden Reading (Caedmon recording TC 1019). For
comparison with the poet's own modest delivery, Dylan Thomas
Reading, vol. 4 (Caedmon, TC 1061) offers a more dramatic
rendition.

W. H. AUDEN, Musée des Beaux Arts, page 279

In Breughel's Landscape with the Fall of Icarus reproduced on
page 279, students may need to have their attention directed to the
legs disappearing in a splash, one quarter inch below the bow of
the ship. One story (probably apocryphal) is that Breughel's
patron had ordered a painting on a subject from mythology, but the
artist had only this landscape painting completed. To fill the
order quickly, Breughel touched in the little splash, gave the
picture a mythological name, and sent it on its way. Question:
How does that story (if true) make Breughel seem a shallower man
than Auden thinks he is?

Besides the Landscape, Auden apparently has in mind two other
paintings of Pieter Breughel the Elder: The Census, also called
The Numbering at Bethlehem (Auden's lines 5-8), and The Massacre of
the Innocents (lines 9-13). If the instructor has access to
reproductions, these works might be worth bringing in; however, the
Landscape seems central to the poem. This painting seems indebted
to Ovid's Metamorphoses, but in Ovid the plowman, shepherd, and
fisherman looked on the fall of Icarus with amazement. The title
of Auden's poem, incidentally, is close to the name of the Brussels
museum housing the Landscape: the Musées Royaux des Beaux Arts.

Edward Mendelson has remarked on the poem in Early Auden (New York: Viking, 1981):

> The poetic imagination that seeks out grandeur and sublimity could scarcely be bothered with those insignificant figures lost in the background or in the crowd. But Auden sees in them an example of Christianity's great and enduring transformation of classical rhetoric: its inversion of the principle that the most important subjects require the highest style. If the sufferings of a carpenter turned preacher mattered more to the world than the doom of princes, then the high style, for all its splendor, was a limited instrument. . . . These casually irregular lines make none of the demands for action and attention that marked Auden's earlier harangues on the urgency of the times, yet beneath the apparent surface disorder a deeper pattern of connectedness gradually makes itself felt. The unassertive rhymes, easily overlooked on a first reading, hold the poem together.

Yet another device of language helps bring unity to Auden's meditation, in P. K. Saha's view. Four clauses begin with how and one phrase begins with anyhow (line 11). These hows vary in meaning; still, the repeated how is the crucial word in the linguistic pattern of the poem ("Style, Stylistic Transformations, and Incorporators," Style 12 [1978]: 18-22.

R. L. BARTH, The Insert, page 280

We would sum up Barth's theme: war blunts the sensibilities of the participant. Like one who begins taking heroin, the new soldier is at first eager for excitement; but with every use, the thrill is of shorter duration.

We didn't know exactly what an insert was, and asked the poet to define it. He replied: "Dropping troops, in this case recon troops, into an area by helicopter--one never knew if it would be a 'hot' LZ or not and was always ready for the worst."

The poet's view of "physical courage" seems ironically at odds with that of von Clausewitz.

Barth's poem invites comparison with other poems by another poet with field experience: Wilfred Owen's "Dulce et Decorum Est" (page 28) and "Anthem for Doomed Youth" (page 341). As in this poem, Barth's protest is stated not in the abstract, but in what lies before the observer's senses. Owen, by contrast, for all his vivid detail, seems continually to be editorializing.

Barth's poems of the Vietnam War may be the best yet written by a combatant. Lately they have been collected in Looking for Peace (Omaha: Abattoir Editions, 1985). The poet has taught English at the University of California, Santa Barbara, and currently teaches at Xavier University in Cincinnati. As Robert L. Barth, he operates a small publishing house at 14 Lucas St., Florence KY 41042, producing books and chapbooks of poetry.

ELIZABETH BISHOP, Filling Station, page 280

Questions for discussion:

1. What is the poet's attitude toward the feeble attempts at
beautification detailed in lines 23-33? Sympathy, contempt, or
what? How is the attitude indicated? (The attempts are doomed,
not only by the gas station's being saturated with oil, but by the
limitations of the family, whose only reading appears to be comic
books and whose tastes run to hairy plants and daisy-covered
doilies. In line 20, comfy is their word, not the poet's own. But
the tone of the poem seems to be good-humored amusement. The sons
are "quick and saucy"--likable traits. The gas station can't be
beautified, but at least its owners have tried. In a futile
gesture toward neatness, they have even arranged the oil cans in
symmetry.)
2. What meanings do you find in the last line? (Somebody
has shown love for all motorists by arranging the oil cans so
beautifully that they spell out a soothing croon, such as what one
might say over and over to an agitated child. But the somebody
also suggests Somebody Up There, whose love enfolds all human
beings--even this oil-soaked crew.)
3. Do you find any similarity between "ESSO--SO--SO--SO" in
"Filling Station" and "rainbow, rainbow, rainbow!" in "The Fish"
(page 72)? (Both lines stand late in their poems and sound
similar; both express the speaker's glimpse of beauty--or at least,
in "Filling Station," the only beauty the people can muster and the
poet can perceive.)

Helen Vendler, discussing the poem in Part of Nature, Part of
Us (Cambridge: Harvard UP, 1980), takes the closing statement to
mean "God loves us all." But Irvin Ehrenpreis disagrees: "The
'--so--so--so' of overlapping labels on stacked cans is supposed to
comfort automobiles as if they were high-strung horses, i.e., like
a mother, not a god." Doily and begonia indicate that some absent
woman has tried to brighten up this gas station for her husband and
her sons (review of Vendler's book in The New York Review of Books,
29 Apr. 1980).
Robert Pinsky has also written of "Filling Station" with high
esteem. He calls the poem a kind of contest between "the meticu-
lous vigor of the writer" and "the sloppy vigor of the family,"
both filling a dull moment and scene with "an unexpected, crazy,
deceptively off-hand kind of elegance or ornament." He particularly admires the poet's choice of modifiers--including the direct,
honest-seeming dirty. "Adjectives," he notes, "according to a
sound rule of thumb for writing classes, do not make 'good descriptions.' By writing almost as though she were too plain and
straightforward to have heard of such a rule, Bishop loads charac-
terizations of herself and her subject into the comfy dog, the dim
doily, the hirsute begonia; the quietest possible virtuoso strokes"
(The Situation of Poetry [Princeton: Princeton UP, 1976] 75-77).
"I've sometimes thought 'Filling Station' would make a good
exercise for acting students," observes critic and teacher David

Walker, "given the number of different ways the first line--and
much of the rest--might be stressed. Is the opening exclamation
solemn and childlike, or prissy and fastidious, or enthusiastic?
All we can identify with certainty, I think, is the quality of
fascination, the intent gaze on the filling station's pure
oiliness." Walker is reminded of Frost's "Design" (page 418) in
that both poets seek to discover "a meaningful pattern in
apparently random details"--but while Frost points toward a
sinister architecture in what he observes, Bishop finds beauty and
harmony ("Elizabeth Bishop and the Ordinary," Field Fall 1984:15).

Brad Leithauser has admired the poem's ingenious sound
effects. At its end, "the cans of oil are arranged like cue cards
to prompt that concluding sentence, the SO--SO--SO grading toward
that 'Somebody loves us all.' Neatly, the message in the oil cans
is reinforced by both the 'so' and the 'softly' in the fourth line
from the end" ("The 'complete' Elizabeth Bishop," New Criterion
Mar. 1983: 38).

WILLIAM BLAKE, The Sick Rose, page 281

WILLIAM BLAKE, The Tyger, page 282

In "The Sick Rose," why is the worm, whose love is rape, in-
visible? Not just because it is hidden in the rose, but also because it is some supernatural dweller in night and storm. Perhaps
the worm is unseen Time, that familiar destroyer--is the rose then
mortal beauty? Those are usual guesses. For an unusual guess, see
E. D. Hirsch, Jr., Innocence and Experience (New Haven: Yale UP,
1964). "The rose's sickness, like syphilis, is the internal result
of love enjoyed secretly and illicitly instead of purely and
openly." In Hirsch's view, the poem is social criticism. Blake is
satirizing the repressive order, whose hypocrisy and sham corrupt
the woman who accepts it. Still, like all the best symbols,
Blake's rose and worm give off hints endlessly, and no one
interpretation covers all of them.

"The Tyger," from Songs of Experience, is a companion piece to
"The Lamb" in Songs of Innocence. But while "The Lamb" poses a
relatively easy question ("Little lamb, who made thee?") and soon
answers it, "The Tyger" poses questions that remain unanswerable.
Alert students may complain that some of Blake's questions have no
verbs--what dread hand and what dread feet did what? While the in-
completeness has been explained by some critics as reflecting the
agitated tone of the poem, it may have been due to the poet's
agitated habits of composition. Drafts of the poem in Blake's
notebook show that, after writing the first three stanzas, he began
the fourth stanza with the line "Could fetch it from the furnace
deep," which would have completed the question in line 12. But
then he deleted it, and wrote in stanza four almost as it stands
now. (See Martin K. Nurmi, "Blake's Revisions of 'The Tyger,'"
PMLA 71 [1956]: 669-85.) Other useful discussions include that of
Hirsch, who thinks the stars are the rebel angels who threw down
their spears when they surrendered; and John E. Grant, "The Art and

282-283 (text pages)

Argument of 'The Tyger'" in Texas Studies in Literature and Language 2 (1960): 38-60.

LOUISE BOGAN, The Dream, page 282

In Louise Bogan: A Portrait (New York: Knopf, 1985), Elizabeth Frank discusses "The Dream," which Bogan wrote in her late thirties after having suffered a series of breakdowns. Bogan herself described the poem as "the actual transcript of 'a nightmare,' but there is reconciliation involved with the fright and horror. It is through the possibility of such reconciliations that we, I believe, manage to live." Thus Frank sees the horse (the night-mare) as "the accumulated power of terror and rage Bogan had only recently confronted during her breakdowns," and the other woman in the poem, who comes to the rescue, as "Bogan's new self, the 'cured' woman, the emergent adult and artist." The glove, according to Frank, "Becomes a symbol of challenge and submission, a token of the poet's strong feminine sexuality--and perhaps many other things as well. Put at the mercy of the beast, who is not only appeased, but in turn enchanted, the glove in the end represents the poet's whole self, triumphant over the lovingly submissive beast."

MARK ALEXANDER BOYD, Cupid and Venus, page 283

Offer a prize to any student who, on a few days' notice, can read this poem aloud. (All it takes is nerve, and a passable Scottish burr.)

The allusions in lines 5-8 will need unraveling. Eros, god of love in Greek mythology (Cupid in Roman), is a youth, the son of Venus, and the lover of the maiden Psyche. Later tradition reduces him to a child and renders him blind or blindfolded. That Venus was born from the sea will be remembered from Botticelli's painting of the goddess on the half-shell, with which some students are probably acquainted.

A Scottish Petrarchan, Boyd shares (belatedly) the tradition that represents the lover as helpless and obsessed--visible in the Wyatt and Surrey versions of Petrarch's line on page 127. Ezra Pound has called this the most beautiful sonnet in the English language, and students may be asked what there is to admire in it.

EMILY BRONTË, Love and Friendship, page 283

This poem appeared in the Brontë sisters' first published book, Poems by Currer, Ellis, and Acton Bell, which came out in 1846. Fannie E. Ratchford, the scholar who found that most of Emily's poems were not reflections of her personal life, as early scholars and biographers had assumed, but rather "pertain to an imaginative country called Gondal, which she created when she was thirteen or fourteen years old and continued to develop as long as

she lived," calls "Love and Friendship" a Gondal poem "unplaced in
the story pattern" ("The Gondal Story," in The Complete Poems of
Emily Jane Brontë, ed. C. W. Hatfield [New York: Columbia UP,
1952]).

In "Love and Friendship" the poet sustains her opening similes
to the end. It is clear that the speaker values the holly more
than the wild rose briar.

GWENDOLYN BROOKS, The Rites for Cousin Vit, page 284

Cousin Vit, a vital, life-loving woman (a prostitute?), is
dead. In this contemporary sonnet, the poet depicts her as too
lively a presence to be confined by the casket, the "stuff and
satin aiming to enfold her, / The lid's contrition nor the bolts
before." To the poet, Cousin Vit appears to be still energetically
moving about: walking, talking, drinking, dancing as of old. The
wonderful Is. that ends the poem emphatically sums up the dead
woman's undying vigor.

GWENDOLYN BROOKS, Sadie and Maud, page 284

As in "The Rites for Cousin Vit," Brooks in "Sadie and Maud"
comes down squarely on the side of those who, like Sadie, "scraped
life / With a fine-tooth comb." Uninhibited by the proprieties,
full of zest and energy, "one of the livingest chits / In all the
land," Sadie lived triumphantly, managing even to pass her zest
(her fine-tooth comb) on to her born-out-of-wedlock children. Poor
Maud, on the other hand, a "thin brown mouse," a paragon of
middle-class virtue, "is living all alone / In this old house."
Both sisters, the poet seems to say, got what they deserved.

OLGA BROUMAS, Cinderella, page 285

Poem and title both carry ironic overtones. "Cinderella" is a
feminist poem, narrated by a woman with certain similarities to
Cinderella, as the first two stanzas make clear. A woman who has
become a success in the world of men, the narrator apparently
represents all women who, grateful to have been allowed into "a
house of men / who secretly / call themselves princes," have had to
pay a high price for their success. Proud of having been found
acceptable, the "woman writer, the lady / umpire, the madam
chairman, anyone's wife" worked overtime, tried to please, felt
privileged to be singled out, to have the "princes" tell them they
were superior to other women.

Unlike the fairy-tale Cinderella, the poet makes clear, these
exceptional women do not live happily ever after. Instead, they
find themselves "in a state of siege." The narrator (and by
implication the feminists she speaks for) comes to the realization
that, in striving so hard to gain respect and admiration from men,
to succeed on their own terms, she has all the while been guilty of

betraying other women, has been "forced / to bear witness, falsely / against my kind, as each / other sister was judged inadequate, bitchy, incompetent, / jealous, too thin, too fat." And her hard-won success, she realizes, is largely illusory: she is a "woman co-opted by promises."

The narrator apparently decides, finally, as have many contemporary feminists, that a "cold stove, a cinder-block pillow, wet / canvas shoes in my sisters', my sisters' hut"--in other words, solidarity with all women--will supply greater health and happiness than lonely acclaim in the world of men.

ELIZABETH BARRETT BROWNING, How do I love thee? Let me count the ways, page 286

This is the penultimate sonnet of forty-four constituting Elizabeth Barrett Browning's Sonnets from the Portuguese, a book that Ezra Pound once called "The second: that is, a sonnet sequence surpassed in English by one other alone. I would argue for that." The sonnets document the poet's growing love for Robert Browning, whom she married, in defiance of her father's wishes, in her fortieth year. "My little Portuguese" was a pet name Robert often used for Elizabeth: hence the title of her book.

Another fine sonnet by Elizabeth Barrett Browning, "Grief," appears on page 166.

ROBERT BROWNING, My Last Duchess, page 286

ROBERT BROWNING, Soliloquy of the Spanish Cloister, page 288

These two dramatic poems, both uttered by speakers we find unsympathetic, may be taken together as memorable works of character drawing. In each poem, Browning places us in the midst of a society thoroughly undemocratic and remote from our own in time. Of the two, only "My Last Duchess" is a typical dramatic monologue. "Soliloquy," as its title indicates, addresses no listener. "My Last Duchess" may be familiar to students from high school literature courses; and if a show of hands indicates that they have met it before, you may wish to spend less time with it. Whether or not it is familiar, it makes a useful companion to "Soliloquy."

Students may be asked to define their feelings toward the Duke and to point to lines in the poem that help define those feelings. Browning stresses the Duke's arrogance ("I choose / Never to stoop. . . . I gave commands; / Then all smiles stopped together") and engages our sympathies for the poor Duchess in lines 21-31, despite the Duke's contempt for her facility to be gladdened. We know one instructor who in teaching this classic takes the tack, "Shouldn't we feel sorry for the Duke, with all his marital troubles?" Students of both sexes are usually provoked to rise and trounce him. Another question: To what extent is the Duke's attitude toward women presumably typical of his society? That the Count,

the visitor's master, would offer a daughter to a man who had just
disposed of his wife, suggests that the Duke is not alone in regarding women as chattels. Still, even for a Renaissance duke he
seems cold-hearted; wives and works of art seem identified as
objects to collect. What were the Duke's commands that stopped the
Duchess's smiles? "That she should be put to death, or he might
have had her shut up in a convent," Browning once explained. But
lines 2 ("Looking as if she were alive") and 46-47 ("There she
stands / As if alive") seem to hint that she was executed. Hypocrisy is still another aspect of the Duke's character: compare his
protest that he lacks skill in speech (lines 35-36) with his artful
flattery of the Count (49-53).

    Like "My Last Duchess," the "Soliloquy" is another poem espe-
cially valuable to combat the notion that poetry can deal only in
love and gladness. Here, the subject is a hatred so intense that
the speaker seems practically demented. In the last stanza, he
almost would sell his soul to the Devil in order to blight a
flowering shrub. A little background information on abbeys, their
organization, and the strictness of their rules may help some class
members. From internal evidence, it is hard to say whether this is
a sixteenth-century cloister or a nineteenth-century one: Barbary
corsairs (line 31) plied their trade from about 1550 until 1816.
The business about drinking in three sips (lines 37-39) may need
explaining: evidently it refers to a symbolic observance, like
crossing knife and fork.

    It might be stressed that the person in this poem is not the
poet: the tone isn't one of bitterness, but of merriment. Comedy
is evident not only from the speaker's blindness to his own faults,
but from the rollicking rhythm and multisyllable comic rimes
(abhorrence / Lawrence; horsehairs / corsair's; Galatians / damna-
tions; rose-acacia / Plena gratia).

    Questions: With what sins does the speaker charge Brother
Lawrence? (Pride, line 23--monogrammed tableware belonging to a
monk!; lust, 25-32; and gluttony, 40.) What sins do we detect in
the speaker himself? (Envy, clearly, and pride--see his holier-
than-thou attitude in stanza 5. How persuasive are his claims to
piety when we learn he secretly owns a pornographic novel?)
"Soliloquy" abounds in ironies, and class members can spend a
lively few minutes in pointing them out.

    For a précis or summing-up of the poem, see page 208 of this
manual.

THOMAS CAREW, Ask me no more where Jove bestows, page 290

    Carew's poem is an eloquent tribute to a lady whose complexion
is so beautiful, the poet says, that it must emanate, with divine
assistance, from the very roses. Her hair is made of sunbeams, her
voice is like the nightingale's, and the stars twinkle in her eyes.
Exaggerated? Yes. Still, what woman, even in the unromantic
1980s, wouldn't relish so lyrical a testimonial to her beauty?

    You might want to ask your class to compare "Ask me no more
where Jove bestows" with "My mistress' eyes are nothing like the

sun" (page 254), where Shakespeare twits the Petrarchan conventions while of course relying as heavily as Carew does upon his readers' ability to appreciate a well-turned conceit.

Herbert J. C. Grierson, in his anthology Metaphysical Lyrics and Poems of the Seventeenth Century (Oxford UP, 1921), waxes poetic over the dividing throat: "One seems to hear and see Celia executing elaborate trills as Carew sits entranced."

There is a famous anecdote about Carew, which may or may not be true. One evening he was lighting King Charles I to the queen's chamber. Entering the room first, the poet saw the queen in the arms of Lord St. Albans. Before the king noticed that anything was amiss, Carew tactfully stumbled, thus extinguishing his candle long enough for the queen to adjust her position. His quick thinking endeared Carew to the queen from that day forward.

FRED CHAPPELL, Skin Flick, page 290

Nastily playful though this poem may be, it makes a serious comment. Students will probably enjoy working through the details of Chappell's comparison between the porn movie's male audience and cowboys surrounded by Indians. (A theme: The more things change, the more they remain the same.) "No water for miles and miles" is a cliché from those grade-C western films now replaced by X-rated fare. Like cowboy movies of the 1940s and 1950s, skin flicks are loveless affairs: "No / Mushy love stuff for them." (Such mush was usually avoided in Hopalong Cassidy horse operas by having the hero ride off into the twilight whenever the heroine invited him to stay awhile and settle down.) In Chappell's poem, lack of water reflects lack of love as surely as it does in the anonymous "Western Wind" (page 276) or in Eliot's Waste Land.

The parallel appears in other ways. Naked bodies are a "different sort of cattle drive." Once Gene Autry was "in the saddle," nowadays it's hard-core porn stars John Holmes or Harry Reems. "The burning bush strikes dumb" points at least three ways: (1) the burning bush or wahoo tree of the West, possibly also sagebrush on the scorching plains; (2) luridly lit pubic hair; (3) the burning bush that astounded Moses in Exodus 3:2-4. In the last line, yet another cliché from western movies takes on new meaning. Like settlers ringed by hostile Indians, pornography addicts are worried and tense, a huddle of men on guard against the outside world.

Chappell, novelist and poet, shared the 1984 Bollingen prize for poetry with John Ashbery. Among his works in poetry are the tetralogy Midquest (Baton Rouge: Louisiana State UP, 1981). He teaches English at the University of North Carolina, Greensboro.

G. K. CHESTERTON, The Donkey, page 291

Questions for discussion:

1. Who is the speaker--some particular donkey? (No, the genetic donkey, looking back over the history of his kind.)
2. To what prehistoric era does Chesterton refer in lines 1-3? (To the original chaos out of which the world was made. The poet apparently imagines it in bizarre, dreamlike imagery: fish with wings, walking forests, fig-bearing thorn.) Chesterton was fascinated by the book of Genesis "because of its beginning in chaos," comments Garry Wills in his introduction to a reprint edition of Chesterton's novel of 1908, The Man Who Was Thursday (New York: Sheed, 1975). The novel hints at a playful God who enjoys returning things to chaos every now and then. Writing about the world of dream in a newspaper article in 1904, Chesterton remarked, "A world in which donkeys come in two is clearly very near to the wild ultimate world where donkeys are made."
3. Whose "ancient crooked will" is meant? The will of the devil in perversely designing the donkey, or the donkey's own venerable stubbornness? (We're not certain.)
4. What fools does the donkey chide in the last stanza? (Anybody who ever abused a donkey, or who thinks donkeys contemptible.)
5. Explain how the allusion in the last stanza is essential to the meaning of the poem.
6. What devices of sound contribute to the poem's effectiveness?

AMY CLAMPITT, The Cormorant in His Element, page 291

In her early sixties, Clampitt is nevertheless a recent arrival on the literary scene, with two critically acclaimed books of poetry to her credit: The Kingfisher (New York: Knopf, 1983) and What the Light Was Like (Knopf, 1985). Her lush diction in "The Cormorant in His Element" almost immediately calls to mind Gerard Manley Hopkins, and one good way to begin discussion of her poem might be to suggest that students compare it with "The Windhover" (page 320). Similarities abound. Both sonnets, Clampitt's perhaps more literally, describe birds that hunt, flying and diving for prey. Both use hyphens to yoke words into striking, surprising combinations. More than once the hyphen appears at the end of a line--even, in Clampitt's poem, before a stanza-break. In both poems the syntax is complex, the tone lofty, the figures of speech extravagant. Hopkins alliterates more; he is in general even less restrained than Clampitt. But the two poets appear to hear similar music inside their heads.

For a start, you may want to be sure that your students can define all the words Clampitt uses in her poem, especially implacably, ramrod, adherence, splayed, vermilion (Hopkins uses gold-vermilion!), involuted, arabesque, inimitable.

How many people in your class have seen cormorants dive? Why
not ask them how accurately they think Clampitt has observed these
strange birds, which, when under water, look almost like fish?
Maybe they can even trace, in words or on the blackboard, the
bird's course as the poet sees it.

It might also be rewarding to have students pick out and
discuss the poem's most striking figures of speech: "bony pot-
bellied arrow," the feet as landing gear, the bird's dive as
arabesque. Be sure they savor "wing-pumping along / implacably"
and "vermilion- / strapped"--and that they know who Houdini was!
(Homo Houdini seems a play on Homo sapiens--implying that the
cormorant's act surpasses that of any stage magician.) The main
thing is that students at least begin to appreciate Clampitt's
Houdinian word magic.

LUCILLE CLIFTON, to the unborn and waiting children, page 292

Clifton once said, "I am a black woman poet, and I sound like
one." In this poem she addresses an unusual audience: "unborn and
waiting children." She begins by reminiscing about her own birth,
which took place (not surprisingly) without her permission. Who
are the "eavesdroppers" she addresses in the last four lines? Are
they other unborn children, listening on the sidelines? She warns
them, as if they had a choice, that to enter a woman's body is
risky. Is she advising them to avoid being born if they can? We
think not. The poem's jaunty tone seems to hint that affliction is
a small price to pay for life.

SAMUEL TAYLOR COLERIDGE, Kubla Khan, 292

The circumstances of this poem's composition are almost as
famous as the poem itself, and, for the convenience of instructors
who wish to read to their students Coleridge's prefatory note, here
it is:

In the summer of the year 1797, the author, then in ill
health, had retired to a lonely farmhouse between Porlock and
Linton, on the Exmoor confines of Somerset and Devonshire. In
consequence of a slight indisposition, an anodyne had been
prescribed, from the effects of which he fell asleep in his
chair at the moment that he was reading the following
sentence, or words of the same substance, in Purchas's
Pilgrimage: "Here the Khan Kubla commanded a palace to be
built, and a stately garden thereunto. And thus ten miles of
fertile ground were inclosed with a wall." The author
continued for about three hours in a profound sleep, at least
of the external sense, during which time he had the most vivid
confidence that he could not have composed less than from two
to three hundred lines; if that indeed can be called
composition in which all the images rose up before him as
things, with a parallel production of the correspondent ex-

pressions, without any sensation or consciousness of effort.
On awaking he appeared to himself to have a distinct
recollection of the whole, and taking his pen, ink, and paper,
instantly and eagerly wrote down the lines that are here preserved. At this moment he was unfortunately called out by a
person on business from Porlock, and detained by him above an
hour, and on his return to his room, found, to his no small
surprise and mortification, that though he still retained some
vague and dim recollection of the general purport of the
vision, yet, with the exception of some eight or ten scattered
lines and images, all the rest had passed away like the images
on the surface of a stream into which a stone has been cast,
but, alas! without the after restoration of the latter!

It is clearly a vulgar error to think the poem a mere pipe
dream, which anyone could have written with the aid of opium. The
profound symbolism of "Kubla Khan" has continued to intrigue
critics, most of whom find that the pleasure-dome suggests poetry,
the sacred river, the flow of inspiration, or instinctual life.
About the ancestral voices and the caves of ice there seems less
agreement, and students might be invited to venture their guesses.
For a valuable modern reading of the poem, see Humphry House,
"Kubla Khan, Christable and Dejection" in Coleridge (London: Hart-
Davis, 1953), also reprinted in Romanticism and Consciousness, ed.
Harold Bloom (New York: Norton, 1970).
Some instructors may wish to bring in "The Rime of the Ancient
Mariner" as well--in which case it may be a temptation to go on to
Jung's theory of archetypes and to other dreamlike poems such as
Yeats's "The Second Coming" (page 217). A fine topic for a term
paper might be, after reading John Livingston Lowes's classic
source study The Road to Xanadu (Boston: Houghton, 1927), to argue
whether it is worth trying to find out everything that may have
been going on in the back of a poet's mind, and to what extent such
investigations can end in certainty.

WILLIAM COWPER, Praise for the Fountain Opened, page 294

Here is a great eighteenth-century hymn, face-to-face with
Emily Dickinson's best-known poem on the right-hand page. Many
students are intrigued to discover that Dickinson's favorite stanza
may have been taken from the hymns she heard in church, and here is
your chance to demonstrate this theory persuasively. Dickinson, of
course, is freer in her off-riming (although Cowper permits himself
to rime prepared with reward). The proof of the influence is in
the singing--if you care to lead the class in song! "Praise for
the Fountain Opened" may be sung to the tune of the more familiar
"O God, Our Help in Ages past," although the music of any other
hymn in common meter will fit. "Because I could not stop for
Death" will go surprisingly well to this tune, too.
Cowper's hymn may be a bit sanguine for contemporary taste,
but it is worth noting that its concerns with death and paradise
are often Dickinson's prime concerns as well. Both hymnists write

135

294-295 (text pages)

in the first person, reporting a spiritual experience as personal.
Dickinson, we think, is clearly the superior dramatist.

EMILY DICKINSON, Because I could not stop for Death, page 295

    Questions for discussion:

    1. What qualities does Dickinson attribute to Death? Why is
Immortality going along on this carriage ride? (For the poet,
death and immortality go together. Besides, Dickinson is
amplifying her metaphor of Death as a gentleman taking a woman for
a drive: Immortality, as would have been proper in Amherst, is
their chaperone.)
    2. Is the poem, as the poet wrote it, in some ways superior
to the version first printed? Is strove perhaps a richer word than
played? What is interesting in the phrase Gazing Grain? How can
grain "gaze"? (It has kernels like eyes at the tips of its stalks.
As the speaker dies, the natural world--like the fly in "I heard a
Fly buzz" on page 208 is watching.) What is memorable in the
rhythm and meaning of the line "The Dews drew quivering and chill?"
(At quivering, the rhythm quivers loose from its iambic tetrameter.
The image of cold dampness foreshadows the next stanza, with its
images of the grave.)
    3. What is the Carriage? What is the House?
    4. Where is the speaker at the present moment of the poem?
Why is time said to pass more quickly where she is now? (Eternity
is timeless.)
    5. What is the tone of the poem? (Complicated!--seriousness
enlivened with delicate macabre humor? Surely she kids her own
worldly busyness in the opening line.)
    William Galperin reads the poem as a feminist affirmation.
Not death, he finds, but immortality is Dickinson's subject. In
the end the poet asserts a triumph possible only because she has
renounced the proposal of Death, that threatening gentleman caller
who might have married her ("Emily Dickinson's Marriage Hearse,"
Denver Quarterly Winter 1984: 62-73).
    Don't fail to have the class try singing this poem and
Cowper's hymn, on the facing page, to the same tune. Whatever the
quality of your rendition, the result will be a class neither you
nor the students will forget!

EMILY DICKINSON, I started Early - Took my Dog, page 296

    It would be unfortunate if students were to regard this poem
as nothing more than a sexual fantasy. Handled with frankness and
tact, it can be an excellent class-awakener. The poet expresses
feelings for the natural world so intense that, like a mystic
choosing erotic imagery to speak of the Beatific Vision, she can
report her walk on the beach only in the language of a ravishing.
The humor of the poem also is essential: The basement-dwelling
mermaids, the poet's self-picture as a mouse.

EMILY DICKINSON, My Life had stood - a Loaded Gun, page 296

This astonishing metaphysical poem (another hymnlike work in common meter) can be an excellent provoker of class debate. Before trying to fathom it, students might well examine its diction. Sovreign Woods ("sovereign" would be the more usual spelling) suggest an estate owned by a king. How do the Mountains reply? By echoing the gun's report. Apparently the smile is the flash from the gun's muzzle; and the Vesuvian face, a glimpse of the flaming crater of the volcano. The Eider-Duck, a sea duck, has particularly soft and silky down which is used in pillows and quilts. The gun's Yellow Eye seems, again, its flash; and the emphatic Thumb is presumably the impact of the bullet that flattens its victim. (Some will say the thumb is a trigger finger, but you don't pull a trigger with your thumb.)

Argument over the meaning of the poem will probably divide the class into two camps. One will see the poem, like "Because I could not stop for Death," as an account of resurrection, with the Owner being God or Christ, who carries away the speaker, life and all, to the Happy Hunting Grounds of Paradise. Personally, we incline toward the other camp. In that view the Owner seems a mere mortal, perhaps a lover. The last stanza reveals that he can die. So taken, the last two lines make more sense. Not having the power to die, the speaker feels something lacking in her. She doesn't wish to outlive her huntsman and be a lonely killer.

Philip Larkin admits the possibility of both views: "This is romantic love in a nutshell, but who is its object? A religious poet--and Emily was this sometimes--might even have meant God" (Required Writing [New York: Farrar, 1984] 193).

Lately a third camp has appeared, proclaiming a feminist interpretation. The poem, as summed up by Adalaide Morris, "tells about a life packed with a potential that the self was not empowered to activate." From this point of view, the poem is overtly political, exhilarating to teach because it recognizes long suppressed animosities ("Dick, Jane, and American Literature: Fighting with Canons," College English 47 [1985]: 477).

But the poem remains tantalizingly ambiguous. You won't know until you go into class what a discussion may reveal.

JOHN DONNE, The Bait, page 297

Izaak Walton, who included "The Bait" in The Compleat Angler, declared that Donne wrote the poem in order to prove that he could write softly and smoothly when he wished.

Writing answers to Marlowe's shepherd apparently was a popular Elizabethan parlor game. (There is also Sir Walter Raleigh's "The Nymph's Reply," page 346.) Donne certainly alters and complicates the tone of Marlowe's gentle Petrarchan pastoral. As a comparison of the figures of speech in the two poems will show, Donne characteristically relies on paradox ("For thou thyself art thine own bait") and on an extended metaphor: loved one is bait; lover, fish. Donne renders Marlowe's concept thoughtier and injects notes

297-298 (text pages)

of grating realism: <u>freeze</u>, <u>cut their legs</u>, <u>coarse</u> hands wrestling
live fish from <u>slimy nest</u>. Donne's lines 13-14 may need paraphrasing. XJK's attempt: if you don't wish to be seen skinny-dipping,
then just eclipse the sun and moon with your superior radiance.

JOHN DONNE, Death be not proud, page 298

    During the Renaissance, when life was short, a man of the
cloth like Donne would have surprised no one by being on familiar
terms with death. Still, "Death be not proud," one of Donne's
"Holy Sonnets," is an almost startling put-down of "poor death."
Staunchly Christian in its sure expectation of the resurrection,
Donne's poem personifies death as an adversary swollen with false
pride and unworthy of being called "mighty and dreadful." (For
another bold personification, see "Batter my heart, three-personed
God [page 40], also one of the 'Holy Sonnets," in which Donne sees
God as ravisher.)
    In "Death be not proud" the poet accuses death of being little
more than a slave bossed around by "fate, chance, kings, and desperate men"--a craven thing that keeps bad company, such as
"poison, war, and sickness." Finally Donne taunts death with a
paradox: "death, thou shalt die."
    Of interest, though perhaps of less than immediate usefulness
in the classroom, are the articles on Donne's religious poetry by
Helen Gardner, Louis L. Martz, and Stanley Archer in <u>John Donne's</u>
<u>Poetry: Authoritative Texts, Criticism</u>, ed. A. L. Clements (New
York: Norton, 1966). All three explore the extent to which Jesuit
methods of meditation might have influenced the "Holy Sonnets."
    It might be instructive for students to compare two personifi-
cations of death: Donne's and Emily Dickinson's in "Because I
could not stop for Death" (page 295), where death appears in the
guise of a courtly gentleman who stops by to take the poet for a
pleasant ride.

JOHN DONNE, The Flea, page 298

    This outrageous poem is a good class-rouser on a dull day, but
we don't urge you to use it unless the class seems friendly. (Some
women students tend to be offended by Donne's levity; men tend to
be put off by his ingenuity.)
    A little familiarity with a seventeenth-century medical notion
may help make Donne's metaphor clear. Conception, it was thought,
took place when the blood of man and woman mingled during inter-
course. That is why Donne declares in line 11 that "we almost, yea
more than married are." Bitten by the flea containing his blood,
the woman may already be pregnant.
    Instructors fond of Donne's knotty poems will be grateful for
Theodore Redpath's valuable crib-book <u>The Songs and Sonnets of John</u>
<u>Donne: An Editio Minor</u> (London: Methuen, 1956; also New York:
University Paperbacks, 1967). Redpath works through the poems line
by line, explicating difficulties. He explains line 18: The woman

would commit "three sins in killing three" in that she'd commit murder in killing him, suicide in killing herself, and sacrilege in killing the flea. Why sacrilege? Because she would be attacking a "marriage temple."

Patricia Meyer Spacks has treated the poem to scrutiny in College English 29 (1968): 593-94.

JOHN DONNE, A Valediction: Forbidding Mourning, page 299

In his Life of Donne, Izaak Walton tells us that Donne wrote this poem for his wife in 1611, when he was about to depart on a diplomatic mission to France.

Much of the meaning of the poem depends upon the metaphor of the compasses in the last three stanzas. There is probably no better way to make sure students understand it clearly than to bring in a draftsman's compass--even the Woolworth's variety--and to demonstrate the metaphor with it. There'll always be someone who thinks Donne means the kind of compass that indicates north.

Some questions for discussion:

1. What is a valediction anyway? (What is a high school "valedictorian"?)
2. Why does the speaker forbid mourning? Do lines 1-4 mean that he is dying? Explain this metaphor about the passing away of virtuous men. (As saints take leave of this world--so sweetly and calmly that one hardly knows they're gone--let us take leave of each other.)
3. In lines 7-8, what is suggested by the words with religious denotations? Profanation (the desecration of a sacred thing), the laity. What is the idea? (Love seems to the speaker a holy mystery. He and his wife are its priests or ministers.)
4. Explain the reference to astronomy in the third stanza. (Earthquakes shake, rattle, and roll; Ptolemaic spheres revolve gently and harmlessly. This takes us to the notion of sublunary lovers in stanza 4. In the medieval cosmos, the heavenly bodies are fixed and permanent, while everything under the moon is subject to change.)
5. Paraphrase stanza 4. (Unlike common lovers, bound to their earthly passions, we have less need of those things that serve sensual love: namely, bodies.)
6. Why is beaten gold an appropriate image in the sixth stanza? What connotations does gold have? (Refined, precious, durable, capable of being extended without breaking.)
7. Comment on the word hearkens, line 31. (As a draftsman's compass will illustrate, the fixed central foot leans forward when the compass is extended, as if, in Donne's metaphor, eager for the other mate's return.)

300-301 (text pages)

JOHN DRYDEN, To the Memory of Mr. Oldham, page 300

With the aid of Dryden's great short poem (and the selections in the book from Swift, Pope, and Johnson), one at least can acquaint students with a little of neoclassical poetry. One can point out, too, that such poetry is not quite dead in America in our own day, as may be seen from the poems of Yvor Winters (page 377) and J. V. Cunningham (page 44, 169). The directness and plainness of Dryden's poem are clear from its very opening, and in teaching it one can question the assumption that neoclassical poetry is written only in bookish and Latinate words.

In teaching Dryden's poem, one can also mention (and define) the elegy, and can refer students to other famous elegies in the text: those of Milton (page 15) and Gray (page 257). If one is going to teach "Lycidas," Dryden's succinct poem might well serve as an introduction. It may be readily compared with "Lycidas" in that it mourns the death of a poet, expresses abhorrence for knaves, and observes a few classical conventions.

A. E. Housman's "To an Athlete Dying Young" (page 323) also may be likened to Dryden's poem in that both poets favor classical conventions: footraces with laurels as crowns and the dead hero's descent into the underworld. Both poets find that premature death can confer benefits. What would Oldham have gained had he survived? More polish as a poet, yet he would have lost much of his force. In reading Housman's poem, students can be helped to recognize its metaphors: the comparison in the first two stanzas of victor's chair and dead lad's coffin, the comparison in line 5 of all human life to a footrace, with death at the finish line. Students might be asked if they know of any living proof of Housman's observation that sometimes the name dies before the man (a truth often shown by the wistfulness of old football players at alumni weekends).

NORMAN DUBIE, The Funeral, page 301

Vermont, where Dubie was born, may well be the setting for this elegy, with its mention of bitter cold and snow and its several allusions to simple rural life (the brook, the springhouse, the marsh, the "offal's pail," the barn, the fragrant bed linen, the horse piss). What is the point of view? It seems to be that of a man looking back though the eyes of the small child he was when his aunt was his companion--and when she died. His memories abound with sensuous details:

> There were rows of butter in small bricks, a mold
> Like ermine on the cheese,
> And cut onions to rinse the air
> Of the black, sickly-sweet meats of rotting pecans.

The aunt must have been very young, perhaps a child herself when she was stricken with cancer. There is no sentimental blubbering here, just understated forthrightness. ("It felt like

140

the zero in brook ice"; "Uncle Peter, in a low voice, said / The
cancer ate her like horse piss eats deep snow.") The cold and snow
underscore the bleak fact of the aunt's death.

Students might be asked to compare this poem with John Crowe
Ransom's "Bells for John Whiteside's Daughter (page 348) and with
Theodore Roethke's "Elegy for Jane" (page 352).

ALAN DUGAN, Love Song: I and Thou, page 301

Except in his title, Dugan doesn't refer to I and Thou, the
work by Martin Buber, Jewish philosopher and Zionist. But in its
theme, Dugan's poem shares Buber's view that a meaningful rapport
with others is necessary in order to endure the human condition.

Dugan's cockeyed homemade house is his life, which he will
endure like a prolonged crucifixion. The house-warming in line 14
may be infancy: the thumb that the baby Dugan sucked purple is
like the bruised thumb of the amateur carpenter whose hammer
slipped. The prime whiskey of rage is the baby's first stimulant:
primal, because indulged in from the start. In the last lines,
trying to crucify oneself is a hopeless task (like trying to ply a
nail scissors with both hands). Some things one can't do for
oneself. Humorous and self-mocking in tone up until the end,
Dugan's "Love Song" ends on a note of grudging tenderness.

T. S. ELIOT, Journey of the Magi, page 302

The speaker is a very old man ("All this was a long time ago
. . ."), looking forward to his death. As his mind roves back over
the past, it is mainly the discomforts and frustrations of his
journey that he remembers, and when he comes to the part we have
been waiting for, his account of the Nativity, he seems still mys-
tified, as though uncertainly trying to figure out what had
happened--"There was a Birth, certainly." Apparently the whole
experience was so devastating that he prefers to omit all further
details. His plight was to recognize Christ as God and yet to be
unable to accept Christ as his savior. Being a king, he did not
renounce his people but they henceforth seemed alien to him,
clutching their discredited gods like useless dolls.

The passage beginning "Then at dawn" (lines 21-28) is full of
foreshadowings, both hopeful and sinister. Besides the symbolic
white horse, the vine leaves suggest Christ, who said to his
disciples, "I am the vine, ye are the branches" (John 15:5). The
tavern customers suggest the Roman soldiers who will drink and cast
dice at the cross.

Although Eliot's dissatisfied Magus isn't one of the kings
portrayed by Yeats in "The Magi" (page 382)--being dissatisfied for
different reasons--it is curious that Eliot may have taken the
dramatic situation of his poem from one of Yeats's stories. In
"The Adoration of the Magi" in Yeats's prose collection Mythologies
(reprinted in 1925, two years before Eliot first published his
poem), three old men call on the storyteller, and, drawing close to

302-306 (text pages)

his fire, insist on telling him of a journey they had made when
young, and of a vision of Bethlehem. Like Eliot's speaker, who
repeats "set down / This set down / This," they demand that their
story be taken down word for word.

Among the useful discussions of Eliot's poem are Elizabeth
Drew's in T. S. Eliot: The Design of His Poetry (New York:
Scribner's, 1949) 118-22, and Grover Smith's in T. S. Eliot's
Poetry and Plays (Chicago: U of Chicago P, 1960) 121-25. More
recently, Daniel A. Harris has characterized the Magus as a
primitive Christian with a "baffled consciousness of mystery." See
his article "Language, History, and Text in Eliot's 'Journey of the
Magi,'" PMLA 95 (1980): 838-56. But Harris's opinions are
questioned by William Skaff in a letter in PMLA 96 (1981): 420-22:
"In 'Journey' Eliot adopts the dramatic mask of the Magus in order
to express his own struggles with literal belief, his real
'religious position of 1927.'"

T. S. ELIOT, The Love Song of J. Alfred Prufrock, page 303

Teaching any basic course in literature, an instructor would
have to be desperate for time not to devote to "Prufrock" at least
a class or two. Eliot's early masterpiece can open such diverse
matters as theme, tone, irony, persona, imagery, figures of speech,
allusion, symbolism, and the difference between saying and suggesting. Most students will enjoy it and remember it.

Questions to raise:

1.   Why the epigraph from Dante? What expectations does it
arouse? (Perhaps that this "song" will be the private confession
of someone who thinks himself trapped and unredeemable, and thinks
it of his hearer, too.)
2.   What facts about J. Alfred can we be sure of? His age,
his manner of dress, his social circles? What does his name suggest? Can you detect any puns in it? (A prude in a frock--a
formal coat.)
3.   What do you make of the simile in lines 2-3? What does
it tell us about this particular evening? (Etherized suggests fog,
also submission, waiting for something grim to happen.) What does
it tell you about Prufrock's way of seeing things? ("A little
sick," some students may say, and with reason.)
4.   What gnaws at Prufrock? (Not just his sense of growing
old, not just his inability to act. He suffers from Prufrock's
Complaint: dissociation of sensibility. In line 105, unable to
join thought and feeling, he sees his own nerves existing at one
remove from him, as if thrown on a screen by a projector.)
5.   Who are "you and I" in the opening line? Who are "we" at
the end? (Some possibilities: Prufrock and the woman he is
attending. Prufrock and the reader. Prufrock and Prufrock--he's
talking to himself, "you" being the repressive self, "I" being the
timid or repressed self. Prufrock and the other eggheads of the

Western world--in this view, the poem is Eliot's satire on the intelligentsia.)

6.   What symbols do you find and what do they suggest? Notice those that relate to the sea, even oyster-shells (line 7). (XJK points out blatantly that water has connotations of sexual fulfillment, and quotes "Western Wind" [page 270]. Eliot hints that unlike Prufrock, the vulgar types who inhabit cheap hotels and fish shops have a love life.)

7.   Try to explain the last three lines.

8.   Now summarize the story of the poem. What parts does it fall into? (Part one: Prufrock prepares to try to ask the overwhelming question. Then in lines 84-86 we learn that he has failed to ask it. In 87-110 he tries to justify himself for chickening out. From 111 to the end, he sums up his static present and hollow future.)

That Eliot may have taken the bones of his plot from Henry James's story "Crapy Cornelia" (1909) is Grover Smith's convincing theory. "This is the story of White-Mason, a middle-aged bachelor of nostalgic temperament, who visits a young Mrs. Worthington to propose marriage but reconsiders owing to the difference in their worlds" (T. S. Eliot's Poetry and Plays [Chicago: U of Chicago P, 1960] 15).

"The meter of 'Prufrock' is peculiar," observes John Heath-Stubbs. "It is not simply free verse, as in [Eliot's] earlier Laforgueian pieces, but in its lines of irregular length, many but not all of which rhyme, suggests a free version of the Dantesque Canzone." This suggestion, and the poem's epigraph from the Inferno, point to Eliot's growing preoccupation with Dante ("Structure and Source in Eliot's Major Poetry," Agenda Spring-Summer 1985: 24).

T. S. Eliot Reading His Poetry (Caedmon recording TC 1045) includes the poet's rendition of "Prufrock."

ROBERT FROST, Stopping by Woods on a Snowy Evening, page 307

Students will think they know this poem from their elementary school textbooks, in which it is usually illustrated as though it were about a little horse, but they may need to have its darker suggestions underlined for them. Although one can present a powerful case for seeing Frost as a spokesman for the death wish, quoting other Frost poems such as "Come In," "To Earthward," and "Into My Own," we think it best to concentrate on this familiar poem and to draw the class to state what it implies. The last stanza holds the gist of it. What would he do if he didn't keep his promises? There is sense, however, in an objection a student once made: maybe he'd just stay admiring the snow for another fifteen minutes and be late for milking. "People are always trying to find a death wish in that poem," Frost told an audience at the Bread Loaf Writers' Conference in 1960. "But there's a life wish there--he goes on, doesn't he?"

Ask students if they see anything unusual about the rime scheme of the poem (rimes linking the stanzas as in terza rima or as in Shelley's "Ode to the West Wind"), and then ask what problem this rime scheme created for the poet as the poem neared its end. How else would Frost have ended it if he hadn't hit upon that magnificent repetition? In 1950 Frost wrote to a friend, "I might confess the trade secret that I wrote the third line of the last stanza of Stopping by Woods in such a way as to call for another stanza when I didn't want another stanza and didn't have another stanza in me, but with great presence of mind and a sense of what a good boy I was I instantly struck the line out and made my exit with a repeat end" (qtd. in Lawrance Thompson, Robert Frost: The Years of Triumph [New York: Holt, 1970] 597-98). On another occasion Frost declared that to have a line in the last stanza that didn't rime with anything would have seemed a flaw. "I considered for a moment winding up with a three line stanza. The repetend was the only logical way to end such a poem" (letter of 1923 to Sylvester Baxter, given by R. C. Townsend, New England Quarterly 36 [June 1963]: 243.)

That this famous poem may be sung to the old show tune "Hernando's Hideaway" (from The Pajama Game) was discovered by college students working as waiters at the Bread Loaf Writers' Conference in 1960.

Paper topic: Read Lionel Trilling's speech at Frost's eighty-fifth birthday dinner, in which Trilling maintained, "I think of Robert Frost as a terrifying poet" ("A Speech on Robert Frost: A Cultural Episode," Partisan Review 26 [Summer 1959]: 445-52; also reprinted in Robert Frost: A Collection of Critical Essays, ed. James M. Cox [Englewood Cliffs: Prentice, 1962]). Referring to "Stopping by Woods" and other Frost poems, state to what extent you agree with Trilling's view or disagree with it.

Frost reads the poem on An Album of Modern Poetry (Library of Congress, PL 20) and on Robert Frost Reading His Own Poems, record no. 1 (EL LCB 1941, obtainable from the National Council of Teachers of English, 1211 Kenyon Road, Urbana, IL 61801). Both recordings also include "Fire and Ice."

ROBERT FROST, The Wood Pile, page 307

A question students might want to ask about this blank verse poem, but don't dare, is: So somebody went off and left a pile of wood all cut and stacked--so what? The quietness of the poem may tempt a careless reader to feel that way. But like the speaker at the beginning of the poem, the student needs to say, "No, I will go on farther--and we shall see."

Evidently this woodpile means much to the poet, or else why would he write a poem about it? It could pass for a symbol, so large and mysterious does it loom in its poem. The speaker wonders about it: who would be such a fool as to do all that work and then go away and forget it, not bothering to enjoy the reward of his toil? Answer (line 35): "Someone who lived in turning to fresh tasks." The woodcutter isn't foolish; he is admirable. (Perhaps a

poet, unless he dwells on past accomplishment, ought to work that
way? Or perhaps not. Clearly the speaker doesn't want to be like
the silly bird in the first part of the poem, "one who takes /
Everything said as personal to himself.")
     Radcliffe Squires: "I read 'the slow smokeless burning of
decay' and I am humbled before the sheer massiveness of time. . . .
Though the wood-pile is decaying, the decay nevertheless in the
whole patient momentum of nature is a conflagration. But is not
the notion of warming a swamp ironical? Does it not merely
emphasize human loss and bleakness?" (The Major Themes of Robert
Frost [Ann Arbor: U of Michigan P, 1963] 39).
     Richard Poirier also sees the final vision of the poem as
bleak: this is a companion piece to "Desert Places" (page 132).
The soliloquy of a lone man in a winter world far from home, "The
Wood-Pile" is "about being impoverished, being on the dump." The
speaker attributes to the small bird his own ego-centered view.
Finding the wood-pile completes his vision of solitude and removal
from the world of men and women. The last line "induces a kind of
awe because it is the acknowledgment of nature as a realm wholly
independent of human need and even perception, and it belongs not
only in what it says but in its very cadence with Wordsworth's
evocation at the end of his sonnet 'Mutability' of 'the
unimaginable touch of time'" (Robert Frost: The Work of Knowing,
[New York: Oxford UP, 1977] 138-44).
     We agree with both critics on at least one point: this is a
magnificent last line. Question: Is it not possible instead to
read the ending of the poem as positive and upbeat? The woodpile
(one might argue) fulfills its purpose after all: it gives
pleasure (at least to speaker and reader); however slightly, it
warms its surroundings, as its cutter meant. The speaker has found
a kind of kinship after all: with that unknown solitary worker in
the wilderness.

TESS GALLAGHER, Under Stars, page 308

     The content of this poem is simple enough. The speaker goes
out in the night to post a letter in her roadside mailbox; she
imagines a millworker and his wife beginning their day before she
herself has gone to bed; and she remembers childhood games played
outside in the dark.
     The poem contains many small, exact details--the white en-
velope, the rain-heavy bushes, the white slices of bread the millworker's wife has laid out for him, to name a few. Yet the most
important details are omitted entirely. The poet does not tell us
who is to receive her letter, whose are the starry voices toward
which she walks, or to what she is returned by all she touches on
the way. Maybe she is purposely vague about these points because
her intent is not to tell a story, but to create for the reader the
kind of pensive mood familiar to those who have ever found
themselves alone under the stars.
     Biographical facts about Gallagher do not really help us find
our way deeper into "Under Stars," the title poem from her third

published book, where it appears last in a section called "The
Ireland Poems." We do learn from James K. Robinson's entry about
her in Contemporary Poets that she traveled in Ireland in 1976. In
this entry, Gallagher comments, 'Only in the language I have made
for myself in the poems am I in touch with all the past, present,
and future moments of my consciousness and unconsciousness. The
poem is the moment of all possibilities where I try to speak in a
concert of tenses, to reflect the intersection of the various
time-zones of actualities and imaginative transformations. I don't
want to disappear into the present tense, the awful NOW. I want to
survive it and to take others with me."

ALLEN GINSBERG, A Supermarket in California, page 309

    A comparison of this poem with Walt Whitman's "I Saw in
Louisiana a Live-Oak Growing" (page 375) and "To a Locomotive in
Winter" (page 13) demonstrates the extent to which Ginsberg, in his
tribute to Whitman, uses very Whitmanlike "enumerations."
Ginsberg's long sentences, use of free verse, parentheses, and
fulsome phrases ("childless, lonely old grubber," "lonely old
courage-teacher," etc.) are further indications that he is paying
tribute to Whitman in part by echoing his style.
    There is in "A Supermarket in California" as well a quality of
surrealism that is Ginsberg's own. The existence of a "Neon fruit
supermarket," the juxtaposition of past and present, the inclusion
of Spanish poet García Lorca (like Ginsberg and Whitman, a
homosexual) "down by the watermelons," and the references to Charon
and to the River Lethe all hover at the edges of dream.
    Questions for discussion: What does Ginsberg mean when he
speaks of "the lost America of love"? What does the poem say about
loneliness? about death? (Whitman's death, in the poem, is as
lonely a journey as Ginsberg imagines his life to have been.)

DANA GIOIA, California Hills in August, page 310

    Gioia has provided this note on his poem:

        "California Hills in August" was conceived as a defense
    of the special beauty of the dry landscape of California and
    the American Southwest. While the poem admits that an out-
    sider might initially find this environment harsh and even
    hostile in the hot summer months, it asks that the landscape
    be seen on its own terms and not judged as some deficient form
    of conventionally verdant summer scenery.
        Strangely, I did not write this poem until I had been
    living in the Northeast for several years. It was only then
    that I realized how foreign the sparse August hills of
    California seemed to most Americans who come from areas which
    are lushly green and overgrown during the summer. Likewise,
    living back East, I finally understood how much the symbolic
    framework of traditional English poetry depended on the

particular kind of climate shared by England and Eastern
America. Until then the seasonal patterns of this poetry with
its snowy winters and green summers had always seemed remote
and artificial to a Westerner like me, raised in a climate
which endowed a radically different sense of Nature's cycles.
I wondered why Western writers had not played with that
paradox more forcefully in their poetry.

These thoughts must have been in the back of my mind when
suddenly I returned home for a family emergency. Two
sleepless days later, after it had been resolved, I took a
noontime walk through some nearby hills. In the strangely
heightened consciousness of physical exhaustion and
dislocating travel, I found myself overwhelmed by the
delicate, sun-bleached beauty of the place. This was a
landscape which I had left long enough ago both to hunger for
as a native and to recoil from as an outsider. Sorting out
these contradictions as I walked home, I heard myself say the
first few lines of the poem. Writing out the opening stanzas
later that day, I realized how image by image this poem had
been forming for a long time in my unconscious.

The poem divides into two uneven parts. The first four
stanzas view the landscape through the eyes of an imaginary
Easterner who sees only the emptiness, deprivation, and
savagery of the place. But then in the final stanza the
speaker suddenly upsets everything said up to this point by
suggesting how a native might see the same place from a
different perspective. Isn't one of the purposes of poetry to
make us see the unexpected beauty of some person, place or
thing we previously took for granted or dismissed? That
transformation was what I hoped to accomplish in "California
Hills in August."

Gioia (the name is pronounced "Joy-a") is a business executive
who finds time to write literary criticism as well as poetry.
Recently he has edited the short stories of Weldon Kees and (with
William Jay Smith) Poems from Italy. At this writing, a first
collection of his poems is about to appear. "California Hills in
August" was first published in The New Yorker.

DONALD HALL, Names of Horses, page 310

Hall is apparently eulogizing not one horse but a long
succession of them, each taking on its predecessors' duties through
the years. The poem enumerates the everyday chores the horses had
to do, "generation on generation," Sundays included. The "man, who
fed you and kept you, and harnessed you every morning" represents
not a single farmer, apparently, but all those on this New
Hampshire farm who cared for and finally buried their horses in the
time-honored way "for a hundred and fifty years." Like all dead
animals (including people), the horses when they die become "soil
makers," useful even in their graves.

The wonderful list in the poem's last line delivers what the title has promised, names of horses. The last one, Lady Ghost, is the most connotative. You might wish to have students explore its suggestions.

First published in The New Yorker, this poem later appeared in Hall's seventh book of poems, Kicking the Leaves (New York: Harper, 1978). The farm in New Hampshire where Hall lives was once a working farm run by his grandparents and, before them, his great-grandparents. Hall has written a prose memoir, String Too Short to Be Saved (Boston: Godine, 1981), about the boyhood summers he spent there with his grandmother and grandfather. "Names of Horses," too, seems to depend heavily on the poet's fond memories of the farm he still loves.

THOMAS HARDY, The Convergence of the Twain, page 311

The discovery in September 1985 of the well-preserved wreck of the Titanic in the North Atlantic, and the subsequent squabble over possession of it, has given this old favorite poem a certain newsiness. Most students will be familiar with the history of this great disaster from recent news reports (or from the popular book and film Raise the Titanic!). Still, a few facts may need to be recalled. The fateful day was April 15, 1912. The pride of the British White Star lines, the Titanic was the world's largest ship in its day, celebrated for luxurious trappings (including Turkish baths and a fully equipped gym). Many of the unlucky passengers were wealthy and famous. One reason the Titanic sank with such cost of life was that the builders, smugly assuming the ship to be unsinkable, had provided lifeboats for fewer than half the 2,200 passengers. (Only 705 survived.) Hardy wrote the poem for the souvenir program of a benefit show for the Titanic Disaster Fund (to aid survivors and the bereaved) given at Covent Garden, May 14, 1912.

Hardy has been seen as an enemy of science and industrialism, those spoilers of rural England, but Donald Davie argues that "The Convergence of the Twain" shows no such animosity. The poem censures vanity and luxury, "but not the technology which built the great ship and navigated her" (Thomas Hardy and British Poetry [Oxford: Oxford UP, 1972]).

Although Hardy personally knew two victims of the disaster, the "Convergence," as J. O. Bailey points out, is not a personal lament; indeed, the drowned are hardly mentioned. The poem is a philosophic argument, with the Immanent Will punishing man for pride: "It acts like the Greek concept of Fate that rebukes hubris" (The Poetry of Thomas Hardy [Chapel Hill: U of North Carolina P, 1970]). Fate, however, seems personified in the poem as the Spinner of the Years, a mere agent of the Will.

Students can concentrate profitably on the poet's choice of words: those that suggest the exotic unnaturalness of the Titanic's furnishings (salamandrine, opulent, jewels . . . to ravish the sensuous mind, gilded). Diction will also point to the metaphor of the marriage between ship and iceberg: the intimate

welding and the consummation. The late Allen Tate was fond of
reading this poem aloud to his friends, with mingled affection and
contempt, and remarking (according to Robert Kent) that it held
"too many dead words, dead then as now, and all the more obtuse for
having been long dead in Shelley. 'Stilly,' for example." From
Hardy's original printed version of the poem, as given in The
Variorum Edition of the Complete Poems of Thomas Hardy, ed. James
Gibson (New York: Macmillan, 1979), it appears that he originally
cast line 6: "The cold, calm currents strike their rhythmic tidal
lyres." Isn't thrid an improvement, even though it is stiltedly
archaic?

THOMAS HARDY, Five Satires of Circumstance, page 313

     This is a selection from the fifteen "Satires of Circum-
stance," a sequence that (at the publisher's insistence) lent its
title to Hardy's poetry volume of 1914. This major collection
appeared in a momentous year for the poet: after his second
marriage and shortly after the outbreak of World War I. Hardy
himself had voiced doubts about putting these bitter items in a
book together with more recent, poignant elegies for his first
wife. He called them "caustically humorous productions which had
been issued with a light heart before the war"; and later remarked
to Edmond Gosse: "The scales had not fallen from my eyes when I
wrote them, and when I reprinted them they had" (letter of 16 Apr.
1918).
     Robert Gittings, a recent biographer, agrees with reviewers of
1914 that the "Satires" would have been better off as short stories
(Thomas Hardy's Later Years [Boston: Atlantic-Little, 1978]
161-63). Yet the astute John Crowe Ransom has been fond of these
caustic items. "They are satires rather than proper tragedies," he
observes, "being poems in which the victims are not entitled to our
sympathy. The joke is upon persons who have to be punished because
they were foolish; because they were more innocent than anybody can
afford to be in this world." The "Satires" show Hardy in a mood of
ferocity that enlarges his range, "though the gentle reader may not
like him any the better" (Introduction, Selected Poems of Thomas
Hardy [New York: Collier, 1966] xxx).
     We admire Hardy's extreme economy in telling these stories, in
centering on moral crises so painful that, unless we laugh, we must
cringe. Together, the "Satires" form a small gallery of various
kinds of irony.
     J. O. Bailey has illuminated the title "Satires of
Circumstance." Earlier, in a novel of 1876, Hardy had used the
phrase in describing a man who "sometimes had philosophy enough to
appreciate a satire of circumstance, because nobody intended it"
(The Hand of Ethelberta, chapter 12). Most of the poems in this
series, Bailey notes, present ironic situations that no one
intended. Some, like "In Church," depend on things accidentally
noticed or overheard (The Poetry of Thomas Hardy: A Handbook and
Commentary [Chapel Hill: U of North Carolina P, 1970] 334).

313-314 (text pages)

"In Church": Irony lies in a contrast between the pulpit personality of the preacher and the vain, self-satisfied actor he is when behind the scenes. One feels for his disillusioned little pupil: a terrible contrast is implied between her before and after views of her idol.

"In the Room of the Bride-elect": Ironies inhere in a contrast between what the parents wanted and what the bride wanted; between the bride's former mind and her mind now; between what the bridegroom knows and what we know.

"In the Cemetery": There's an ironic discrepancy between how the dead should be treated and this shuffling-about of their remains; between what the mothers assume and what the "man of the cemetery" knows. "In tone a poem of cynical humor, but Hardy's compassion is implied" (Bailey 337). The custodian's expressed view is certainly not the poet's. Ironically, this poem recalls a classic British folk ballad, "They're Digging Up Father's Grave to Build a Sewer."

"In the Nuptial Chamber": An ironic contrast lurks between the happy serenade and this horrific revelation. What a remarkably forthright bride! Wonderful detail: how, in line 2, the music turns her into a sinister ghost. As a child, Hardy had delighted in a country band organized by his father and grandfather; no doubt this combo serenaded many newlyweds. Compare the ironic situation of this poem with that in James Joyce's great story "The Dead" (in Dubliners).

"Over the Coffin": It would seem that Hardy agreed with the first wife . . . that divorce because of wounded pride or public opinion brings greater misery than tolerance. The irony of the first wife's wrong choice is deepened by the suggestion that the dead man is eavesdropping" (Bailey 339).

SEAMUS HEANEY, Sunlight, page 314

What is a sunlit absence? Absence of motion, perhaps, on a sunny afternoon in the country. This poem's diction is arresting; students who pay attention to it, with the aid of a dictionary if necessary, will be amply rewarded. The poet manages to be both accurate and surprising in such phrases as helmeted pump, slung bucket, and plaque of heat. (The dictionary defines plaque as "a flat plate, slab, or disk that is ornamental or engraved for mounting." Imagine a plaque of heat coming at you and you know that this was one hot stove!)

The woman in the poem says nothing. How, then, does the poet bring her alive? Ask your class to notice that her hands scuffled over the bake board and that she has measling (measly? thus "contemptibly small, meager"?) shins. Encourage students on the basis of these and additional details to characterize the woman Heaney portrays.

Why, in this poem, are two clocks better than one? (Two clocks double the impact of the poem's quiet power.)

The simile that ends the poem deserves special notice. What does a tinsmith's scoop in the meal bin have to do with love? Why

is the scoop "sunk past its gleam"? Like the woman herself,
perhaps, the love which underlies the performance of her everyday
tasks is plain, quiet, simple, "past its gleam"--but solidly
grounded, like the scoop in the bin.

Richard Murphy, in The New York Review of Books, 30 September
1976, has remarked of "Sunlight":

> Every word in it rings true to the culture, to my memory of
> Ireland in the past, to its sad beauty. The play of light and
> shadow in this poem, the spaces filled by sunlight, the woman
> baking bread, the tick of two clocks work like a revelation as
> in the art of Vermeer. I'm thinking of the Officer and
> Laughing Girl at the Frick, where a dark moment of time is
> suspended forever in a ray of light that pours through an open
> window, crosses a blank wall under a map of Holland, and is
> caught up by a girl's ecstatic smile.

ANTHONY HECHT, The Vow, page 315

The fear that too powerful a blend of Jewish and Irish spirits
caused the miscarriage is foreshadowed in the opening lines: "The
mirth of tabrets ceaseth," as does the joy of the Irish minstrel
harp. (Ceaseth gives the line an Old Testament ring.) Apparently
the poem reflects part of the poet's life: Hecht and his first
wife, Patricia Harris, were married in 1954; they had two sons.
"The Vow" was first printed in 1957.

Does the speaker accept the dream-child's tragic view that the
best of all fates is not to be born? Evidently not, or he wouldn't
make the vow. The bone gates (line 13) are not only the classical
gates of horn, but literally the mother's pelvic girdle. Stanza 3
seems a weak one in an otherwise powerful poem. In rhetoric,
diction ("Mother, . . ."), and imagery, it recalls the earlier
Robert Lowell (see for instance "Christmas Eve Under Hooker's
Statue" in Lord Weary's Castle).

In the last stanza, the metallurgical metaphor will probably
need explaining. Gentile and Jewish parents will be tried (refined, perfected) by the flames of their love. Possibly Hecht has
in mind amalgamation--the only gold-refining process that uses a
furnace--in which mercury and crude gold unite, then separate under
high heat to produce pure gold.

Hecht has recorded "The Vow" for The Spoken Arts Treasury of
100 Modern American Poets, vol. 15 (SA 1054).

GEORGE HERBERT, Love, page 316

Herbert's poem is often read as an account of a person's
reception into the Church; the eaten meat, as the Eucharist.
Herbert's extended conceits or metaphors are also evident in "The
Pulley" (page 94) and "Redemption" (page 207).

For discussion: compare "Love" with another seventeenth-
century devotional poem, Donne's "Batter my heart" (page 40).

What is the tone of each poem? Herbert may seem less intense, almost reticent by comparison. Douglas Bush comments, "Herbert does not attempt the high pitch of Donne's 'Divine Poems.' His great effects are all the greater for rising out of a homely, colloquial quietness of tone; and peace brings quiet endings--'So I did sit and eat'" (English Literature in the Earlier Seventeenth Century [New York: Oxford UP, 1945] 139).

Herbert, by the way, is an Anglican saint--according to Anthony Hecht, the only one who does not also appear in the Roman Catholic calendar.

ROBERT HERRICK, Delight in Disorder, page 317

Herrick's lovely poem is easy to paraphrase badly ("sloppiness is sexy"), and students will need to see the meanings of its words. Wantoness does not mean licentiousness; and Herrick is not condemning it (a wrong impression some students may get at first by recalling Robert Graves's "Down, Wanton, Down!" [page 38]). It means a natural and pleasing wildness, that freedom enjoyed by (in poetic diction) "wanton breezes" or "a wanton brook." Enthralls is a wonderful word; literally, the lace keeps the stomacher in check, keeping it pressed against the bosom; in another sense, the lace charms the garment. (The poet seems to attribute to the clothes his own kindled feelings.)

Delightful disorder is a principle of Herrick's poetry. Great master of metrical verse that he is, he knows that a poem "too precise in every part" (perfectly conforming, say, to an iambic pattern) would seem studied and monotonous. "Delight in Disorder," of course, contains many departures from absolutely regular iambic tetrameter. Herrick states his prosodic principle in a poem about his poetry, "A Request to the Graces":

Teach it to blush, to curtsie, lisp, and shew
Demure, but yet, full of temptation too.
Numbers ne'er tickle, or but lightly please,
Unless they have some wanton carriages.

ROBERT HERRICK, To the Virgins, to Make Much of Time, page 317

Roses would have suited Herrick's iambic meter--why is rose-buds richer? Rosebuds are flowers not yet mature, and therefore suggest virgins, not matrons. There may be a sexual hint besides: rosebuds more resemble private parts than roses. But in this poem, time flies; the rosebuds of line 1 bloom in line 3. Rose-buds is also rhymically stronger than roses, as Austin Warren has pointed out: it has a secondary stress as well as a primary. Warren has recalled that when he first read the poem in college in 1917, he misread rose-buds as roses, kept misreading it ever after, and only a half-century later realized his mistake and found a new poem in front of him. "In untutored youth, the sentiment and the rhythm suffice: the exactness of the language goes unnoticed. And in later life a remembered favorite escapes exact attention because we think we know it so well" ("Herrick Revisited," Michigan Quarterly Review 15 Summer 1976: 245-67).

Question for discussion: What do you think of Herrick's advice? Are there any perils in it?

MICHAEL HOGAN, Spring, page 318

It takes a great leap of human sympathy, we think, to see both from the point of view of prisoners (lines 7-12) and from that of a prison guard (13-16), who daydreams that his rifle is a fishing pole and who yearns to be elsewhere. Note the irony that plays between the beginning and the end of the poem. Small boys pretend they have rifles, while the guard, who actually has one, wistfully pretends his rifle is something else. The inside world of compound and quadrangle stands in sharp contrast to the world outside, where children play and trout swim in streams--and yet the poet, by imagining, by observing what is before him, combines both worlds into one.

Hogan's images of spring are unconventionally bleak: cracking ice, birds returned to peck at scraps, the old cons in jackets too thin to protect them from the cold. The grimness of these early images leaves us vulnerable to surprise in the poem's energy-packed and powerful last line.

This poem was written while Hogan, in Arizona State Prison, was a student in Richard Shelton's writing workshop. He has since won a Pushcart prize, a PEN Prison Writing Award, and a fellowship from the National Endowment of the Arts.

GARRETT KAORU HONGO, The Hongo Store / 29 Miles Volcano / Hilo, Hawaii, page 318

Hongo, born in Hawaii in 1951 and educated at Pomona College and the University of California, now teaches at the University of Missouri in Columbia. "The Hongo Store," apparently based on family lore as well as an old photograph, is gently humorous in tone. The father's saying "Be quiet" to the crying baby, the fact that the family car is an Edsel, the father's panicky defiance of the advice on the radio, and his broken English, all evoke gentle smiles. Yet an air of genuine thankfulness and relief pervades the final stanza. The family's only damage from the volcano's rumblings is a broken store window.

Among Hongo's strengths as a poet are his verbs. The volcano and the bells thud, the baby squalls, the radio squeals, the car grinds, the news barks and crackles. Such sensuous language makes it easy for the reader to take in Hongo's world.

GERARD MANLEY HOPKINS, Spring and Fall, page 319

Hopkins's tightly wrought syntax may need a little unraveling. Students may be asked to reword lines 3-4 in a more usual sequence ("Can you, with your fresh thoughts, care for leaves like the things of man?") and then to put the statement into more usual words. (An attempt: "Do you, young and innocent as you are, feel as sorry for falling leaves as for dying people?") Lines 12-13 may need a similar going-over and rough paraphrase. ("Neither any human mouth nor any human mind has previously formed the truth that the heart and spirit have intuited.") "Sorrow's springs are the same"--that is, all human sorrows have the same cause: the fact that all things pass away. A world of constant change is "the blight man was born for": an earth subject to death, having fallen from its original state of a changeless Eden. The difficulties of a Hopkins poem result from a swiftly thoughtful mind trying to jam all possible meaning into a brief space (and into words that are musical).

Wanwood is evidently a term the poet coined for pale autumn woods. W. H. Gardner, editor of Hopkins's poems, finds in it also the suggestion of "wormwood"--bitter gall, also wood that is worm-eaten. The term leafmeal reminds him of "piecemeal," and he paraphrases line 8: "One by one the leaves fall, and then rot into mealy fragments."

John Crowe Ransom's "Janet Waking" is another poem in which a sophisticated poet contemplates a grieving child. How do the poems differ? Ransom tries to convey the intensity of Janet's grief over her dead hen; Hopkins is content to talk to Margaret, like a priest trying to console her, and to philosophize.

Hopkins's great lyric ought to survive George Starbuck's brilliant travesty (page 236). The two are worth comparing in case students assume that what matters in poetry is the message alone, that particular words have no consequence. It will be a dull student who doesn't notice that Hopkins selects his words with greater precision and suggestiveness than does Starbuck (who is, of course, deliberately putting the idea crudely). Starbuck obviously is having a good time translating "Spring and Fall" into the American vernacular. His parody may be useful as a way into a number of crucial matters: the diction of a poem and how language indicates it. Who or what is the butt of Starbuck's ridicule? Is it Hopkins and his poem; or the speaker himself, his crudeness, his hard-boiled simplemindedness? (Howard Moss performs a comparable reduction of a sonnet of Shakespeare's on page 84.)

GERARD MANLEY HOPKINS, Thou art indeed just, Lord, if I contend, page 320

Like Milton in his sonnet on page 337, Hopkins begins with a complaint. Unlike Milton he seems, at last, far from being reconciled to the Lord's will; and tension between his faith and the testimony of his experience threaten to (but do not quite) overpower him. In the octet, to be sure, Hopkins is not merely speaking for himself: he is paraphrasing Jeremiah, who also complains that God lets scoundrels prosper. One of Hopkins's so-called "Terrible Sonnets," the poem ends not with any sense of deliverance, but with a prayer.

In line 1, why is the Lord said to be just? Well, at least he gives the poor suffering mortal a hearing. "When I have a friend like you, who needs an enemy?" seems the near-despairing thrust of lines 5-9. Although in the sestet the speaker sees the possibility of change, drawing hope from the fact that nature is renewed in spring, nature only reminds him once more of his own impotence and sterility. Birds build nests, but he can't.

In this as in other Hopkins poems, close reading is essential, but will reveal a few vexing difficulties. In line 2, "but, sir, so what I plead is just," the so what can give trouble--more so than the way Hopkins worded the line originally: "but, sir, what I shall speak is just." Syntax is inverted in lines 12-13 to stress the no and the two nots.

Norman MacKenzie has suggested that this poem could have been entitled "Bitterness in Spring," and thinks the poet's envy of the fresh wind (which shakes those lucky birds) suggests lack of poetic inspiration. (You might contrast this tormented poem with Hopkins's rapturous "Pied Beauty" [page 75] and with "The Windhover" [next], in which the sheer plod of the religious life is triumphantly justified.) It is ironic, notes MacKenzie, "that one of [Hopkins's] most enduring poems should be based on the conviction that no work of his would ever endure" (A Reader's Guide to Gerard Manley Hopkins [Ithaca: Cornell UP, 1981] 204).

GERARD MANLEY HOPKINS, The Windhover, page 320

"The best thing I ever wrote," said Hopkins. If your students have enjoyed "Pied Beauty" (page 75) or "God's Grandeur" (page 133) without too much difficulty, then why not try "The Windhover," despite its famous ambiguities? Some students may go afield in reading the opening line, and may take I caught to mean that the poet trapped the bird; but they can be told that Hopkins, a great condenser, probably means "I caught a glimpse of."

Dispute over the poem often revolves around whether or not the windhover is Christ and around the meaning of Buckle! Most commentators seem to agree that the bird is indeed Christ, or else that Christ is like the bird. (Yvor Winters, who thought the poem "minor and imperfect," once complained, "To describe a bird, however beautifully, and to imply that Christ is like him but greater, is to do very little toward indicating the greatness of Christ.") Some read Buckle! as a plea to the bird to descend to earth; others, as a plea to all the qualities and things mentioned in line 9 (Brute beauty, valor, act) to buckle themselves together into one. Still others find the statement ending in Buckle! no plea at all, but just an emphatic observation of what the poet beholds. If Christ is the windhover (other arguments run), in what sense can he be said to buckle? Two of the answers: (1) in buckling on human nature and becoming man, as a knight buckles on armor; (2) in

having his body broken on the cross. Students can be asked to seek
all the words in the poem with connotations of royalty or chival-
ry--suggestive, perhaps, of Christ as King and Christ as noble
knight or chevalier. Why the sheer plod? Hopkins reflects (it
would seem) that if men will only buckle down to their lowly duties
they will become more Christlike, and their spiritual plowshares
will shine instead of collecting rust. Hopkins preached a sermon
that expressed a similar idea: "Through poverty, through labor,
through crucifixion His majesty of nature more shines." The
embers, we think, are a metaphor: moist clods thrown by the plow
going down the sillion. Hopkins likes to compare things to hearth
fire: for instance, the "fresh-firecoal chestnut-falls" in "Pied
Beauty."

For detailed criticism, one might start with Norman H.
MacKenzie, A Reader's Guide to Gerard Manley Hopkins (Ithaca:
Cornell UP, 1981). MacKenzie provides facts from ornithology and
his own kestrel-watching: no other birds are so expert in
hovering, body horizontal, tail and head pointing down as they
study the ground for prey. To hang stationary in the air over one
spot, they must fly into the wind "with rapidly quivering
(wimpling, line 4) wings, missing a few beats as gusts die,
accelerating as they freshen"--responding to variations in the wind
with nearly computer speed. Once in about every eight hovers, the
kestrel will dive, not inertly but with wings held tense and
high--it doesn't "buckle" in the sense of collapse. If it finds no
victim, the bird swings and banks and takes an upward "stride," to
hover once more. Hopkins's "how he rung upon the rein" doesn't
mean that the kestrel climbs in a spiral. No gyring Yeats-bird,
he.

Despite his fondness for Old and Middle English, Hopkins
luckily refrained from calling the windhover by its obsolete name:
fuckwind or windfucker. (No, that f is not a long s.) Thomas
Nashe in Lenten Stuffe (1599) speaks of the "Kistrilles or
windfuckers that filling themselves with winde, fly against the
winde evermore." See windfucker in the Oxford English Dictionary.
(For the dumbfounding discovery, thanks to David Lynch, who
copyedited Introduction to Poetry, 6th ed.)

A. E. HOUSMAN, Terence, this is stupid stuff, page 321

Questions for discussion:

1. Terence is the poet, addressed in the opening lines by a
friend. What is the friend's complaint?
2. For whom does the poet recommend ale instead of poetry?
Lines 21-22 echo Milton's invocation at the beginning of Paradise
Lost, in which Milton calls on the Muse to aid him in writing his
epic poem, that he may "justify the ways of God to men." Is it
Housman's view that "malt does more than Milton can / To justify
God's ways to man," or is this his mocking version of someone
else's view?

3.   What defense of his poetry ("the stuff I bring for sale")
does the poet offer? How does the story of Mithridates support his
point?

A. E. HOUSMAN, To an Athlete Dying Young, page 323

For a comment on this poem, see the note in this manual on
Dryden's "To the Memory of Mr. Oldham," page 300.

LANGSTON HUGHES, Dream Deferred, page 323

Simile by simile, Hughes shows different attitudes, including
violent protest, that blacks might possibly take toward the long
deferral of their dream of equality. Students might be asked what
meanings they find in each comparison. The sugared crust (line 7)
is probably the smiling face obligingly worn by Uncle Toms.
The angry, sardonic tone of the poem is clearly different from
the sorrowful tone of Dudley Randall's "Ballad of Birmingham" (page
347).
Hughes's poem supplied the title for Lorraine Hansberry's
long-running Broadway play A Raisin in the Sun (1958), in which the
Youngers, a family descended from five generations of slaves, come
to a Chicago ghetto in hopes of fulfilling their dream.
Donald Ritzhein has written a moving account of what the poem
has meant to him, starting when his mother cut it out of a
newspaper and pasted it to his bedroom door. "By the time I got to
high school . . . I still didn't know a lot about the misery of
deferred dreams. . . . I knew a little more about them when I heard
Martin Luther King, Jr., talk about dreams in Washington. I
finally felt a little of what it's like to defer dreams when John
F. Kennedy was killed" ("Langston Hughes: A Look Backwards and
Forwards," Steppingstones, a little magazine published in Harlem,
Winter 1984: 55-56). Have you any black student who would care to
write about what the poem has meant to her or him?

LANGSTON HUGHES, Subway Rush Hour, page 324

"Subway Rush Hour" is strikingly different in tone from "Dream
Deferred." In this short depiction of rush hour in the subway, the
poet seems to send an optimistic message: that were blacks and
whites ever to mingle closely with one another on equal terms,
there would be "no room for fear." Notable in the poem is Hughes's
imagery. Within his sixteen-word limit he evokes three of the five
senses: smell, touch, and sight.

324-325 (text pages)

DAVID IGNATOW, Get the Gasworks, page 324

What is the tone of this poem by a Brooklyn-born poet? In his vigorous glimpses of tough, wisecracking, fast-paced city life (summed up in the metrical line "gaswork smokestack whistle tooting wisecracks"), Ignatow evidently admires the grimy kids who go on playing ball in the streets, even though one of their number died. Compare Elizabeth Bishop's affection for the "quick and saucy / and greasy sons" in "Filling Station," page 280.

Students might also be asked how the gasworks are shown to be a symbol for America. (Even the kids' speech is like gas; and the gasworks, like American living and thinking, are practical.)

The poem seems Ignatow's poetic manifesto. He wants a kind of poetry written in speech ("You've got America, boy; He gets it over the belly, all right"), a poetry that will take in actual life, however grimy. The poet depicts that life with humor and affection and, like papa flinging his newspaper, favors a passionate response to it.

RANDALL JARRELL, The Death of the Ball Turret Gunner, page 325

The speaker seems an unknown citizen like Auden's (page 23). Jarrell's laconic war poem is complex in its metaphors. The womb is sleep; the outside world, waking; and the speaker has passed from one womb to another--from his mother into the belly of a bomber. His existence inside the ball turret was only a dream, and in truth he has had no mature life between his childhood and his death. Waking from the dream, he wakes only to nightmare. In another irony, the matter-of-fact battle report language of the last line contrasts horribly with what is said in it. How can the dead gunner address us? Clearly the poet had written his epitaph for him--and has done so as Jarrell said he wrote "The Woman at the Washington Zoo," "acting as next friend."

RANDALL JARRELL, Well Water, page 325

This late poem, from Jarrell's collection The Lost World (1965), seems to us one of his finest lyrics. The well at the bottom of the world is a metaphor, not a real well, however actual its cold, drinkable water is made to seem. This fictive well is probably a personal myth of the poet's invention, although it sounds like something out of one of the folk or fairy tales Jarrell so loved: like the mill at the bottom of the sea that supposedly grinds forth salt.

A problem: What is the girl's request? We guess it is one more typical, mildly annoying but ingratiating part of the dailiness of life. "Since you're up . . ." seems almost an echo from a series of whisky advertisements current at the time: "Since [or While] you're up, get me a Grant's."

Perhaps Jarrell kept this poem just short of fourteen lines lest anyone accuse him of trying to write a sonnet. On occasion,

158

he voiced his distrust of elaborate forms--although, curiously, the
title poem of The Lost World is in terza rima.
     Another poet who celebrates the wonder of the everyday is
Elizabeth Bishop in "Filling Station" (page 280).

BEN JONSON, On My First Son, page 326

     This heartbreaking poem from Jonson's Epigrammes, requested by
several instructors, repays close reading. What is "the state
[man] should envy?" Death. Why the dead child should be envied is
made clear in the lines that immediately follow (7-8). The final
couplet is difficult in its syntax, and contains a pun on like in a
sense now obsolete. The speaker vows, or prays (vow, along with
votive, comes from the Greek euchesthai: "to pray"), that anyone
whom he loves may not live too long. The seriousness of Jonson's
wit is shown in this colossal pun: like meaning "thrive, do well,
get on" as well as "to be fond." See like in the OED for other
illustrations:

     Shallow to Falstaff: "By my troth, you like well and bear
     your years very well" (Henry IV, P.2, 3.2.92).

     "Trees generally do like best that stand to the Northeast
     wind" (Holland's Pliny, 1600).

     "Poems Arranged by Subject and Theme" in this manual lists the
book's eleven other poems about fathers and children. In this
Anthology section, see especially the father-and-son poems by
Phillips, Shu Ning Liu, and James Wright ("Autumn Begins in Martins
Ferry, Ohio").

DONALD JUSTICE, On the Death of Friends in Childhood, page 326

     There is more emotional distance, less grief in this poem than
in Ben Jonson's. Neither does the speaker in "On the Death of
Friends in Childhood" seem to be mourning one specific loss. The
"Friends" he mentions suggest friends in general, perhaps other
people's as well as his own. Yet, though time has softened the
impact of long-ago losses, the narrator urges that we remember dead
childhood friends and what was shared with them.

JOHN KEATS, Ode on Melancholy, page 326

     Here is the briefest of Keats's great odes. The lushness and
profusion of the imagery will be clear enough, but students will
need to read with care to get the plain prose sense.
     The first stanza offers students some timely advice: when
subject to a fit of melancholy, don't seek comfort in drugs. Such
stuff only deadens the spirit and the senses. (A fact to recall is
that Keats, who had studied medicine, probably was professionally

326-328 (text pages)

familiar with the opiates and sedatives he mentions.) "Wakeful
anguish" is preferable to numb comfort. Far better (advises stanza
2) to go to nature and the great outdoors, and a lover, for a
correlative of what one feels. To behold the goddess Melancholy
face to face is a privilege available only to those who work hard
at bursting the grape of joy against their sensitive palates:
e.g., as Keats did in poetry. Such a vision will appear only to
those with clear and undrowsy senses. To be impaled by this
dangerous deity, to have one's soul hung up as one of her trophies
(like a stuffed moosehead on a wall?) strikes us as ludicrously
strange.

As in the closing stanza of "To Autumn," a theme of this poem
(lines 21-26) is that the beauty of the world (and, here, that of a
lover) is transitory--hence a source of melancholy to one who
thinks on it. That is why Melancholy sets up shrine "in the very
temple of delight." To the sensitive, pleasure and gloom are never
far apart.

If you want a painstaking exegesis, Helen Vendler's The Odes
of John Keats (Cambridge: Harvard UP, 1983) is recent and
readable.

JOHN KEATS, On First Looking into Chapman's Homer, page 327

Questions for discussion:

1.   What are the realms of gold? Can the phrase have
anything to do with the fact that early Spanish explorers were
looking for El Dorado, a legendary city of treasure in South
America?
2.   Does Keats's boner about Cortez mar the poem?
3.   Did you ever read anything that made you feel like a
stout Cortez? If so, what?

JOHN KEATS, To Autumn, page 328

Although "To Autumn" was to prove the last of the poet's
greatest lyrics, we have no evidence that Keats (full of plans and
projects at the time) was consciously taking leave of the world.
On September 21, 1819, three days after writing the poem, Keats in
a letter to his friend John Hamilton Reynolds spoke of his delight
in the season: "I never lik'd stubble fields so much as now--Aye
better than the chilly green of the Spring. Somehow a stubble
plain looks warm--in the same was that some pictures look warm--
this strikes me so much in my Sunday's walk that I composed upon
it."
Questions for discussion:

1.   In the opening stanza, what aspects of autumn receive
most emphasis? To what senses do the images appeal?
2.   In the first two stanzas, autumn is several times
personified (lines 2-3, 12-15, 16-18, 19-20, 21-22). Who are its

different persons? (Conspiring crony, careless landowner, reaper,
gleaner, cider presser.)
      3.   In the third stanza, how does the tone change?   Has
there been any progression in scene or in idea throughout the poem?
(Tone: calm serenity. In the first stanza, autumn is being
prepared for; in the second, busily enjoyed; in the third, calmly
and serenely contemplated. There is another stanza-by-stanza
progression: from morning to noon to oncoming night. Like the
soft-dying day, the light wind sometimes dies. The gnats in wailful choir also have funereal, mourning suggestions, but the stanza
as a whole cannot be called gloomy.)
      4.   What words in stanza 3 convey sounds? (Songs, music,
wailful choir, mourn, loud bleat, sing, treble, whistles, twitter.
What an abundance of verbs! The lines convey a sense of active
music making.)
      5.   Do you see any case for reading the poem as a statement
of the poet's acceptance of the facts that beauty on earth is
transitory and death is inevitable? (Surely such themes are
present; the poem does not have to be taken to mean that the poet
knows he himself will soon perish.)

      For an unusually grim reading of the poem, see Annabel M.
Patterson, "'How to load . . . and bend': Syntax and Interpretation in Keats's To Autumn, PMLA 94 (1979): 449-58. Finding that
the poem "undermines" our traditional notion of Autumn, Patterson
argues that Keats subversively portrays the goddess as deceptive,
careless, and demanding. Her proffered ripeness leads only to last
oozings and stubble-plains--dead ends not to be desired. In the
poet's view (as she interprets it), "Nature is amoral and not to be
depended upon." Try this argument on the class. Do students
agree? Whether or not they side with Patterson, they will have to
examine the poem closely in order to comment.

GALWAY KINNELL, Saint Francis and the Sow, page 329

      One way to approach this poem might be to have students ponder
and evaluate its striking images: the "brow / of the flower"
(lines 7-8), "the earthen snout" (line 17), "the spiritual curl of
the tail" (line 18), and "the blue milken dreaminess spurting and
shuddering / from the fourteen teats" (lines 21-22). It seems
evident that the poet has looked closely at a real sow. His
observations are poetic but exact.
      Saint Francis of Assisi has long had tremendous appeal because
of his legendary love for all God's creatures. He called the
animals his brothers and sisters, and if anyone could have enhanced
the "self-blessing" (self-approbation?) of a brokenhearted sow, it
would have been he. "Saint Francis and the Sow" is a life-
affirming, even tender poem. It begins with the general statement
of a simple idea: that since everything flowers from within,
"self-blessing" is important. When it flags, ". . . sometimes it
is necessary / to reteach a thing its loveliness." Starting with
line 12 the poem illustrates the general idea with the specific

329-330 (text pages)

example of Saint Francis retelling the sow "in words and in touch"
it is lovely. Students will probably agree that the poem's
systematic enumeration of the sow's attributes and its gentle,
Saint-Francis-like appreciation for a creature not often described
as "lovely" have the desired effect of persuading us to view the
sow through Saint Francis's eyes.

CAROLYN KIZER, The Intruder, page 329

     In "The Intruder," Kizer successfully juggles several con-
flicting feelings. Perhaps overriding them all is the tender
regard the poet feels for her nature-loving mother, a compassionate
woman "preferring the strange to the tame." Thus, when she first
saw the wounded bat, the mother reacted by regarding it as "rather
sweet," even though Kizer's vivid images more than adequately
convey the alien ugliness of the little creature: he was
"fluttering, bleeding" and had a "hard feral glint." At the sight
of the "pallid, yellow" lice that "cosily sucked and snoozed," even
the kind mother recoiled. Yet, in the end, she had to wash "the
pity from her hands."
     Kizer's title is richly suggestive. The bat is an intruder
simply by being in a house, where wild things don't belong. At
another level, his very grotesqueness is an intrusion upon the
mother's pity for him and her well-meaning love of the "wild and
natural."
     The knottiest part of Kizer's poem is perhaps the long
sentence that opens the third stanza. In order to make sure that
your students understand it, you might ask them to paraphrase that
sentence. A successful attempt might read: What remained of my
mother's compassion for wild creatures was a dark, sticky puddle of
blood on the floor. To the inhabitants of the wild, our
benevolence is as foreign as our traps and bullets--and just as
likely to invite attack.

TED KOOSER, Flying at Night, page 330

     What does the poet mean when he says, "Beneath us, constella-
tions"? In its usual sense, the word constellations means "stellar
groups," and these appear not beneath but above us. Constellations
here is evidently a metaphor for the configurations of lights that
signal the presence of cities passed over by the plane flying at
night. The yard light seems richly suggestive of one distant
farmer's effort, against formidable odds, to ward off not only
cosmic loneliness but death: the death of his way of life as "the
cities, like shimmering novas, / tug with bright streets at lonely
lights like his"; his own inevitable physical death; and even the
death of our galaxy, which will, like the one mentioned in lines 2
and 3, die "like a snowflake falling on water."
     Kooser is vice-president of an insurance company in Lincoln,
Nebraska.

PHILIP LARKIN, Home is so sad, page 330

Larkin's considerable achievement in "Home is so Sad" is that he so beautifully captures the ring of ordinary speech within the confines of a tight a b a b a rime scheme and iambic pentameter. Note the slant rimes in the second stanza: as, was, and vase.

In an interview, Larkin has recalled a letter he received from a middle-aged mother who had read his poem: "She wrote to say her children had grown up and gone, and she felt precisely this emotion I was trying to express in the poem" ("Speaking of Writing XIII: Philip Larkin," [London] Times 20 Feb. 1964: 16). Bruce Martin finds the poem written not from a mother's point of view, but from that of a son who used to live in this house himself. The speaker projects his own sadness into it: it has remained pathetically changeless. What has changed is himself and others who once lived here (Philip Larkin [Boston: Twayne, 1978] 52).

DMK, taking a different view, thinks it quite possible to read the poem as though (as in Larkin's well-known "Mr. Bleaney" from the same collection, The Whitsun Weddings) the former inhabitants of this house have died. The speaker is left unidentified, an impersonal seeing-eye; and so your students, too, will probably come up with differing interpretations.

Is Larkin's poem sentimental? Hard-eyed and exact in its observations, aided by the colloquialism of line 7, "A joyous shot at how things ought to be," it successfully skirts the danger. Students might like to discuss the three words that follow: "Long fallen wide." Does Larkin mean that the home was an unhappy one, or merely ordinary in its deviation from the ideal? Or is it that the arrow--the "joyous shot"--has fallen merely in the sense that, meant to be full of life, the home is now "bereft / Of anyone to please"?

PHILIP LARKIN, A Study of Reading Habits, page 331

This is one of Larkin's most frequently misunderstood poems, according to David Timms. Critics have taken it for an attack on reading itself--and if critics have done so, what will your students do?

To begin, help them recognize the poem's ironic point of view. This isn't the poet himself speaking, but an invented character --"an ordinary man," Larkin calls him (on a recording of The Whitsun Weddings [Hessle, Yorkshire: Listen Records, 1965]). The speaker, now in his maturity, can see (according to Timms) that his life has grown more and more like a paperback novel, one in which he is neither hero nor villain but just a minor, slightly despicable character. "The undependable dude and the cowardly storekeeper are 'far too familiar' because the speaker realizes that they are the characters he most resembles." In reaction, he tries ineffectually "to blunt the point of this insight by a show of bravado--that last line." And the speaker, of course, is right: the books he used to read are indeed a load of crap: not War and Peace or the Iliad, but pulp-paper western stories ("'Church Going'

331-332 (text pages)

Revisited," Phoenix Autumn/Winter 1973-74: 19-20; and Timms's Philip Larkin [Edinburgh: Oliver, 1973] 94-95).

The poem satirizes, in Bruce Martin's view, "the simpleminded approach to reading taken by most people. The character's disappointment with books reveals not only his disillusionment with life . . . but the fallacy of reading to find a mirror of oneself" (Philip Larkin [Boston: Twayne, 1978] 90).

No, this isn't exactly Larkin talking. Students might care to know that the poet is no enemy of books: he has published eleven of his own, writes book reviews, and is a librarian by profession (at the University of Hull, in charge of about 600,000 books and a staff of a hundred). Still, perhaps the speaker in this poem somewhat resembles the poet himself. Larkin has testified that, as a boy, he was an avid reader of detective stories. In adolescence he started wearing glasses (Martin 14).

A criticism leveled at Larkin (by A. Alvarez and others) is that his poems are depressingly negative. He has obliquely replied: "The impulse for producing a poem is never negative; the most negative poem in the world is a very positive thing to have done" ("A Conversation with Philip Larkin," Tracks Summer 1967: 9). As Andrew Motion has observed of Larkin's apparently angry or bitterly satirical poems, "their rage or contempt is always checked by the assuaging energy of their language and the satisfactions of their articular formal control" (Philip Larkin [New York: Methuen, 1982] 59).

D. H. LAWRENCE, A Youth Mowing, page 331

Students enjoy figuring out the dramatic situation: the young mower apparently doesn't yet know that the speaker is pregnant by him. Why is she sorry for him? The lad is like a handsome wild animal; now he'll have to be tamed and become responsible. Imagery of scythe strokes and sharp breaths (lines 2-3) suggests love-making.

What is the speaker, whose language is that of a Nottingham-shire peasant, doing beside the Isar? Lawrence is evidently trying to render German peasant speech into English, like Ezra Pound making a Chinese farmer say, "Yaller bird, let my crawps alone." Is the attempt effective in Lawrence's poem? Like the gamekeeper in Lady Chatterly's Lover, the young woman who carries the dinner pail falls into dialect when most affectionate.

The poem dates from the time when Lawrence and Frieda von Richthofen Weekley had eloped to the Continent.

IRVING LAYTON, The Bull Calf, page 332

Sentimental poets frequently shed tears over concrete objects, while (in their imagery and diction) failing to open their eyes to the physical world. Such is not the case in Layton's "The Bull Calf," in which the poet tells us that he weeps only after having portrayed the dead calf in exact detail ("one foreleg over the other").

Layton's poem develops a series of contrasts. In the first section, the calf's look of nobility ("the promise of sovereignty," "Richard II") is set against his immaturity. The "fierce sunlight," in an implied metaphor, is compared to the calf's mother: taking in maize, licking her baby. In line 14, the "empty sky," suggestive of the calf's coming death, seems the turning point of the poem. In the remainder, the calf, which had been portrayed at first as full of life and pride, becomes an inanimate object, "a block of wood," a numb mass that emits ugly sounds when handled ("a sepulchral gurgle"). But in the closing lines, introducing still another contrast, Layton seems to show the calf as a living sleeper, or perhaps a statue or finished work of art.

Probably the best-known living poet in Canada, Layton was born in Rumania and came to Montreal early in life. Standing outside both British and French communities, Layton's perspective often has been that of an outsider, a Jew, a satirist, and a revolutionary. The Selected Poems of Irving Layton, with an introduction by Hugh Kenner (New York: New Directions, 1977), is an attempt to widen his audience south of the border.

DENISE LEVERTOV, The Ache of Marriage, page 333

In this poem, Levertov's view of marriage seems a less than happy one: husband and wife are denied communion, or sharing. They are imprisoned together in darkness (the belly of Leviathan) "looking for joy, some joy / not to be known outside" marriage. Thus trapped, they seem unlikely to find the joy they seek.

Of interest is the poet's use of two other words with Biblical connotations: communion (from which Levertov's couple, like non-Christians, are excluded) and ark (in the poem, scarcely the refuge that Noah's ark was, therefore ironic).

This ambiguous poem set off a marital spat between the authors of this manual. The preceding two paragraphs are DMK's; XJK doesn't see the poem as all that negative. For him, Noah's ark has happy connotations: it offers a comfortable, womby cruise toward a blissful resting place. Agreed, the couple in Levertov's poem live in intense discomfort, craving a joy they have not yet found. But is their ache pure pain? Perhaps there is pleasure in it.

Try these clashing views on your students. Let them ponder and discuss the ultimate phrase in the poem, that richly musical "ark of / the ache of it."

PHILIP LEVINE, To a Child Trapped in a Barber Shop, page 333

Levine's ironies may need underscoring. He is not, of course, berating the scared child (he is advising him to let the fearful cops rescue him), nor does the poet really think that drinking a little hair tonic would be a terrible crime "against property and the state," however bad it might be for the child's digestion. The

poem is actually addressed to the reader--one of the "we" who have
lived through similar terrors. The ironic statements stop with the
fourth stanza, and in the last three stanzas we can take what the
poet tells us at face value. Most children fear barbers (or hair-
dressers) at first, and yet their fears prove groundless. Everyone
growing up has to go through an ordeal, the poet seems to be
saying, and life isn't so terrible as it looks through a child's
eyes.

The poem has a subtle form besides its look of symmetry. It
is roughly in syllabic verse, with a rime scheme (including some
off-rimes).

ROBERT LOWELL, Skunk Hour, page 334

Students should have no trouble in coming up with the usual
connotations of skunk, but they may need help in seeing that the
title is a concise expression of Lowell's theme. This is an
evil-smelling hour in the speaker's life; and yet, paradoxically,
it is the skunks themselves who affirm that life ought to go on.
After the procession of dying and decadent people and objects in
the first four stanzas, the mother skunk and her kittens form a
triumph: bold, fecund, hungry, impossible to scare. Although they
too are outcasts (surrounded by their aroma as the poet is surrounded by his madness and isolation?), they stick up for their
right to survival.

The poem is rich in visual imagery. In the mind's eye, there
are resemblances between the things contained in stanza 5 (the Ford
car and the hill's skull), also the objects set in fixed rows
(love-cars, tombstones, beached hulls). Water and the sea (by
their decline or absence) are to this poem what they are to Eliot's
Waste Land. Even the Church is "chalk-dry"; its spire has become a
spar like that of a stranded vessel.

This poem is intensively analyzed in The Contemporary Poet as
Artist and Critic: Eight Symposia, ed. Anthony Ostroff (Boston:
Little, 1964). Richard Wilbur, John Frederick Nims, and John
Berryman comment on the poem, after which Lowell comments on their
comments. Lowell calls the opening of the poem "a dawdling, more
or less amiable picture of a declining Maine sea town. . . .
Sterility howls through the scenery, but I try to give a tone of
tolerance, humor, and randomness to the sad prospect." He sees the
skunk hour itself as a sort of dark night of the soul and refers
readers to the poem by Saint John of the Cross. Lowell's night,
however, is "secular, puritan, and agnostical." Lowell notes that
the phrase red fox strain was intended only to describe the color
of vegetation in the fall on Blue Hill, a mountain in Maine.

Elizabeth Hardwick, Lowell's wife when "Skunk Hour" was
written, has affirmed that all the characters in the poem were
actual--"were living, more or less as he sees them, in Castine
[Maine] that summer. The details, not the feeling, were rather
alarmingly precise, I thought. But fortunately it was not read in
town for some time" (quoted by Ian Hamilton, Robert Lowell: A
Biography [New York: Random, 1982] 267).

Sandra M. Gilbert, who sees the poem as "richly magical,"
reads it for its embodiment of myth. She explores it as a vision
of Hell, pointing out that its events happen not on Halloween, but
"somewhere in Hallowe'en's ritually black and orange vicinity."
(The fairy decorator's shop is "sacramentally orange.") The summer
millionaire has departed in fall, like a vegetation deity--Osiris
or Attis. Nautilus Island's witchlike hermit heiress is Circe,
Hecate, Ishtar, Venus, "the goddess of love turned goddess of death
in an All Soul's Night world" ("Mephistophilis in Maine: Rereading
Lowell's 'Skunk Hour,'" A Book of Rereadings, ed. Greg Kuzma
[Lincoln: Pebble and Best Cellar, 1979] 254-64).

CHRISTOPHER MARLOWE, The Passionate Shepherd to His Love, page 335

How do you teach a poem that seems so remote from the twentieth century? You might begin by asking whether it is so remote
after all. What do contemporary swains promise their loved ones?
Things, clothes, good times, a lovely neighborhood. Certainly
remote from most contemporary love songs, however, is the tone of
Marlowe's poem: a rare and appealing innocence. In demonstrating
this quality to your students, try comparing this famous love lyric
to one more complex and ironic: Donne's deliberate variation on
"The Passionate Shepherd," "The Bait" (page 297), or Raleigh's
"The Nymph's Reply" (page 346). Either will make Marlowe's poem an
excellent foil. (For a note comparing the various tones of these
three poems, see the entry for Raleigh (page 175 in this manual.)

GEORGE MEREDITH, Lucifer in Starlight, page 336

The name Lucifer (Latin for "light-bringing") comes from
Isaiah 14:12: "How art thou fallen from heaven, O Lucifer, son of
the morning!" Early interpreters of Scripture thought this line
meant the fallen archangel; later translators changed Lucifer to
day star. Students may not be aware that Lucifer is a name both
for the Devil and for the planet Venus as the morning star. (Venus
is sometimes the evening star, too, but only as the morning star is
it called Lucifer.)
Meredith, however, seems well aware of the name's duality.
Although his sonnet can be read first as an account of the Miltonic
fiend's taking a new flight (and meeting chagrin), it is also
satisfying to read the poem as a description of Venus as a planet.
We are told that Lucifer uprose and sank. Amid the stars, his huge
bulk--a black planet--crosses Africa and shadows the Arctic,
arriving at a middle height in the sky. The last two lines are
puzzling, but seem to refer both to God's law and to the orderly
path each star and planet follows as it circles the sun.
An Italian sonnet, "Lucifer in Starlight" illustrates a clear
division in meaning between octave and sestet. In lines 1-8, the
fiend appears triumphant and domineering: this is his night to
howl. In lines 9-14, however, he crumples in defeat once more; or,

167

if Lucifer is also the morning star, he rises in the octave and sets in the sestet.

JAMES MERRILL, Laboratory Poem, page 336

   If you have any students who assume that poetry deals only with the pleasant and the beautiful (and how widespread this assumption is!) then you may find Merrill's clinical love poem a useful thing to surprise them with. Try paying attention to its language in particular: the outrageous pun taking heart in the opening line, the kymograph (a device with a revolving drum that records pulsations such as muscle contractions or heartbeats), her solutions tonic or malign (stimulants or sedatives, preservatives or poisons?). Merrill's language is exact in the extreme, a love poem written with loving care. (After all, why should love be banned from a laboratory?)
   Discussion will probably focus on the last stanza. Of the "exquisite disciplines," at least one of them is Naomi's research. The turtle's heart, violently removed, becomes a fact in a theorem. Like turtles, Charles realizes, some people give their lives for some abstract perfection, whether science, art, or any knowledge in whose service one may die. There is lovely irony in the contrast between Naomi's coldly clinical dissections (she has to "take heart," build up her nerve to perform them) and the human situation ("easy in the presence of her lover").

CHARLOTTE MEW, Fame, page 337

   Sense seems to demand a period after the word care in line 15 of "Fame," and we have put one there even though the poem when reprinted does not usually sport one.
   Mew's thwarted life, marked by insanity in her family, a difficult invalid mother, frustrated lesbian passions, and her suicide at 59, is as well documented in Penelope Fitzgerald's biography of the poet, Charlotte Mew and Her Friends (London: Collins, 1984), as it can be, considering Mew's lifelong reticence about herself and her family. Her poems, as Val Warner points out in the introduction to Charlotte Mew: Collected Poems and Prose (Manchester: Carcanet, 1981), reflect a soul always at war with itself. "The theme of natural beauty is also present throughout the work. Alida Monro [Mew's friend] found her 'nostalgia for the country and her real, full enjoyment of life in London . . . typical of the warring pair within her'--desire and negation, passion and renunciation." This "warring pair" is evident in "Fame." With one side of her nature the speaker loves fame and asks:

              But could I spare
   In the blind Earth's great silences and spaces,
        The din, the scuffle, the long stare
        If I went back and it was not there?

Ultimately, though, she rejects fame and its excitement for an odd
pastoral calm, "one little dream":

> A frail, dead, new-born lamb, ghostly and pitiful and white,
> A blot upon the night,
> The moon's dropped child!

James Wright says of Mew, "This poet died in 1928. The story
is that she did away with herself, but the truth is that she wrote
maybe 6 of the best poems of the 20th century. She's a superb
poet, and a great woman. Thomas Hardy felt the same" (Poetry Pilot
[New York: Academy of American Poets] Sept. 1978). In her own day
Mew was also admired by Virginia Woolf, John Masefield, and Sieg-
fried Sassoon. Yet, ironically, her poems did not circulate widely
and she never received her share of the acclaim she writes about in
"Fame." Since 1953 there have been sporadic attempts to give the
poet her due. Perhaps the recent collection of her work, and the
biography, signal the beginning of a new appreciation of her
output.

JOHN MILTON, When I consider how my light is spent, page 337

While this famous sonnet is usually taken to refer to the
poet's lost eyesight, some critics have argued that it is not about
blindness at all. The familiar title "On His Blindness" was not
given by Milton, but by a printer a century later.

Questions for discussion:

1.   If the poem is not about blindness, what might it be
about? (Possible suggestions: Milton's declining powers of
poetry; Milton's fame as a Puritan apologist.)
2.   Is talent a pun referring to Milton's talent for writing
poetry? What other meanings of the word seem appropriate in this
poem? In the New Testament parable (Matthew 25:14-30), the hidden
talent is money that should have been earning interest. That
Milton is thinking primarily of work and business can be plausibly
argued; other words in the poem convey such connotations--spent,
true account, day-labor, and perhaps useless, which suggests the
Medieval Latin word for interest, usuria.
The theme of frustration in life (and reconciliation to one's
lot) is dealt with differently in Shakespeare's "When, in disgrace
with Fortune and men's eyes" (page 355).

N. SCOTT MOMADAY, The Delight Song of Tsoai-talee, page 338

A poem to read aloud. A model that student poets might be
asked to emulate. Let them choose an emotion (whether delight or
gloom or another), and in the same "I am . . ." frame, find
metaphors to state it. The poet's own metaphors, evidently coming

from memory and tribal culture, will not be easily imitable. They
add up to a sensuous paean to the universe.

Navarre Scott Momaday, a Kiowa Indian who took a doctorate at
Stanford with Yvor Winters, received the 1969 Pulitzer Prize for
fiction for his autobiographical The Way to Rainy Mountain. The
Gourd Dancer (New York: Harper, 1976), with Momaday's own
drawings, contains most of his work in poetry. He is professor of
English at the University of Arizona in Tucson.

MARIANNE MOORE, The Mind is an Enchanting Thing, page 339

About this poem the poet has written, "One of the winters
between 1930 and 1940, Gieseking gave at the Brooklyn Academy a
program of Handel, Bach, and Scarlatti, the moral of this poem
being that there is something more important than outward rightness. One doesn't get through with the fact that Herod beheaded
John the Baptist, 'for his oath's sake'; as one doesn't, I feel,
get through with the injustice of the deaths died in the war, and
in the first world war" (note on the poem in Kimon Friar and John
Malcolm Brinnin's anthology Modern Poetry [New York: Appleton,
1951]).

These remarks, and the poem's appearance in 1944, have led
critics to call "The Mind is an Enchanting Thing" a war poem. What
to make of the poet's statement? To put it baldly, perhaps she
means that nobody but a bigoted Herod would condemn a superb German
musician for being German and for playing splendid German and
Italian music, even in the 1930s. The drift of the poem is that it
takes the mind to recognize beauty and, to do so, the mind must
pierce through the heart's illusions (and prejudices?). In her
tribute to the mind's "conscientious inconsistency," perhaps Moore
recalls Emerson's adage, "A foolish consistency is the hobgoblin of
little minds." Still, one needn't speculate about the poem's
wartime relevance in order to see it as a restatement of the poet's
favorite poet's theme, "Beauty is truth, truth beauty." Only the
mind can apprehend things truly; like Gieseking's violin and like
the apteryx's beak, it is a precision instrument.

Class discussions of this poem tend to be slow, but good and
ruminative. Many students greatly admire the poem, and some
instructors report getting outstanding papers about it.

What form is the poem written in? Syllabics, with lines
arranged in a repeated stanza pattern--like Dylan Thomas's "Fern
Hill" (page 369), which students may be invited to compare. Once,
in an interview, Donald Hall asked Moore, "Do you ever experiment
with shapes before you write, by drawing lines on a page?" "Never,
I never 'plan' a stanza," she replied. "Words cluster like chromo-
somes, determining the procedure. I may influence an arrangement
or thin it, then try to have successive stanzas identical with the
first." Asked "How does a poem start for you?" she answered, "A
felicitous phrase springs to mind--a word or two, say-- . . .
'katydid-wing subdivided by sun / till the nettings are legion.' I
like light rhymes, inconspicuous rhymes" (interview in The Paris

Review [Winter 1961], reprinted in A Marianne Moore Reader [New
York: Viking, 1961]).

Hall discusses the poem helpfully, too, in his study Marianne
Moore (New York: Pegasus, 1970). He admires the poet's ability to
weave a single word through the length of the poem, subtly changing
its meaning: "The word eye, for example, is first the eye of the
mind, then the eye of the memory, then the eye of the heart, suggesting three ways of 'seeing' that do not involve sight, but insight."

HOWARD NEMEROV, Storm Windows, page 340

"Storm Windows," written in the 1950s before combination
windows were as common as they are today, may call for a little
classroom reminiscing on the instructor's part about the spring and
fall rituals of exchanging storm windows for screens and vice
versa. As those who have lifted such windows up and down well
know, this was a fairly strenuous outdoor job that needed doing
when season and weather were right. Many older houses still have
such windows.

Storm windows, of course, herald the onset of winter, a fact
significant in establishing the bleak tone of this poem. Who is
the "you" in "Storm Windows"? It seems to be someone with whom the
poet is communicating imperfectly, perhaps someone from whom he is
painfully parted. The tone of the poem is wistful, infused with a
parched yearning unrelieved by the heavy, wintry rain. The blurred
windows stand in the way, barriers between the dry grass underneath
them and the rain above.

The storm windows, minutely observed objects in the real
world, are richly symbolic. Lying on the ground and preventing the
rain from wetting the grass beneath them, they are aptly expressive
of "missed desires." In addition, because the windows are "brimful
of bouncing water," their "swaying clarity" beautifully conveys how
memories, clear and inexact at the same time, waver to the surface
of the speaker's mind. The windows can also be regarded, perhaps,
as barriers to perfect communication in a relationship that has
been interrupted, even as the task of hanging windows has been
interrupted by a storm.

JOHN FREDERICK NIMS, Love Poem, page 340

For a lively comparison, teach this with Alan Dugan's "Love
Song: I and Thou" (page 301). Both love poems proceed through
comedy. Nims is kidding his loved one affectionately, of course,
and the mingled tone of his tribute, both tender and chiding, also
recalls Swift's wonderful "On Stella's Birthday" (page 29).
Another subject common to Nims and Dugan is incompetence, although
Nims's lady is good with "words and people and love." In Dugan's
poem the incompetent is the speaker himself.

341-342 (text pages)

SHARON OLDS, The One Girl at the Boys Party, page 341

This poem whimsically describes a talented little girl, "her math scores unfolding in the air around her," during a pool party at which all the other guests are boys. They in lines 2 and 15, their in lines 18 and 19 seem to refer only to the boys. In lines 5, 7, and 11, the word they apparently includes the girl. You might ask students to note the pairs of adjectives that affirm the child's strength and composure: she is "smooth and sleek" (line 3), her body is "hard and / indivisible as a prime number" (lines 5-6), her face is "solemn and / sealed" (lines 16-17). The adjectives make clear the narrator-mother's respect for her brilliant daughter. Notable too is the metaphor of wet ponytail (itself a by-now-dead metaphor!) as pencil (line 12). That and the "narrow silk suit / with hamburgers and french fries printed on it" remind us that she is in some ways a very typical little girl.

It is the mathematical figures of speech that make this poem unique. Why not ask students to point out and discuss them? Are they apt? Do they ever appear forced? Which ones succeed best?

WILFRED OWEN, Anthem for Doomed Youth, page 341

Metaphorically, this sonnet draws a contrast between traditional funeral trappings and the actual conditions under which the dead lie on the field of battle: with cannon fire instead of tolling bells, rifle bursts instead of the patter of prayers, the whine of shells instead of choirs' songs, the last lights in dying eyes instead of candle-shine, pale brows (of mourning girls, at home?) instead of shrouds or palls, the tenderness of onlookers (such as the poet?) instead of flowers--an early draft of the poem reads, "Your flowers, the tenderness of comrades' minds"--and the fall of night instead of the conventional drawing down of blinds in a house where someone has died.

For another Owen war poem, see "Dulce et Decorum Est" (page 28). For other war poems, see in this manual "Poems Arranged by Subject and Theme."

The poet's revisions for this poem, in four drafts, may be studied in the appendix to C. Day Lewis's edition of Owen's Collected Poems (London: Chatto, 1963). In its first draft, the poem was called "Anthem for Dead [not Doomed] Youth," and it went, in our reading of the photographed manuscript:

> What minute bells for these who die so fast?
>   Only the monstrous anger of our guns.
> Let the majestic insults of their iron mouths
>   Be as the priest-words of their burials.
> Of choristers and holy music, none;
>   Nor any voice of mourning, save the wail
> The long-drawn wail of high, far-sailing shells.
>   What candles may we hold for these lost souls?
> Not in the hands of boys, but in their eyes
> Shall many candles shine, and [?] will light them.

172

Women's wide-spreaded arms shall be their wreaths,
And pallor of girls' cheeks shall be their palls.
Their flowers, the tenderness of all men's minds,
And every dusk, a drawing-down of blinds.

ROBERT PHILLIPS, Running on Empty, page 342

Phillips, born in Delaware, now lives in Katonah, New York.
He writes fiction and criticism as well as poetry, and has edited
the letters and the late and uncollected poems of Delmore Schwartz.
he sent us the following comment about "Running on Empty":

> "Running on Empty" is fairly autobiographical. I was
> stunned at how grudgingly my father let me use the family
> car once I'd obtained my driver's license at age 16. It
> seemed to me he withheld this symbol of my new freedom and
> attainment just as he withheld his affection. So when I
> finally had use of the car, I went hog-wild in celebration
> and release.
> The landscape is Sussex County, Delaware--extremely
> flat country bisected by Route 13 (nicknamed "The Dual"
> because it is composed of twin lanes dually parallel in an
> inexorable straight line). I was pushing my luck speeding and
> refusing to refuel in an act of rebellion against my father's
> strictness (which may explain why the 12th line reads "defying
> chemistry" rather than the more accurate "defying physics"--
> my father taught high school chemistry, and even in the class-
> room I was subject to his discipline).
> I'm rather pleased with the way the poem picks up rhythm
> and begins to speed when the car does (5th-7th stanzas). And
> I hope students relate to the central images of car and boy,
> one of which can be mechanically refueled and replenished,
> one of which cannot.

To us the word chemistry in line 12 carries additional meaning, as in "behavior or functioning, as of a complex of emotions"
(The American Heritage Dictionary). In this sense, too, the
narrator was surely in defiance of his father's chemistry.

SYLVIA PLATH, Daddy, page 342

There are worse ways to begin teaching this astonishing poem
than to ask students to recall what they know of Dachau, Auschwitz,
Belsen (line 33), and other Nazi atrocities. "Every woman adores a
Fascist"--what does Plath mean? Is she sympathizing with the
machismo ideal of the domineering male, lashing his whip upon sub-
jugated womankind? (No way.) For an exchange of letters about the
rightness or wrongness of Plath's identifying with Jewish victims
of World War II, see Commentary (July and October 1974). Irving
Howe accuses Plath of "a failure in judgment" in using genocide as
an emblem of her personal traumas.

342-345 (text pages)

Incredible as it seems, some students possess an alarming fund of ignorance about Nazis, and some might not even recognize the cloven foot of Satan (line 53); so be prepared, sadly, to supply glosses. They will be familiar with the story of Dracula, however, and probably won't need much help with lines 71-79. Plath may be thinking of Nosferatu, F. W. Murnau's silent screen adaptation of Bram Stoker's novel Dracula, filmed in Germany in 1922. Hitler's propagandists seized on the Nosferatu theme and claimed that the old democratic order was drinking the country's blood. Plath sees Daddy as doing the same to his daughter.

SYLVIA PLATH, Morning Song, page 345

Plath's image of the cloud being effaced seems almost a pre-monition of her own death. But "Morning Song" is rich in humor: the wonderful self-portrait of the cow-heavy mother, the baby's cries coming out in balloons (as in a comic strip?). The title refers to the child's crying (music to wake up by!), as well as to the poem itself.

EZRA POUND, The River-Merchant's Wife: a Letter, page 345

After the death of Ernest Fenollosa, a scholar devoted to Chinese language and literature, Pound inherited Fenollosa's manu-scripts containing rough prose versions of many Chinese poems. From one such draft, Pound finished his own version of "The River-Merchant's Wife." Fenollosa's wording of the first line went:

My hair was at first covering my brows (child's method of wearing hair)

Arthur Waley, apparently contemptuous of Pound for ignoring dictionary meanings of some of the words of the poem, made a translation that began:

Soon after I wore my hair covering my forehead . . .

Pound's version begins:

While my hair was still cut straight across my forehead . . .

Pound, says the recent critic Wai-lim Yip, has understood Chinese culture, while Waley has not, even though he understands his dictionary. "The characters for 'hair/first/cover/forehead" conjure up in the mind of a Chinese reader exactly this picture. All little Chinese girls normally have their hair cur straight across the forehead." Yip goes on to show that Pound, ignorant of Chinese as he was, comes close in sense and feeling to the Li Po original. (Ezra Pound's Cathay [Princeton: Princeton UP, 1969] 88-92.)

What is the tone of the poem? What details make it seem
moving and true, even for a reader who knows nothing of Chinese
culture?

SIR WALTER RALEIGH, The Nymph's Reply to the Shepherd, page 346

This classic, sour reply to Marlowe's Shepherd counters the
conventional promises of pastoral poetry with notes of unpleasant
realism: its references to winter and old age. The heavily
alliterative lines containing antitheses hold striking power ("When
rivers rage and rocks grow cold," "A honey tongue, a heart of
gall," "In folly ripe, in reason rotten"). Raleigh reverses the
usual carpe diem theme: time passes, joys fade, age nears--there-
fore, let's not love!
    This trio of poems (Marlowe's "Passionate Shepherd" [page
335], Raleigh's reply, and Donne's "The Bait" [page 297]) are a
study in clashing tones. Marlowe's bubbles lightheartedly, Donne's
smirks with wry wit, Raleigh's rather severely dissects pastoral
conventions and frowns at their shallowness, sounding a wistful
note in the last stanza. (Oh, if only that shepherd could be
believed!)
    The poem may interest students of today in that male Raleigh
bravely attempts to reason as the woman speaker might: seeing
through the shepherd's sugary, summery promises and (in stanza 5)
casting doubt on the worth of the trinkets he proffers. Is she a
feminist forerunner?
    Who was Raleigh? Everyone knows his name. His highly
dramatic career as soldier, courtier, author of A History of the
World, and frustrated New World explorer deserves at least sketchy
recall. A favorite of Elizabeth, who bestowed upon him huge
estates in Ireland, Raleigh planned and executed the expedition to
America that sadly ended with the lost colony on Roanoke Island,
Virginia. Unluckily, Raleigh angered the queen by a marriage she
disliked, but redeemed himself by taking rich booty from Spanish
merchant ships and by embarking on an expedition to Guiana in
search of El Dorado, the legendary city of gold. James I charged
him with treason, but released him to make another try for El
Dorado. The city of gold remained legendary, and Raleigh returned
to England to face the treason charge again and to lose his head on
the block.

DUDLEY RANDALL, Ballad of Birmingham, page 347

Randall's poem is an authentic broadside ballad: it not only
deals with a news event, it was once printed and distributed on a
single page. "I had noticed how people would carry tattered
clippings of their favorite poems in their billfolds," the poet has
explained, "and I thought it would be a good idea to publish them
in an attractive form as broadsides" (Interview in Black World,
Dec. 1971). "Ballad of Birmingham" so became the first publication
of Randall's Broadside Press, of Detroit, which has since expanded

347-348 (text pages)

to publish books and issue recordings by many leading black poets, including Gwendolyn Brooks, Don L. Lee, and Nikki Giovanni.

The poem seems remarkably fresh and moving, though it shows the traits of many English and Scottish popular ballads (such as the questions and answers, as in "Edward," and the conventional-sounding epithets in stanza 5). Randall presents without comments the horror of the bombing--in the mother's response and in the terrible evidence--but we are clearly left to draw the lesson that if the daughter had been allowed to join the open protest, she would have been spared.

Four black girls were killed in 1963, when a dynamite blast exploded in Birmingham's Sixteenth Street Baptist Church. In September 1977 a Birmingham grand jury finally indicted a former Ku Klux Klansman, aged 73, on four counts of first-degree murder.

JOHN CROWE RANSOM, Bells for John Whiteside's Daughter, page 348

This is an excellent poem with which to set off a discussion of sentimentality--a quality of much bad poetry that Ransom beautifully avoids. What conventional sentiments might be expected in response to a small child's death? Usual expressions of grief. But how does the poet respond? With disbelief and astonishment, delight in remembering the little girl alive, with vexation--even outrage--that she is dead.

Between what Ransom says and what he might have said gapes the canyon of an ironic discrepancy. "It is not a poem," Robert Penn Warren has said, "whose aim is unvarnished pathos of recollection. . . . The resolution of the grief is not on a compensatory basis, as is common in the elegy formula. It is something more modest. The word vexed indicates its nature: the astonishment, the pathos, are absorbed into the total body of the mourner's experiences and given perspective so that the manly understatement is all that is to be allowed. We are shaken, but not as a leaf" (see "John Crowe Ransom: A Study in Irony," Virginia Quarterly Review 11 [1935]: 93-112).

Vivienne Koch has underscored the colloquial phrase brown study ("a state of serious absorption or abstraction"--Webster's New Collegiate). A child in a brown study seems alien, for her nature includes "speed" and "lightness." "The repetition in the last stanza of 'brown study' in conjunction with the key word vexed clinches the unwillingness of the narrator to accept the 'little lady' as departed" ("The Achievement of John Crowe Ransom," Sewanee Review 58 [1950]: 227-61). Warren's essay, Koch's, and other good ones are reprinted in John Crowe Ransom: Critical Essays and a Bibliography, ed. Thomas Daniel Young (Baton Rouge: Louisiana State UP, 1968).

James Wright has recalled a four-line parody of this poem that he wrote in collaboration with four or five other undergraduates, Ransom's students at Kenyon College (interview with Wright in The Pure Clear Word, ed. Dave Smith [Urbana: U of Illinois P, 1982] 12):

Balls on Joan Whiteside's Stogy

There was such smoke in our little buggy
And such a tightness in our car stall--
Is it any wonder her brown stogy
Asphyxiates us all?

HENRY REED, Naming of Parts, page 348

This is one of the most teachable poems ever written. There
are two voices: the voice of the riflery instructor, droning on
with his spiel, and the voice of the reluctant inductee, distracted
by the springtime. Two varieties of diction and imagery clash and
contrast: technical terms opposed to imagery of blossoming nature.
Note the fine pun in line 24, prepared for by the rapist bees in
the previous line. Note also the connotations of the ambiguous
phrase point of balance (line 27)--a kind of balance lacking from
the recruits' lives?
Students need to be shown the dramatic situation of the poem:
the poor inductee, sitting through a lecture he doesn't want to
hear. One would think that sort of experience would be familiar to
students, but a trouble some instructors have met in teaching this
poem is a yearning to make out of it a vast comment about Modern
Civilization.
The poet himself has recorded the poem for An Album of Modern
Poets, 1 (Library of Congress, PL 20). Dylan Thomas reads "Naming
of Parts" even more impressively in his Reading, Vol. IV: A Visit
to America and Poems (Caedmon, TC 1061).

ADRIENNE RICH, Aunt Jennifer's Tigers, page 349

The poet herself has made revealing mention of this poem in a
College English essay reprinted in Adrienne Rich's Poetry, ed.
Barbara Charlesworth Gelpi and Albert Gelpi (New York: Norton,
1975):

Looking back at the poems I wrote before I was 21, I'm
startled because beneath the conscious craft are glimpses of
the split I even then experienced between the girl who wrote
poems, who defined herself in writing poems, and the girl
who was to define herself by her relationships with men.
"Aunt Jennifer's Tigers," written while I was a student,
looks with deliberate detachment at this split. In writing
this poem, composed and apparently cool as it is, I thought
I was creating a portrait of an imaginary woman. But this
woman suffers from the opposition of her imagination,
worked out in tapestry, and her life-style, "ringed with
ordeals she was mastered by." It was important to me that
Aunt Jennifer was a person as distinct from myself as possi-
ble--distanced by the formalism of the poem, by its objec-

tive, observant tone--even by putting the woman in a different generation.

Rich's feminism clearly was beginning to emerge, however, as
far back as 1951, when this poem was first published. It is apparent in the poem that the poet perceived something wrong with the
passive role assigned to women. The pride, confidence, and fear-
lessness ("masculine" virtues, whatever the sex of the tigers) of
Aunt Jennifer's imaginary creations contrast sharply with Aunt
Jennifer herself--a frail lady with fluttering fingers, terrified
hands. Worth comment is the poet's use of the word ringed--sug-
gesting "encircled"--to refer both to the wedding ring that "sits
heavily upon Aunt Jennifer's hand" and to "ordeals she was mastered
by," specifically marriage and being expected to conform. Although
she goes down in defeat, her tigers triumph.
        Question for discussion: Is Aunt Jennifer's plight that of
the woman artist in our society? (Because of the wedding ring's
weight, she must struggle to ply her instrument, the ivory needle.)
        Compare Aunt Jennifer with the dead woman who once embroidered
fantails in Wallace Stevens's "The Emperor of Ice-Cream" (page 67).
For another, in some ways comparable, contrast between a dull world
of reality and the colorful life of the imagination, see Stevens's
"Disillusionment of Ten O'Clock" (page 64), in which

        Only, here and there, an old sailor,
        Drunk and asleep in his boots,
        Catches tigers
        In red weather.

Mary Slowik discusses this and other early poems of Rich in
"The Friction of the Mind," Massachusetts Review Spring 1984:
142-60.

ADRIENNE RICH, Diving into the Wreck, page 350

        Although it is always risky to read a poem as a personal
statement, perhaps this wreck may be (among other things) the wreck
of the poet's marriage. (The poet's husband, from whom she was
separated, died in 1970.) Like a diver, the speaker "came to see
the damage that was done / and the treasures that prevail." The
climax of the poem occurs in line 77: the two spouses (mermaid and
merman) merge identities. Pronouns become confounded in line 87.
The object of the dive has been to find the truth: "the wreck and
not the story of the wreck / the thing itself and not the myth."
The last stanza is a negative kind of triumph. The speaker returns
to the surface bearing the same workaday equipment she submerged
with, and having successfully avoided lying to herself about the
wreck of their lives. She has made no myth out of it.
        This reading of the poem may be overly biographical; others
have seen the poem differently. Wendy Martin, in an essay on
Rich's poetry, thinks the wreck is the wreck of male-dominated
civilization. ("From Patriarchy to the Female Principle," in

<u>Adrienne Rich's Poetry</u>, cited above.) Erica Jong (in "Visionary Anger," in the same gathering) sees the poem's diver as an androgyne, the "mentally bisexual" artist or new woman whose name now goes unlisted in the book of "the old myths of patriarchy . . . that split male and female irreconcilably into two warring factions." The wreck is the world, which needs to be salvaged.

However dissimilar in theme, Hardy's "The Convergence of the Twain" (page 311) is worth comparing to Rich's poem for its similar view of a wreck, its undersea creatures, and its backward glance at history.

THEODORE ROETHKE, Elegy for Jane, page 352

By piling up figures of speech from the natural world, Roethke in "Elegy for Jane" portrays his student as a child of nature, quick, thin, and birdlike. A wren, a sparrow, a <u>skittery pigeon</u>, Jane has a <u>pickerel smile</u> and neck curls <u>limp and damp as tendrils</u>. She waits <u>like a fern, making a spiny shadow</u>. She has the power to make shade trees and (even more surprising) mold burst into song. For her, leaves change their whispers into kisses.

Then she dies. The poet acknowledges that for him there is no consolation in nature, in the "sides of wet stones" or the moss; his grief is not assuaged. Because he mourns the girl as teacher and friend, no more, he recognizes a faint awkwardness in his grief as he speaks over her grave:

> I, with no rights in this matter,
> Neither father nor lover.

Roethke, writing about this poem in <u>On the Poet and His Craft</u> (Seattle: U of Washington P, 1965) 81-83, reminds the reader that it was John Crowe Ransom (to whose "Bells for John Whiteside's Daughter" [see page 348] this poem has often been compared) who first printed "Elegy for Jane." Roethke discusses his use of enumeration, calling it "the favorite device of the more irregular poem." He calls attention to one "of the strategies for the poet writing without the support of a formal pattern," a strategy he uses in "Elegy for Jane": the "lengthening out" of the last three lines in the first stanza, balanced by the progressive shortening of the three lines at the poem's end.

Some readers have interpreted "Elegy for Jane" as the work of a man who never had children of his own; but in fact Roethke as a young man had fathered a daughter for whom he felt great affection. Although "neither father nor lover" of Jane, he at least could well imagine a father's feelings.

THEODORE ROETHKE, The Waking, page 352

As the poet tells us, he thinks we think by feeling; and his sonorous villanelle is probably more rewarding if taught for its rhythms, sound, and form than if taught for its literal sense, theme, or subject (not that it doesn't have any). Examined word by word in a sober hunt for its sense, it is likely to bind students in despair; but if you want to try, a few questions follow (and we must confess not to be at all sure of the answers). What "waking" is the poem about? Does "I wake to sleep" mean "I wake in order to sleep," or "I wake up to find I'm still asleep," or what? Why is the lowly worm climbing the winding stair? (Is it the stair of evolution that the worm ascends--to become man, the awakened animal?) What is "another thing" that Nature will do to us? (Age us, kill us, or make us fall in love?) What is "this shaking"? (Shaking with the rhythms of the dance, or shaking with palsy in old age?) What does "What falls away is always" mean? (Attempt at a paraphrase: whatever chance befalls us, some kind of permanence will remain.)

Students may be asked to compare Roethke's villanelle with Dylan Thomas's "Do not go gentle" (page 171). Is either poem (like some villanelles) an elaborate and trivial exercise? We think Thomas's poem a better one than Roethke's. It is unified thematically, and its refrain lines seem to occur more naturally.)

PAUL RUFFIN, "Hotel Fire: New Orleans," page 353

A native of Mississippi who now teaches English at Sam Houston State University, Ruffin provides this comment on his poem:

> On the evening news a few years back I watched the account of a dreadful New Orleans hotel fire in which several people died. In one vivid scene the victims were forced into a corner room several stories up where they had to face our two greatest fears, burning and falling. They appeared at the smoke-filled window, looked back toward the fire, then crawled one by one onto the ledge, clung momentarily, and dropped to their deaths. With that fire pressing them, there seemed almost a kind of faith as they turned loose into the smoky air.

This memorable poem appears in Ruffin's collection Lighting the Furnace Pilot (Peoria: Spoon River Poetry, 1980), and we thank Cleatus Rattan of Cisco Junior College for pointing it out to us. Its metaphors and similes invite patient unraveling.

The first stanza of Ruffin's poem serves as background for the second. By devoting six lines to the inborn fear of falling, the poet heightens the ghastliness of the second stanza, in which the people choose to fall because they fear fire, "an old and certain death," even more.

What are "that natural window" and "the fire / that tempers us for the sun"? Both apparently refer to the experience of being born, going from the darkness of the womb to the light of the world outside. Both also suggest the New Orleans fire and the means its victims used to escape it: passage through a dreaded window, then through a holocaust. At birth, presumably, we trust in the earth beyond the womb to sustain us--but those who leap from the hotel

window flail "like children / who know the earth has failed them."
It takes one act of faith to be born; another, to leap to death.
The last line of the poem is a serious pun: an apt play on the
expression a leap of faith.

WINFIELD TOWNLEY SCOTT, Mrs. Severin, page 353

Questions for discussion:

1.   What kind of person is Mrs. Severin? (An elderly
eccentric who now lives alone, so fat she can hardly fit into the
cast-off clothes people give her. Open and naive and straightforward, garrulous--"naturally" she talked later of her
confrontation with the Lord--brave, devout. Don't infer from line
18 that she is a drug user.)
2.   How do others see her? (They laugh at her, or regard her
as a bore and a nuisance. She has lost or alienated all her family
and friends.)
3.   How does the poet see her? (With love and admiration,
with humor as well. Like Mrs. Birchfield in stanza 2, he can see
her as a figure of fun. But her laying herself bare to the Lord is
the "brave" and lonely act of a kind of desert saint. Like the
rest of Mrs. Severin's listeners and nonlisteners, the Lord remains
mute. Maybe He can't get a word in edgewise.)
     Scott, of the generation of midcentury American poets that
included Berryman, Bishop, Jarrell, Lowell, Roethke, and (still
surviving) Ciardi, Wilbur, and Shapiro, is the subject of an
excellent, compassionate biography by Scott Donaldson, Poet in
America: Winfield Townley Scott (Austin: U of Texas P, 1972).

ANNE SEXTON, To a Friend Whose Work Has Come to Triumph, page 354

     On February 1, 1960, Sexton wrote about "To a Friend Whose
Work Has Come to Triumph" in a letter to poet W. D. Snodgrass: "I
wrote a not so good poem to you. It was two weeks ago that I wrote
it and I have almost forgotten it was to YOU (of all people). I
guess I was thinking about your problem (the one that has to do
with being a success. Thinking that it was important to have
touched the sun. That what you've done is all that matters, no
matter what happens next)" (see Anne Sexton: A Self-Portrait in
Letters, ed. Linda Gray Sexton and Lois Ames [Boston: Houghton,
1977]). It was in 1960 that Snodgrass won a Pulitzer Prize for
Heart's Needle, his first book of poems.
     This book's other poem about Icarus, W. H. Auden's "Musée des
Beaux Arts" (page 279), deals with the tragic result of Icarus's
experiment, his fall into the sea--and the world's indifference to
his fate. Sexton's sonnet dwells instead on the wonder and joy of
his rise to the sun ("Think of the difference it made!"), insisting
that no matter what happens next, nothing can ever cancel out the
glory of Icarus's achievement--or, by implication, Snodgrass's.

The parallel Yeats poem (page 381) makes no reference to Icarus, of course, but, like the other two, ponders success and failure. Yeats's point seems to be that it is better to fail in a noble cause than to succeed in a dishonest one. Sexton's title echoes Yeats's, but as opposed to the emphasis on failure in both the Auden and the Yeats poems, Sexton's explores brilliant success, as her title suggests: It is better to succeed and die in a daring cause than, like the sensible, conservative daddy, to settle for a more humble accomplishment.

WILLIAM SHAKESPEARE, That time of year thou mayst in me behold, page 355

WILLIAM SHAKESPEARE, When, in disgrace with Fortune and men's eyes, page 355

Shakespeare's magnificent metaphors probably will take some brief explaining. How is a body like boughs, and how are the bare boughs like a ruined choir loft? Students will get the general import, but can be helped to visualize the images. "Consumed with that which it was nourished by" will surely require some discussion. Youth, that had fed life's fire, now provides only smothering ashes. The poet's attitude toward age and approaching death stands in contrast to the attitudes of poets (or speakers) in other poems of similar theme: sweet acceptance of old age in Burns's "John Anderson my jo, John" (page 245); admiration for the exultant sparrows in William Carlos Williams's "To Waken an Old Lady" (page 377); defiance in Yeats's "Lamentation of the Old Pensioner" (page 226).

Figures of speech are central to "That time of year," but barely enter into "When, in disgrace" until the end, when the simile of the lark is introduced. The lark's burst of joy suggests that heaven, called deaf in line 3, has suddenly become keener of hearing. Critical discussion of both sonnets goes on: valuable is Shakespeare's Sonnets, edited with analytic commentary by Stephen Booth (New Haven: Yale UP, 1977).

WILLIAM SHAKESPEARE, When daisies pied and violets blue, page 356

WILLIAM SHAKESPEARE, When icicles hang by the wall, page 356

Students are usually pleased to add the word cuckold to their vocabularies. (The origin of the word is uncertain, but it evidently refers to the cuckoo's habit of laying its eggs in other birds' nests.) Both songs take birdcalls for their refrains. How is the owl's call evocative of winter? Despite the famous harsh realism of the winter scene, discussion may show that winter isn't completely grim, nor is summer totally carefree.

Bertrand Bronson has a good discussion of these two poems in Modern Language Notes 63 (Jan. 1948): 35-38.

KARL SHAPIRO, The Dirty Word, page 357

Shapiro's theme, which the class may be asked to make explicit, is that the dirty word one secretly loves in childhood is seen in maturity to be powerless. Is it a paradox that the word-bird is said to outlive man, and yet later the speaker tells us he murdered it? It would seem, rather, that at these two moments in his poem Shapiro sees the word from two different points of view. In one sense, the word will continue to live after the speaker's death because (figuratively) it is freed from the cage of his mind and also because (literally) words live longer than their speakers do. In the last paragraph the speaker means that he neutralized the bird's magic. Simply by growing up, he abolished its power over him.

Arranged in paragraphs rather than in conventional lines of poetry, "The Dirty Word" may lead some students to ask why this is poetry, not prose. It is a good opportunity to point out that poetry is a name we can apply to any language we think sufficiently out of the ordinary and that poetry is not determined merely by arranging lines in a conventional order on a page. To a much greater extent than a prose writer usually does, Shapiro expresses himself through metaphor. Besides the central metaphor of word as bird, there are the metaphors of mind as cage, brain as bird food, self as house, skull as room, secret thoughts as closet, vocabulary as zoo, feathers as language. The poem needs to be heard aloud, for it is full of unprosaic sounds: rimes (sweet meat, bird . . . word); alliterations (buried, body, bird; worn, wing; murdered, my, manhood); and internal alliterations (ripping and chopping, walls of the skull). It is also rich in bizarre and startling imagery.

STEPHEN SHU NING LIU, My Father's Martial Art, page 357

Born in China, Stephen Shu Ning Liu has lived in this country since 1952 and currently teaches at Clark County Community College in Las Vegas. In Breaking Silence, An Anthology of Contemporary Asian American Poets edited by Joseph Bruchac (New York: Greenfield Review, 1983) he remarks:

My philosophy in writing poetry is that poetic language should be simple, clear and direct. Like fresh air and wholesome bread, poetry is for the crowd; and the poet, since he is just another human being, does not necessarily have a tattoo or a weird hairdo. A poet should work alone and leave group exercise to the football players.

In "My Father's Martial Art," the father has apparently died ("the smog / between us deepens into a funeral pyre"). His son remembers him and his skill with the martial arts, learned during a three-year stay in a monastery. The poignant final stanza makes evident the speaker's love and longing for his absent father. "But

don't retreat into night, my father" calls to mind another elegy
for a father, Dylan Thomas's famous "Do not go gentle into that
good night" (page 171).

CHARLES SIMIC, Butcher Shop, page 358

"Butcher Shop" is a constellation of metaphors. Associating
the everyday instruments of a butcher's trade with things we
wouldn't expect--things whose connotations are emotionally power-
ful--Simic works a kind of nighttime transformation. The light recalls a convict struggling to escape. Knives recall church,
cripple, and imbecile. Most pervasive of the metaphors in the poem
is the river of blood (lines 8 and 14). In a sense, we are
nourished by a river of blood when we dine on the flesh of animals.
Perhaps (like convict, cripple, and imbecile) the animals too are
sufferers. Perhaps all of these victims in chorus lift the
mysterious voice that the poet hears in the closing line.

CHRISTOPHER SMART, For I will consider my Cat Jeoffrey, page 359

Telling us more about cats than Carl Sandburg (page 78) and
T. S. Eliot (in "Prufrock," lines 15-22, page 303) put together,
Smart salutes Jeoffrey in one of several passages in Jubilate Agno
that fall for a little while into some continuity. This fascinating poem, and the whole work that contained it, have come down to
us in a jumble of manuscripts retrieved from the asylum, sorted out
brilliantly by W. H. Bond in his edition of Smart's work (Cambridge: Harvard UP, 1954). Some of Smart's gorgeous lines seem
quite loony, such as the command to Moses concerning cats (lines
34-35) and the patriotic boast about English cats (line 37). Other
statements, as Bond points out, are not madness but only misinfor-
mation: the ichneumon (or Icneumon, line 63) is not a pernicious
rat, but a weasellike, rat-killing mammal.
Read aloud, Smart's self-contained poem in praise of Jeoffrey
can build a powerful effect. In its hypnotic, psalmlike repetition, it might be compared with the section of Whitman's "When
Lilacs Last in the Dooryard Bloom'd" quoted on page 174.
Talking with Boswell of Smart's confinement, Dr. Johnson observed,

> I did not think he ought to be shut up. His infirmi-
> ties were not noxious to society. He insisted on people
> praying with him; and I'd as lief pray with Kit Smart as
> with any one else. Another charge was, that he did not
> love clean linen; and I have no passion for it.

A possible paper topic: "Smart's Cat Jeoffrey and Blake's
Tyger: How Are These Poems Similar in View?"

WILLIAM JAY SMITH, American Primitive, page 361

We might expect a painter called an American primitive to be naive, unsophisticated, and childlike in his view. So is the speaker who draws this verbal scene. Not only do the references to Daddy seem juvenile, but so does the line "the screen door bangs, and it sounds so funny." (Smith, incidentally, has written much fine verse for children in addition to his more serious poetry, and he understands the way a child thinks and speaks.) There is, of course, an ironic distance between the speaker's point of view and the poet's. Irony is enforced, too, by contrast between the grim event and the bouncy rhythm and use of feminine rimes.

Another possible way of looking at the poem is that Daddy himself is the primitive: the primal dollar-worshipping American. The capitalization of Dollar (as in the familiar phrase "the Almighty Dollar") may support this view. We are not told why Daddy died, an apparent suicide, but it is evident that riches did not buy him life. Besides inviting comparison with Sylvia Plath's ironic poem about the death of a terrible "Daddy" (page 342), Smith's mock-elegy may be set beside Wallace Stevens's "The Emperor of Ice-Cream" (page 67), with students asked to compare the two in tone and in subject matter.

W. D. SNODGRASS, The Operation, page 361

Awaiting surgery, the speaker feels himself enacting myths and taking part in rituals. Students will see this if asked to sort out all the speaker's comparisons of himself to others: a sacrificial victim being shaved, a child (as if returned to childhood by the razor), Pierrot, a girl making her first communion, a "blank hero" (an antihero who will not act, but will be acted upon). While it is possible to make too much of the poem's myth and symbolism, Robert Phillips is surely right in suggesting that the poet in the hospital is undergoing a kind of purification, and metaphorically is being reborn. The hospital, says Phillips, is a world "in which one dies to become resurrected, is cut to become whole" (The Confessional Poets [Carbondale: Southern Illinois UP, 1973]). Phillips also observes that "The Operation" is probably the great original that launched what Anne Sexton once called the My-stomach-laced-up-like-a-football school of poetry.

"The Operation" is an excellent poem to read aloud slowly, with attention to its meaningful sound effects: the old woman "arched to her gnarled stick," the rather menacing and mysterious "cargoes under dark tarpaulins." In the development of its narrative, it is an interesting poem to set next to Robert Lowell's "Skunk Hour" (page 334). In "The Operation" we have a fearful procession of awful details, building to the crucial moment when the narrator feels death (or madness) imminent ("shackled and spellbound," declares Snodgrass; "my mind's not right," says Lowell). Both poems are resolved on a note of triumph and repose. In both, the closing image is of an object out of the world of

361-362 (text pages)

nature, slightly sullied by contact with civilization but blooming
(or feeding) and going on--as the poet at last seems able to do.
     The poem has been dissected carefully by Paul L. Gaston, who
finds in it an "archetypal rite of passage: ritual preparation,
the journey to the ordeal, the departure from the present world,
and eventual rebirth into a world turned upsidedown." But such a
reading isn't compulsory. "The Operation" describes a commonplace
experience--"many readers will find its details familiar. What is
singular is the poet's insistence on discovering meaning in an
experience that, were it not his, would be routine" (W. D. Snodgrass [Boston: Twayne, 1978] 40-42).

GARY SOTO, Black Hair, page 362

     This is the title poem in Black Hair (Pittsburgh: U of Pitts-
burgh P, 1985), Soto's fourth book of poems. A Chicano, the poet
teaches in the Departments of Chicano Studies and English at the
University of California, Berkeley.
     "Black Hair" seems to tell of a childhood memory. The eight-
year-old boy watches a playground baseball game in July and identifies with its hero, Hector Moreno--most obviously in the final
stanza. Notable are the poem's figures of speech, and you might
begin discussion of "Black Hair" by having students identify some
of them and comment on their aptness. July is a "ring of heat / We
all jumped through"; the boy's collection of baseball cards is an
altar; the boy, a Mexican, is "a stick / Of brown light," his hair
a "black torch"; his mother is "the terror of mouths / Twisting
hurt by butter knives." (What does that mean?)
     Interesting too is the clarification in lines 21-25. The boy
was "brilliant with [his] body" in humbler ways than the first line
had led us to believe. In his imagination, though, as the last
lines make clear, he was brilliant with his body as if he and
Hector Moreno were running the bases as one.

WILLIAM STAFFORD, At the Klamath Berry Festival, page 363

     Questions for discussion:

     1.   What is ironic in the performance of traditional dances,
by a scout troop on an Indian reservation, for an audience
including a sociologist? What does the sociologist signify? What
is the significance of the fact that other Indians are gambling
outside, turning their backs on the dances? Sum up the poet's
theme.
     2.   Why is the war chief bashful? How do you account for his
behavior ("listening and listening, he danced after the others
stopped")? (Listening past the noise of the gamblers to the quiet
of mountains and river, he gets caught up in the old dance in spite
of himself, and thoughtfully keeps dancing, forgetful of himself
and of the modern world.)

186

3. How would you scan "He took two steps"? The poet introduces the statement four times--what is the effect of this repetition? (It makes for a row of heavy stresses followed by a pause.
The poet is approximating the rhythm of the war chief, who makes
heavy footfalls, pauses, then goes on with his dance.)

TIMOTHY STEELE, Timothy, page 363

Apparently this poem refers to the poet's boyhood in Vermont.
It seems translucently clear until the last stanza. What is the
"lonely and concealed" thing now risen? The answer lies back in
stanza 1: stiff grass at the field's edge that the mower missed.
Somehow, the haying operation has freed it, brought it out in the
open. That it was once "sorrowing" might seem a contrived pathetic
fallacy, but not if we dwell on the title metaphor of the poem.
Evidently the boy Timothy identifies with his namesake: all the
hay, both cut and uncut. By this mowing, he too has been delivered
into happiness. The poem tells us nothing of his own adolescent
sorrows, but shows him now, like the revealed stiff stems, happily
flourishing in the open field. (This is only our reading of this
lovely poem. You may not care to settle for it.)
    Like Gjertrud Schnackenberg (see page 209) Steele is a scarce
bird: a younger poet whose work is entirely in meter and rime. At
this writing, his largest collections are Uncertainties and Rest
(Baton Rouge: Louisiana State UP, 1979) and The Prudent Heart (Los
Angeles: Symposium, 1983). A third has been scheduled by Random
House. Steele studied under J. V. Cunningham at Brandeis and now
teaches at UCLA.

WALLACE STEVENS, Peter Quince at the Clavier, page 364

    Questions for discussion:

    1. We know that it is Peter Quince who speaks to us in the
opening section; what are we to make of what follows? (We are to
laugh when he sits down at the clavier. The story of Susanna is to
be a tale told by a clown, not a faithful and serious recital; nor
are we to take the clown's anguish [lines 5-15] in total earnest.)
    2. Point out all the onomatopoeia you can find in the poem.
Why is it appropriate to a poem whose imagery is largely taken from
music?
    3. "Music is feeling, then, not sound" (line 4). How is the
truth of this statement demonstrated in the rest of the poem?
(Each character in the poem has a theme song. Whenever we hear the
music of the elders, as in lines 12-15 and 39-40, it is like that
of a coarse jazz band, or like show-off violinists excitedly plucking their violins instead of playing them: "pizzicati of Hosanna"
--praise not of God, but of Susanna. The elders are unimaginative
men, coarse sensualists bound to the physical world. All they can
hear is "Death's ironic scraping," not Susanna's music of immortality. Other theme songs are audible. Susanna, as she lolls in
her bath, touches "springs" of melody--an autoerotic suggestion?

The simpering Byzantine maids titter like tambourines. All have
their appropriate music.)
    4.   "Beauty is momentary in the mind-- / The fitful tracing
of a portal; / But in the flesh it is immortal." Is this statement
nonsense? What sense can you make of it? (Stevens weaves a metaphor: the beauty of a woman is like music. Not that bodily beauty
lasts forever; instead, it becomes a legend, and so continues to
inspire works of art that live on in human memory.)

    Harold Bloom has found an affinity between "Peter Quince" and
Robert Browning's dramatic monologue "A Toccata of Galuppi's." In
Browning's poem, a man apparently playing the music of the Venetian
composer on the clavichord finds himself remembering Venetian
gallants and ladies, and their long-vanished lust. But in
Stevens's opening lines, says Bloom, "it is Stevens who speaks
directly of his own desire." This desire "deprecates itself, by an
identification with the desire of the elders for Susanna rather
than with the more refined and repressed desire of Susanna herself,
in section II" (Wallace Stevens, The Poems of Our Climate [Ithaca:
Cornell UP, 1977] 36).
    A difficult and demanding comparison: Stevens's notion that
"beauty is momentary in the mind" and John Ashbery's concept of art
as "a fine forgetfulness" in "City Afternoon" (page 277).

MAY SWENSON, Question, page 366

    The poem called "Question" is really a series of questions
that add up to one big one: what will happen to me once death has
overtaken my body? Singular and tentative, the poet's view of life
after death cannot be called conventionally Christian; but that she
sees the individual human spirit as living on into eternity seems
clear.
    The poet introduces three metaphors for the body: house,
horse, and hound, the three bound together by both consonance (h
and s are repeated) and assonance (ou in house and hound). Line 4,
"when you are fallen," follows from all three metaphors.
    In stanzas 2 and 3, Swenson extends each metaphor separately,
in the order in which they are first mentioned. Stanza 4 begins by
referring again to the house metaphor but veers off in a startling
new direction when the poet imagines herself with "wind for an
eye." How can this be? The effect of the phrase is to emphasize
dramatically the disembodied state the poet envisions.
    The element of surprise continues in the last two lines and
introduces a paradox:

    With cloud for shift
    how will I hide?

The lines suggest that, though having become pure spirit, the poet
with "cloud for shift" will be as visible as when she inhabited her
body.

JONATHAN SWIFT, A Description of the Morning, page 366

This slice of eighteenth-century London life seems replete
with human failings: Betty (a conventional name for a servant)
sleeping with her master and trying to hide the evidence, prisoners
released from jail in order to steal. Swift's couplets describe
not the highborn but the common people, for whom a hackney coach
heralded dawn in place of mythology's grander chariot driven across
the sky by Phoebus Apollo. Although Swift crams his lines with
images of city dirt and human corruption, the humor of his poem
implies considerable affection for London's streets and sinners.
If students see no humor in his view, let them compare this poem
with another poem about eighteenth-century streets, Blake's angry
"London" (page 62), or a rhapsodic, Romantic description of a
London morning, Wordsworth's "Composed upon Westminster Bridge"
(page 378).

ALFRED, LORD TENNYSON, Dark house, by which once more I stand,
page 367

In Memoriam, section 7. "This is great poetry," wrote T. S.
Eliot, "economical of words, a universal emotion related to a particular place; and it gives me the shudder that I fail to get from
anything in Maud" (Introduction to Poems of Tennyson [London:
Nelson, 1936]). The dark house was indeed a particular place--
"67, Wimpole Street," as Tennyson noted--the house of Henry Hallam.
The poem contains at least two allusions, whether or not we are
expected to pick them up: "And then it started, like a guilty
thing" (Horatio describing the ghost in Hamlet, 1.1.148); and "He
is not here, but is risen" (Luke 24:6). In line 11 of one
manuscript version, Tennyson wrote dripping instead of drizzling.
Why is drizzling superior? The highest moment in the poem occurs
in the last line in the two spondees, at least equal in their
effect to Yeats's "And the white breast of the dim sea" ("Who Goes
with Fergus?" page 122).
For some of these notes we are indebted to Christopher Ricks's
matchless edition of The Poems of Tennyson (New York: Norton,
1969).

ALFRED, LORD TENNYSON, Ulysses, page 367

The following inadequate précis, meant to make lovers of
Tennyson's poem irate, might be quoted to students to see whether
they agree with it: a hardy old futzer can't stand life in the old
folks' home, and calls on his cronies to join him in an escape,
even though the whole lot of them are going to break their necks.
For criticism, see Paull F. Baum, Tennyson Sixty Years After
(Chapel Hill: U of North Carolina P, 1948), 92-94; and John
Pettigrew, "Tennyson's 'Ulysses': A Reconciliation of Opposites,"
Victorian Poetry 1 (Jan. 1963): 27-45.

DYLAN THOMAS, Fern Hill, page 369

Fern Hill is the farm of Thomas's aunt, Ann Jones, with whom he spent boyhood holidays. In line 2 the poet cites a favorite saying of his father's, "Happy as the grass is green." The saying is echoed again in line 38. As students may notice, Thomas likes to play upon familiar phrases and transform them, as in line 7, "once below [not upon] a time."

It came as a great shock when we first realized that this poem, which XJK had thought a quite spontaneous burst of lyric energy, is shaped into a silhouette, and that the poet contrived its form by counting syllables. Such laborious working methods were customary for Thomas. John Malcolm Brinnin has recalled seeing more than 200 separate and distinct versions of "Fern Hill"--a fact worth conveying to students who think poets simply overflow.

We take the closing line to express Thomas's view of his own poetry, lyrical and rule-bound at the same time: a song uttered in chains. Of course, the last line also means that the boy in the poem was held in chains by Time, the villain, who informs the whole poem (except for stanzas 3 and 4, which see childhood as Eden). Students may be asked to trace all the mentions of Time throughout the poem, then to sum up the poet's theme. William York Tindall, who offers a line-by-line commentary, makes a fine distinction: "Not how it feels to be young, the theme of 'Fern Hill' is how it feels to have been young" (A Reader's Guide to Dylan Thomas [New York: Noonday, 1962]). And we'd add, "how it would have felt to grow old, if the boy had realized he wouldn't live forever."

According to Tindall (in a lecture), Thomas used to grow huffy whenever asked if he were an admirer of Gerard Manley Hopkins. Still, to hear aloud both "Fern Hill" and Hopkins's "Pied Beauty" (page 75) is to notice much similarity of sound and imagery. Hopkins studied Welsh for a time, while Thomas never did learn the language; but both at least knew of ancient Welsh poetry and its ingeniously woven sound patterns.

Thomas's magnificent (or, some would say, magnificently hammy) reading of this poem can be heard on Caedmon recording TC 1002 (cassette 51002).

JOHN UPDIKE, Ex-Basketball Player, page 370

Updike's ex-basketball player suffers the fate that Housman's athlete escapes by dying young. Flick Webb has to live on, unsung, in "fields where glory does not stay." The man whose "hands were like wild birds" now uses those hands to pump gas, check oil, and change flat tires. "Once in a while, / As a gag, he dribbles an inner tube." In his spare time, he sits in Mae's luncheonette and "just nods / Beyond her face toward bright applauding tiers / Of Necco Wafers, Nibs, / and Juju Beads." (Are today's students still familiar with those brand names?)

Updike's light tone does not obscure the pathos of Flick's situation. (Students might be asked if they know anyone like Flick Webb.) Though Updike has written notable light verse, he says of

this early poem, his second to be accepted by The New Yorker, that
it "is 'serious' and has enjoyed a healthy anthology life, though
its second stanza now reads strangely to students. . . . That is,
they have never seen glass-headed pumps, or gas stations with a
medley of brands of gasoline, or the word Esso" (foreword to a new
edition of Updike's first book, The Carpentered Hen [New York:
Knopf, 1982]).

See how quickly your class can identify the poem's form as
blank verse.

HENRY VAUGHAN, The Retreat, page 371

Like Dylan Thomas, Vaughan was a Welshman proud of his
country; like William Carlos Williams, he led a long and quiet life
as a small-town doctor in the district where he was born. Often
compared with the work of George Herbert (whose "pious convert"
Vaughan once declared himself to be), his poems tend to be less
technically skilled. Still, as J. William Hebel and Hoyt Hudson
remark, "he achieves illuminating figures and enlightening epithets
quite beyond Herbert's reach" (Poetry of the English Renaissance
[New York: Appleton, 1929] 1025-26). One such figure may be (in
"The Retreat," line 20) "Bright shoots of everlastingness"; another
may be the celebrated opening of "The World":

     I saw eternity the other night
     Like a great ring of pure and endless light.

Vaughan, in the view of Douglas Bush, "has a peculiar quiet power
unlike that of any other poet." His central theme (evident in "The
Retreat") is the idea, traditional in Christian Neoplatonism, of
the exiled soul's yearning to go back to its original Heavenly
home, the world of light in which it had existed before birth.
Jailed in the flesh, the soul may yet reenter Heaven "by regaining
the unsullied vision of 'angel-infancy'" (English Literature in the
Earlier Seventeenth Century [New York: Oxford UP, 1952] 146).

Students, once they grasp this old idea, may find it novel and
interesting! Most of Vaughan's language and imagery will be clear.
Possible trouble spots:

     *The odd implied metaphor in lines 4 and 22 (Heaven and earth
are running tracks);
     *aught (5), meaning "anything";
     *"shady city of palm trees" (26): a Biblical echo, Jericho
being so called in Deuteronomy 34:3, but Vaughan to be sure means
Heaven;
     *"when this dust falls to the urn" (31), referring to the
custom of urn burial.
     *Why does the soul stagger? From its long stay in the world,
which numbs, drags one down into sensuousness, impedes one's walk
(or run) toward Eternity.

372-375 (text pages)

DAVID WAGONER, Staying Alive, page 372

Relevant to this poem is the fact that Wagoner has lived since 1954 in the Pacific Northwest. Those students knowledgeable about wilderness survival may be asked whether Wagoner's advice in "Staying Alive" is practical enough to benefit anyone actually lost in the woods.

Because several lines in the poem seem to hint at another, deeper level of meaning, a second question is worth posing: to what extent is the poet in "Staying Alive" providing a guide not only through the wilderness but through life? In line 10, for instance, he says, "Spit out all bitterness." Line 13 goes on to advise, "It may be best to learn what you have to learn without a gun." In line 26 we are told, "The bottom of your mind knows all about zero." Invite students to examine these and other insights in the poem for their possible application to survival, not only in the wilderness, but anywhere.

EDMUND WALLER, Go, Lovely Rose, page 374

In some ways quieter than Marvell's "To His Coy Mistress" (page 8) or Herrick's "To the Virgins, to Make Much of Time" (page 317), this poem has the same theme: carpe diem. "Go, Lovely Rose" merits admiration for its seemingly effortless grace and for the sudden, gently shocking focus on our mortality in the poem's final stanza.

Students may enjoy reading Ezra Pound's imitative tribute to Waller: the "Envoi" to Hugh Selwyn Mauberley, beginning "Go, dumb-born book . . . ," in Personae, Pound's collected shorter poems (New York: New Directions, 1949).

WALT WHITMAN, I Saw in Louisiana a Live-Oak Growing, page 375

Whitman often regards some other living thing and sees himself reflected in it. In "Live-Oak" (one of the Calamus poems), the tree becomes his mirror in line 4; and one might expect the poem, like "A Noiseless Patient Spider" (page 228), to extend the comparison. But the poem takes a surprising twist: Whitman himself cannot abide the oak's solitude. (This poem has not been shown to refer to any particular friends or events in the poet's life.)

Pablo Neruda's tribute to Whitman may well be applied:

There are many kinds of greatness, but let me say (though I be a poet of the Spanish tongue) that Walt Whitman has taught me more than Spain's Cervantes: in Walt Whitman's work one never finds the ignorant being humbled, nor is the human condition ever found offended (qtd. in Gay Wilson Allen in Poetry Pilot, Nov. 1976).

RICHARD WILBUR, Museum Piece, page 375

Does the fact that the French Impressionist painter hangs his
pants on a canvas by El Greco mean that he scoffs at the great
Spaniard's work? Not at all--Degas just doesn't treat art with
dull reverence, the way museum-goers do. His sleep, we may assume,
follows from the weariness of a day's work, unlike the museum
guard's sleep, the result of boredom. We take this poem to make a
witty case for seeing works of art with fresh, loving irreverence.
Qualities of good art are defined in line 12: "Beauty joined to
energy."
    The opening lines amply show how a poem can have a complex
music: the g-alliterations in line 1; guardians, art, impartially;
the internal alliteration of the l in patrol, halls, impartially;
the s-sounds; the o-sounds in lines 1-6; the initial d's and p's of
the second stanza. All weave the lines together in a net of sound,
drawn tight by the insistent rimes. To write inside so demanding a
form may cost strain, but Wilbur, like a dancer, makes the
difficult act seem graceful by his energy.
    Questions for students: What is this poem saying? How do you
define good art?

WILLIAM CARLOS WILLIAMS, Spring and All, page 376

    Questions for discussion:

    1.   Why cannot Williams's attitude toward spring be called
"poetic" and "conventional"? What is his attitude toward the
approaching season? By what means is it indicated? Consider
especially lines 14-15 and 24-25, and the suggestions of contagious
in the opening line. (Spring is stealing over the land as a
contagious disease infects a victim. But spring is not a disease:
it has a "stark dignity.")
    2.   An opinion: "This poem clearly draws from the poet's
experience as a pediatrician who had attended hundreds of newborns,
and whose work was often to describe with clinical exactness the
symptoms of his patients." Discuss. (Lines 16-18 especially seem
to contain a metaphor of newborn infants. The adjectives mottled,
dried, sluggish could occur in a physician's report. In lines 9-13
also, the description of bushes, trees, and vines seems painstak-
ingly exact in its detail.)
    Recalling his life as writer and physician in an article for a
popular magazine, Williams once told how poems would come to him
while driving on his daily rounds. "When the phrasing of a passage
suddenly hits me, knowing how quickly such things are lost, I find
myself at the side of the road frantically searching in my medical
bag for a prescription blank" ("Seventy Years Deep," Holiday Nov.
1954: 78). "By the road to the contagious hospital" was one such
poem, originally recorded on prescription blanks (Roy Miki,
"Driving and Writing," in William Carlos Williams: Man and Poet,
ed. Carroll F. Terrell [Orono: National Poetry Foundation, 1983]
113).

376-377 (text pages)

Scholars have speculated that the brief lines of many of Williams's poems may have been decreed by the narrow width of a prescription blank, but we don't buy that guess. Had he wanted longer lines Williams would have turned the blanks sideways, or composed in smaller handwriting.

WILLIAM CARLOS WILLIAMS, To Waken an Old Lady, page 377

Questions for discussion:

1. By which words or phrases does Williams suggest the physical ravages of old age? What very different connotations do the phrases broken / seedhusks and shrill / piping carry, as well as the suggestions of feeble and broken senility? (Broken husks suggest a feast, piping suggests merriment.)
2. What is the dark wind? Can a wind be literally dark? (No, it can't, Williams means dark in the sense of sinister or menacing. This wind is like the passage of time that buffets or punishes.)
3. What is the dictionary definition of tempered? What does the word mean in this poem?

YVOR WINTERS, At the San Francisco Airport, page 377.

Students might be asked to compare the language of this poem with that of a neoclassical poem such as Dryden's "To the Memory of Mr. Oldham" (page 300). Both poems demonstrate that it is possible for a poet to write of a subject of personal concern and yet to select a diction relatively devoid of imagery, tending to be general and abstract. (For the result to be good poetry, the abstract words have to be accurate, as in these illustrations.)
Of all the terms in Winters's poem, the most tangible things named are light, metal, planes, and air. It is not to Winters's purpose here to number the streaks on any tulip; his concerns take in knowledge and passion, being and intelligence. At the outset Winters indicates that to see perfectly with one's physical eyes may be, in a sense, to see falsely and imperfectly. The glittering metal of the planes is a menacing distraction. He restates this observation in lines 16-17: "The rain of matter upon sense / Destroys me momently." It is not until the third stanza, when the poet is able to see beyond the immediate moment, that he achieves understanding. In the last line we are back to the original paradox, stated another way: to be awake in a merely physical light is not to be awake at all.
Like Winters's criticism, the poem praises will, reason, and intelligence. We admit, though, to some reservations about it. In lines 18-20, the diction becomes so abstract as to seem grandiose. We might wish to know more about the situation. Why is the girl leaving? Where is she going? But if we accept the poet's lofty tone--in which seeing one's daughter off on an airplane becomes

an event as momentous as the launching of Cleopatra's barge--it
seems an impertinence to ask.

In his fine study of Winters, the English poet and critic Dick
Davis has written sympathetically of this poem:

> The farewell is given the deeper implication of the
> father's watching his daughter move out of his immediate care
> and influence into the world of her own life. . . . "That
> which you dare not shun" suggests the child's future journey
> through life, on which the poet cannot accompany her. The
> understated stoicism of the end is very moving, particularly
> if we recall that this was virtually Winters's last serious
> poem. . . . The closing image is not only a fine evocation of
> the father left alone, momentarily fixed in private thought,
> withdrawn from the airport's public glare, but it suggests too
> that light of the intellect which had become Winters's chief
> concern, the intellect which sees and understands but knows
> that it is cut off from the life it loves and watches.
> (Wisdom and Wilderness: The Achievement of Yvor Winters
> [Athens: U of Georgia P, 1983] 146-47).

This beautiful, knotty, generation-spanning poem has lasted in
the Introduction to Poetry ever since the book's first edition.
Today, as in the 1960s, its appeal to students seems to reach deep.

WILLIAM WORDSWORTH, Composed upon Westminster Bridge, page 378

Imaginary conversation:

Instructor: What do you make of the title? Is this a poem
composed upon the subject of a bridge, or a poem composed
while standing on a bridge's sidewalk?
Student: The latter, obviously.
Instructor: How do you know?
Student: His eye is located up on the bridge. Otherwise he
couldn't see with such a wide-angle lens.
Instructor: You genius! To the head of the class!

Whose is the "mighty heart"? Wordsworth is describing the
city as a sleeping beauty about to awaken. Of course, the
brightness of the scene is increased by the poet's being out for
his stroll before a hundred thousand chimneys have begun to smoke
from coal fires preparing kippers for breakfast. Charles Lamb, in
a letter to Wordsworth, had chided the poet that the urban emotions
must be unknown to him, so perhaps this famous sonnet is an answer
to the charge.

Compare "The World Is Too Much with Us" (page 217) for a different Wordsworth attitude toward commerce; or compare Wordsworth's
London of 1807 with Blake's "London" of 1794 (page 62)--practically
the same city, but a different perspective. (Wordsworth up on the
bridge at dawn, letting distance lend enchantment; Blake down in

the city streets by night, with the chimney sweep, the teenage
whore, and the maimed veteran.)

JAMES WRIGHT, A Blessing, page 378

At first, students are likely to regard "A Blessing" as "a
delicate poem about the kinship between men and horses," as Ralph
J. Mills sees it (Contemporary American Poetry [New York: Random,
1965]). They will be right, of course; but to take them a step
further, they can be asked what blessing the poem refers to, and to
ponder especially its last three lines. In a sense, the image of
stepping over barbed wire into an open pasture (line 7) anticipates
the idea of stepping out of one's body into--what? Any paraphrase
is going to be clumsy; but Wright hints at nothing less than the
loneliness of every creature alive. Although they are together,
the two ponies are lonely to an extreme and are apparently over-
joyed to see people. By implication, maybe the speaker and his
friend are lonely together as well. In lines 15-21 the speaker, to
his astonishment, finds himself falling in love with one of the
ponies; he sees her beauty as that of a girl. At this point, we
might expect him to recoil and cry, "Good grief! what's the matter
with me?"--but he persists and becomes enlightened, at least for a
moment. Only his physical body, he realizes, keeps him alone and
separated. What if he were to shed it? He'd bloom.
A master of open form, Wright knows how to break off a line at
a moment when a pause will throw weight upon sense: "Suddenly I
realize / That if I stepped out of my body I would break / Into
blossom."
Maybe the best way to teach "A Blessing" is just to read it
aloud, and then say nothing at all.

JAMES WRIGHT, Autumn Begins in Martins Ferry, Ohio, page 379

Martins Ferry is the poet's native town. "Dreaming of
heroes," the speaker sits in the high school stadium, the only
place in town where heroes are likely to appear. Certainly the
heroes aren't the men portrayed in lines 2-4: beery, gray-faced,
ruptured, worn out by their jobs in heavy industry. These are the
same "proud fathers" who, ashamed of their failures (including
their failures as lovers to their wives), won't go home but prefer
to hang around taverns. Without fathers to supply them with hero
figures, their sons set out to become heroes themselves on the
football field. The season of their "suicidal" ritual is fittingly
the season of the death of the year. Will they become heroes?
Most likely they'll just break their necks.
Perhaps the fathers were once football heroes themselves, as
George S. Lensing and Ronald Moran point out in Four Poets and the
Emotive Imagination (Baton Rouge: Louisiana State UP, 1976), a
study that discusses nearly the whole of Wright's work. "From this
there is the suggestion that the futures of the current community

heroes may be as bleak as the present time assuredly is for the
fathers."

Did Wright mean to protest the violence of football--at least,
football of the Martins Ferry kind? Not according to the poet
himself, who once played on an Ohio River Valley semipro team.
Although the high school games were "ritualized, formalized
violence," they had positive qualities: "the expression of
physical grace," "terrific aesthetic appeal." Wright's own high
school produced not just lads doomed to frustration (like their
fathers), but at least one football hero: Lou Groza, placekicker
for the Cleveland Browns. (Wright made his remarks in an interview
reprinted in The Pure Clear Word: Essays on the Poetry of James
Wright, ed. Dave Smith [Urbana: U of Illinois P, 1982] 3-4.)

In the same critical anthology, Robert Hass sees football in
the poem as a harvest ritual, which, like all good harvest rituals,
celebrates sexual potency and the fruitfulness of the earth (two
positive qualities apparently not conspicuous in Martins Ferry).
"Even the stanzaic structure of the poem participates in the
ritual. The first two stanzas separate the bodies of the men from
the bodies of the women, and the third stanza gives us the boys
pounding against each other, as if they could, out of their wills,
effect a merging (210).

SIR THOMAS WYATT, They flee from me that sometime did me seke, page
379

Surely Wyatt knew what he was about. Sounding the final e's
helps to fulfill the expectations of iambic pentameter in lines 2,
12, 15, 17, 20, and 21, lines that otherwise would seem to fall
short. In other lines, however, Wyatt appears to make the rhythm
deliberately swift or hesitant in order to fit the sense. Line 7
("Busily seeking with a continual change") seems busy with extra
syllables and has to be read quickly to fit the time allotted it.
Such a metrical feat seems worthy of Yeats, as does line 11, in
which two spondees ("loose gown," "did fall") cast great stress
upon that suddenly falling garment.

What line in English love poetry, by the way, is more engaging
than "Dear heart, how like you this?" And when have a lover's
extended arms ever been more nicely depicted? (This line may be
thrown into the teeth of anyone who thinks that, in descriptive
writing, adjectives are bad things.)

WILLIAM BUTLER YEATS, Crazy Jane Talks with the Bishop, page 380

Piecing together a history from this Crazy Jane poem and
others, John Unterecker has identified the Bishop as a divinity
student who had courted Jane in his youth. She rejected him in
favor of a wild, disreputable lover: Jack the journeyman. As soon
as he got enough authority, the Bishop-to-be had Jack banished, but
Jane has remained faithful to her lover (at least, in spirit).
(See A Reader's Guide to William Butler Yeats [New York: Noonday,

1959].) In this poem, the Bishop's former interest in Jane has
dwindled to a concern for her soul only. Or has it? Perhaps the
Bishop, no doubt a handsome figure in his surplice, may be demonstrating Yeats's contention that fair needs foul. Jane is living
in lonely squalor. The grave, she says, can affirm the truth that
her friends are gone, for it holds many of them; and her own empty
bed can affirm that Jack is gone, too, Still, she firmly renounces
the Bishop and his advice.

Each word of the poem is exact. Love has <u>pitched</u> his mansion
as one would pitch a tent. The next-to-last <u>line</u> ends in two
immense puns: <u>sole or whole</u>. The Bishop thinks that soul is all
that counts, but Jane knows that both soul and hole are needed.
Such puns may be why Yeats declared (in a letter) that he wanted to
stop writing the Crazy Jane series: "I want to exorcise that slut,
Crazy Jane, whose language has become unendurable."

What does Yeats mean by the paradoxical statement in the last
two lines? Perhaps (1) that a woman cannot be fulfilled and remain
a virgin--that, since fair and foul are near of kin, one cannot
know Love, the platonic ideal, without going through the door of
the physical body; and (2) that the universe is by nature a yin/
yang combination of fair and foul (or, as Yeats would have it in <u>A
Vision</u>, a pair of intertwining gyres). Crazy Jane may be crazy,
but in Yeats's view she is a soothsayer.

WILLIAM BUTLER YEATS, For Anne Gregory, page 380

Anne Gregory was the granddaughter of Lady Gregory, the poet's
friend and patron. The poem is cast as a dialogue between her and
another speaker, presumably the poet.

What is the tone of this poem? Tender, loving, gently teasing
--but also deeply serious. Yeats doesn't say that Anne in herself
isn't lovable; his point is that only God, being pure spirit, is
capable of loving soul independent of body. Men, being mortal,
can't help loving the physical attributes of a woman, too. This
poem is one of many written in Yeats's middle or late years in
which the inextricable oneness of body and soul is affirmed.
Another is "Crazy Jane Talks with the Bishop," page 380.

The metaphor of Anne's "great honey-colored / ramparts" is
worth scrutiny. Ramparts, as singers of the national anthem will
recall, are embankments or turrets circling a fort or castle,
protecting it from attack. Perhaps the poet thinks of Anne's
wonderful hair in somewhat the way that Campion regards a young
girl's eyebrows as "bended bows" defending her innocence, in "There
is a garden in her face," page 254.

WILLIAM BUTLER YEATS, The Lake Isle of Innisfree, page 381

As a young man in London in 1887-91, Yeats found himself
hating the city and yearning for the west of Ireland. He recalled:
"I was going along the Strand and, passing a shop window where
there was a little ball kept dancing by a jet of water, I

remembered waters about Sligo and was moved to a sudden emotion
that shaped itself into 'The Lake Isle of Innisfree'" (Memoirs [New
York: Macmillan, 1972] 31). In London (he recalled in his Autobiography), he sometimes imagined himself "living in imitation of
Thoreau on Innisfree, a little island in Lough Gill." The nine
bean rows of the poem were evidently inspired by Thoreau's bean
patch.

Yeats's lines provide rich rows of sound for the student to
hoe: assonance (from I . . . arise in the first line through the
o-sounds in the closing stanza), onomatopoeia (lapping), initial
alliteration, internal alliteration (arise, Innisfree; hear,
heart's core). Sound images of bees, cricket, linnet, and lake
water are predominant. Whatever noises come from roadway or
pavement, however, are left unspecified.

Perhaps, in London, Yeats thought himself one of Ireland's
prodigal sons. At least, A. Norman Jeffares has noticed in the
first line an echo from the parable of the prodigal son (Luke
15:18): "I will arise and go to my father" (A Commentary on the
Collected Poems of W. B. Yeats [Stanford: Stanford UP, 1968] 35).

In later years, according to John Unterecker, Yeats was
shocked that "The Lake Isle" had become his most popular poem. He
had taken a dislike for its "Biblical opening lines." But audi-
ences always demanded it of him, and his sonorous reading of the
poem is available on a recording (Spoken Arts, 753).

WILLIAM BUTLER YEATS, To a Friend Whose Work Has Come to Nothing,
page 381

Yeats's poem and Anne Sexton's (page 354) represent in a way
opposite sides of the same coin in that both deal with success and
failure. Yeats in his poem urges Lady Gregory, who at first
thought the poem was written for Hugh Lane (see A. Norman
Jeffares's A Commentary on the Collected Poems of W. B. Yeats
[Stanford: Stanford UP, 1968] 132), to "be secret and exult" even
though she has failed. Sexton too urges exultation--but exultation
in the face of success rather than of failure. Sexton speaks out
against the fear of success, Yeats against success falsely won.

In class, you might want to call attention to the skill with
which Yeats, within tight formal limits, maintains a conversational
tone throughout his poem.

WILLIAM BUTLER YEATS, The Magi, page 382

After writing a lesser poem than this--"The Dolls," in which
dolls hurl resentment at a "noisy and filthy thing," a human baby--
Yeats had a better idea. "I looked up one day into the blue of the
sky, and suddenly imagined, as if lost in the blue of the sky,
stiff figures in procession" (Yeats's note at the back of his
Collected Poems). Like dolls, the Magi seem frozen, somewhat in-
human ("rain-beaten stones"), unfulfilled. They are apparently

382-384 (text pages)

troubled that Christ, whose birth was a miracle, died as a man. In
hopes of regaining the peace of the Nativity, they pursue a second
journey.

Bestial will seem to students an odd word to apply to a stable
floor, unless they catch its literal sense: "belonging to beasts."
But they will also need to see that its connotations of brutality
fit the poem and interact with Calvary's turbulence. Compare "The
Magi" with the rough beast in "The Second Coming" (page 217), a
poem written after Yeats had more fully worked out his notion that
historical events move in a cycle of endless return. ("Leda and
the Swan," page 133, can be brought in, too, if there is time for
it.)

In comparing Yeats's unsatisfied wise men to Eliot's in
"Journey of the Magi" (page 302) good questions to ask include,
Which poet writes as a Christian? How can you tell?

ANTHOLOGY: CRITICISM

This additional anthology is designed not to give you anything
more to teach, but to supplement your teaching resources. While
there isn't anything you'll need to do about it, this anthology of
criticism offers additional possibilities for paper topics and some
broad, general subjects for discussion. It provides, moreover,
brief texts of certain famous critical statements that some
instructors have said they would like to have available. These
include Plato's account of Socrates' theory of inspiration and his
banishment of poets from the Republic, Aristotle on imitation,
Sidney on nature, Samuel Johnson on the superiority of universal
truths to tulips' streaks, Wordsworth on emotion in tranquility,
Coleridge on the imagination, Shelley's view of poets as
"unacknowledged legislators," Emerson on the relation of thought to
form, Poe on long poems, Frost on the "sound of sense," and Eliot
on personality. All seem part of the permanent baggage of received
critical ideas that the reader who cares deeply for poetry will
tote along.
     The Anthology is arranged in chronological order. Most of the
extracts at the more recent end of the anthology have not yet
become permanent, but are (we hope) lively critical notions that
may interest students, cause them to reflect and perhaps to argue.
Here are a few topics (for either writing assignments or class
discussion) suggested by these selections, including the classic
ones.

PLATO, Inspiration, page 385

     1.   According to Socrates, what is the source of poets' in-
spiration? How is it possible for "the worst of poets" to sing
"the best of songs"?
     2.   Can readers be inspired as well? (Yes, and critics such
as Ion. This is the point of the metaphor, the magnet that
attracts iron rings and makes magnets of them, too, early in this
passage.)

PLATO, Socrates banishes poets from his ideal state, page 386

     1.   What is the tone of this dialogue? (In banishing poets,
Socrates appears to have a smile on his lips. As the passage ends,
he is trying to find a way to let them return.)

386-389 (text pages)

2.   What distinction does Socrates draw between admissible
poetry and inadmissible poetry? What danger to the Republic does
he find inherent in epic and lyric verse? (The danger is that
feeling and emotion will be encouraged to unseat reason. Therefore, only hymns to the gods and praises of famous men, legitimate
and useful expressions of feeling, are to be allowed.)
3.   Compare Socrates' view of poets with Shelley's (page
391).

ARISTOTLE, Two causes of poetry, page 388

In your own words, sum up what Aristotle appears to mean by
imitation. Can it be charged that he reduces poetry to journalism,
poems to mere descriptions of the world? (But mere descriptions
don't embody harmony and rhythm—two equally essential sources of a
poem.)

SIR PHILIP SIDNEY, Nature and the poet, page 389

Is Sidney of one mind with Aristotle on the subject of imitation? (No, he says, in this particular passage, that poets don't
imitate nature, they create something better than nature has ever
conceived!)

SAMUEL JOHNSON, The business of a poet, page 389

1.   Do poets, in Johnson's view, appear to be Muse-inspired
utterers of surprising statements not their own? (Look back once
more on Socrates's remarks on inspiration.)
2.   What, then, is a poet's task as Johnson sees it?
3.   Write a one-paragraph review of a book of imagist poetry
(including, say, Ezra Pound's "In a Station of the Metro" [page
70], H. D.'s "Heat" [page 80], and Elizabeth Bishop's "The Fish"
[page 72]—this last a later poem, but owing much to imagism) as
Dr. Johnson might have written it. Would he condemn such poets for
numbering the streaks of the tulip instead of articulating universal ideas?

WILLIAM WORDSWORTH, Emotion recollected in tranquility, page 390

1.   In Wordsworth's description of the poetic process, how
does a poet usually go about writing a poem?
2.   Take another look at Wordsworth's poem "I Wandered Lonely
as a Cloud" (page 17). What light does this statement cast upon
it? What lines in the poem seem to describe the same process of
poetic composition?

SAMUEL TAYLOR COLERIDGE, Imagination, page 390

1.   This won't be easy, but try to state in your own words
Coleridge's doctrine of the imagination, as you understand it from
this passage. What does the mind of a poet do in composing a poem?
(Coleridge's doctrine is more fully set forth in the Biographia
Literaria, chapter 13. But this concise description, without
special philosophical terms, of the synthesizing power of the
imagination will serve, perhaps, to give the beginning student the
essence of it.)
2.   Name a poem, by any poet, in which you find what
Coleridge might call "the balance or reconcilement of discordant
qualities." (Suggestion: "The Love Song of J. Alfred Prufrock,"
in which Eliot certainly blends unlikely, conflicting matter--
visions of loveliness such as the mermaids with ratty and sordid
urban imagery.)

PERCY BYSSHE SHELLEY, Unacknowledged legislators, page 391

How is Shelley's view of the value of poetry different from
that of Socrates in the statement about banishing poets from the
Republic? How does Shelley's thinking resemble that of Socrates in
the remarks on inspiration?

RALPH WALDO EMERSON, Meter-making argument, page 392

Have you read any poems in this book that appear to be the
work of mere musicbox heads, like Emerson's acquaintance? (Perhaps the best illustration of a poem that seems all sound, and no
sense, is the extract from Thomas Holley Chivers on page 243.)

EDGAR ALLAN POE, A long poem does not exist, page 392

Do you agree or disagree? If Poe is right, should we discard
The Odyssey, The Divine Comedy, and "Lycidas"? If he is wrong,
then how do you account for the fact that certain long poems
contain patches of deadly dullness?

ROBERT FROST, The sound of sense, page 393

1.   Experiment: Let someone in the class follow Frost's in-
structions, go out into the hall, and try speaking these or other
sentences in a soft voice through a closed door. What element (if
any) can the hearers still recognize?
2.   Point to sentences in Frost's poems that sound as though
written according to his ideas. Any Frost poem will do.

394-396 (text pages)

WALLACE STEVENS, Proverbs, page 394

    1.   Explain any of these remarks that seem cryptic.
    2.   Make up a few proverbs (about poetry) of your own.

WILLIAM CARLOS WILLIAMS, The rhythm persists, page 394

    Williams's own poetry is often regarded as an influential model of vers libre, or free-form verse. What isn't free or formless about it? How do Williams's remarks help you perceive what he is doing in his poem?

WILLIAM CARLOS WILLIAMS, The crab and the box, page 395

    What is the point of the poet's blast against sonnets? Would you agree or disagree that a twentieth-century sonnet (such as MacLeish's "The End of the World" [page 167]) can be called a crab in a box?

EZRA POUND, Poetry and music, page 395

    Do you agree? Or are there any poems you know that aren't particularly musical but are worth reading? Give examples.

T. S. ELIOT, Emotion and personality, page 395

    Why does Eliot think Wordsworth (in his remarks on emotion recollected in tranquility) is wrong? Compare these two poets' statements.

YVOR WINTERS, The fallacy of expressive form, page 396

    1.   Winters is reacting against critics who charge that traditional metrical verse is no good because it doesn't capture the nervous, start-and-stop pace of city traffic; because it doesn't reflect the sprawling formlessness of our rapidly changing society. What is his defense of formal poetry?
    2.   How do you suppose Winters would react to Dr. Williams's remarks about the crab and the box?

RANDALL JARRELL, On the charge that modern poetry is obscure, page 396

    1.   To the reader who protests that modern poetry is obscure, Jarrell replies, "That's not the reason you don't read it." What does he imply the reason actually is?

2.   Compare Jarrell's remarks on obscurity in poetry to
Coleridge's. Isn't it possible, for reasons given by Coleridge,
that certain contemporary poems may indeed be obscure?

SYLVIA PLATH, The magic mountains, page 397

1.   What discovery does Plath say she has made? How does it
change her attitude toward writing a poem?
2.   Compare her discovery with the contention of William
Carlos Williams, "No ideas but in things."

BARBARA HERRNSTEIN SMITH, Closure and anti-closure, page 397

1.   What does the critic appear to mean by <u>closure</u> and <u>anti-</u>
<u>closure</u> in poetry?
2.   What similarity does she find between poetry and other
forms of contemporary art?
3.   Compare Smith's remarks to William Carlos Williams's on
rhythm in poetry (page 394). What limits do both writers set on
"openness" in poetry? According to both, what is to stop a "free
verse" poet from freeing a poem all the way?

Smith's <u>Poetic Closure: A Study of How Poems End</u> (Chicago: U
of Chicago P, 1968), is a provocative critical book well worth
reading in its entirety. In the passage reprinted in the text, one
of the author's arguments has been greatly condensed from pages
240-44. Professor Smith kindly read and approved this
condensation.

SUPPLEMENT

WRITING ABOUT LITERATURE

WRITING ABOUT A POEM

These sections in the text are provided for the instructor whose students complain, "I've never written about poetry before-- what am I supposed to do?"

This material need not take up a great amount of time in class; it is here mainly to give students a few illustrations of decent papers and some pointers on method and mechanics. If the instructor likes, it can be assigned for outside reading at the time of the first writing assignment. (Perhaps the more general "Writing about Literature" might be good to assign even sooner.) To make sure that students are at least aware that this material exists, it might be dealt with very briefly in class, with a few minutes devoted to any questions students may have about it and about the expected format of their papers.

Some instructors like to assign few papers and to exact polished prose from their students. Others prefer to keep students scribbling away constantly, on the assumption that the practice is valuable, whether or not the instructor reads all of their output word by word. Some instructors who favor the latter approach tell us that they simply assign poems in the book that have questions after them, and ask students to answer the questions in writing outside of class. These papers are collected and the instructor later skims through them, selecting a few lively points from them to read in class and discuss. (The papers are not returned.)

Once--at the end of a class in which discussion had waxed hot over the question, Is "Naming of Parts" an antiwar poem or isn't it?--XJK made the mistake of telling students to go home and write their own opinions down on paper. The result was to cool future class discussions: students were afraid that if they animatedly talked up, they would be told to write.

Students often come into a poetry course laboring under the suspicion that anybody who thinks and writes about poetry is heart- less or obtuse and is tearing the wings off a beautiful butterfly, and that poetry is simply to be felt. To bring such doubts out into the open and perhaps allay them, Michael Fixler, at Tufts, has an excellent first writing assignment: in about 1,000 words discuss the preferability of experiencing a poem rather than thinking, talking, or writing about it. Is the first possible without the second? If so, then why do we think, talk, and write?

206

ROBERT WALLACE, The Girl Writing Her English Paper, page 415

This fine poem has no purpose here but to interrupt the editorial prose and help put students in a writing mood. But it is worth reading with an eye to its metaphors: Crumpled up drafts are like the wreckage of Eden (lovely hyperbole!); writing about a poem is like plowing furrows.

Interestingly, Wallace has discussed the process of writing this poem, which once ended in a stanza since deleted:

> Consider, if you don't believe in poems,
> how pensively she attends
> words of a man long dead.

Later, reading the poem to an audience, the poet found himself distrusting that last stanza. "The point of the poem was not to club anybody for not liking poetry, but to express all my feelings of awe and astonishment at the girl's utterly absorbed love of a poem." The stanza about starlight now seemed to him more trustworthy. "So real was her love for the poem, so real was her concentration that (as stanza 4 said) the factual room with its firelight and lamplight might simply vanish and the reality of the poem and her culturing labor would continue to exist." For Wallace's discussion of the poem in full, together with its successive worksheets, see his textbook Writing Poems (Boston: Little, 1982) 338-48.

Here are notes on the two poems contained in "Writing about a Poem."

ROBERT FROST, Design, page 418

"Design" is fruitful to compare in theme with Walt Whitman's "A Noiseless Patient Spider" (page 228). One could begin by comparing the early versions of the two poems, Whitman's "The Soul, reaching" and Frost's "In White" (given on pages 229 and 433). What are the themes of these versions? It is more difficult to tell from these vaguer, more general statements. In rewriting, both poets seem not only to have made their details more specific, but also to have defined their central ideas.

If you wish to deal with this section in class, you might have students read "Design," then the two student papers about it (pages 418 and 423). What did these writers notice about the poem that you didn't notice? What did you notice about it that they left out?

Besides Jarrell's classic explication, many other good discussions of the poem can be consulted. Elizabeth Drew has a succinct explication in Poetry: A Modern Guide to Its Understanding and Enjoyment (New York: Norton, 1959), and there is a more detailed reading by Richard Ohmann in College English 28 (Feb. 1967): 359-67.

426-432 (text pages)

ABBIE HUSTON EVANS, Wing-Spread, page 426

The student's evaluation seems just to us. While "Wing-Spread" is not so vivid a cameo as "Design," nor so troubling in its theme, and while it contains trite rimes (except for beryl / peril), we think it a decent poem and admirably terse.

Insufficiently recognized (like most poets), Evans was born in 1881 and (as far as we know) is still alive at this writing. Her Collected Poems was published in 1970 by the University of Pittsburgh Press. There are dozens of poems better than "Wing-Spread" in it.

SUGGESTIONS FOR WRITING

These suggestions for paper assignments supplement the list of topics on pages 431-32 in the book.

Topics for Brief Papers (250-500 words)

1. A précis (French, from Latin: "to cut short") is a short abstract or condensation of a literary work that tries to sum up the work's most essential elements. Although a précis, like a paraphrase, states the poet's thought in the writer's own words, a paraphrase is sometimes as long as the original poem, if not longer. A précis, while it tends to be much briefer than a poem, also takes in essentials: theme, subject, tone, character, events (in a narrative poem), and anything else that strikes the writer as important. A précis might range in length from one ample sentence to a few hundred words (if, say, it were condensing a long play or novel, or a complex longer poem). Here, for instance, is an acceptable précis of Robert Browning's "Soliloquy of the Spanish Cloister":

> The speaker, a monk in a religious community, voices to himself while gardening the bitter grudge he has against Brother Lawrence, one of his fellow monks. He charges Lawrence with boring him with dull talk at mealtime, sporting monogrammed tableware, ogling women, drinking greedily, ignoring rituals (unlike the speaker, who after a meal lays knife and fork in a cross--which seems overly scrupulous). Having vented his grudge by slyly scissoring Lawrence's favorite flowering shrubs, the speaker is now determined to go further, and plots to work Lawrence's damnation. Perhaps he will lure Lawrence into misinterpreting a text in Scripture, or plant a pornographic volume on him. So far gone is the speaker in his hatred that he is even willing to sell his soul to the devil if the devil will carry off Lawrence's; and so proud is the speaker in his own wiles that he thinks he can cheat the devil in the bargain. Vespers ring, ending the meditation, but his terrible grudge seems sure to go on.

208

As the detailed précis makes clear, Browning's poem contains a chronicle of events and a study in character. The précis also indicates the tone of the poem and (another essential) its point of view.

Students might be supplied with a copy of the above material to guide them and be asked to write précis of four or five poems, chosen from a list the instructor compiles of six or eight poems in the Anthology.

2. Pick a short poem rich in figures of speech (Plath's "Metaphors," say, or Burns's "Oh, my love is like a red, red rose," or Keats's "On First Looking into Chapman's Homer"). Rewrite it, taking for your model Howard Moss's deliberately bepiddling version of Shakespeare's "Shall I compare thee to a summer's day?" Eliminate all figurative language and turn the poem into language as flat and unsuggestive as possible. (Just ignore any rime or rhythm in the original.) Then, in a paragraph, sum up what your barbaric rewrite suggests to you about the nature of poetry.

3. Evaluate a poem, briefly referring to particulars in the poem to support your opinion of it.

4. Take some relatively simple poem (such as William Carlos Williams's "This Is Just to Say" or Donne's "A Burnt Ship") and write a burlesque critical interpretation of it in which you discover all sorts of symbols, myths, and profundities in the poem that it doesn't contain. While allowing your ability to read into a poem to run wild, do not invent anything that you can't somehow support from the text of the poem itself. At the end of your paper, append a sentence or a paragraph summing up what your burlesque indicates about how to read poems, or how not to.

5. Find a poem that you like, one not in this book so it may be unfamiliar to other members of the class. Insert into it a passage of five or six lines that you yourself write in imitation of it. Your object is to lengthen the poem by a bit of forgery that will go undetected. Type out the whole poem afresh, inserted lines and all, and have copies duplicated for the others in the class. Then let them try to tell your forged lines from those of the original. A successful forgery will be hard to detect, since you will have imitated the poet's language, handling of form, and imagery--indeed, the poet's voice.

Topics for More Extensive Papers (600-1,000 words)

1. This is a two-part exercise in analyzing writing for connotations.

First, analyze a piece of writing whose words very obviously convey suggestions. In a recent newspaper or magazine, find an advertisement that tries to surround a product with a certain aura. For instance, an ad for a new car might describe the car in words that suggest some powerful jungle animal ("purring power," "ready to leap"). Such language implies that whoever buys the car controls a savage force, that the car is sleek and beautiful as a panther, and so on. (Likely hunting grounds for such ads are magazines printed on slick paper, aimed toward the more affluent:

431-432 (text pages)

The New Yorker, Glamour, Playboy, Sports Illustrated, and others.)
Clip or photocopy the ad so that you can turn it in along with your
paper. Circle words in it that seem to you full of suggestions and
explain what the words suggest to you.

Second, take a more subtle piece of writing: an excellent
poem rich in connotative language. This book abounds in such
poems: among them, Marianne Moore's "The Mind is an Enchanting
Thing" and Shakespeare's pair of sonnets glimpsing spring and
winter, "When daisies pied and violets blue" and "When icicles hang
by the wall." As you did with the ad, indicate words in the poem
that seem to you especially rich in suggestions and try to state
what they suggest. For an example of such an analysis, see the
list of connotations of words in Blake's "London" (pages 63-64).
Your instructor can help you decide whether to make your analysis
in the form of a list or an essay.

2. Compare or contrast two poems (or compare and contrast
them.) Such a paper might be an examination of a theme (or other
element) that you find in both poems. Sample topics:

"Reflections on Fascism in Cohen's 'All There Is to Know about
Adolph Eichmann' and Plath's 'Daddy'"
"Robinson's 'Richard Cory' and Paul Simon's: The Same
Individual?"

For many more pairings of comparable poems, see the back-of-the-
book Anthology, where the note "Compare" after a poem will direct
you to another poem somehow like it (usually in theme).

3. Relate a personal experience of poetry: a brief history
of your attempts to read it or to write it; a memoir of your experience in reading poetry aloud; a report of a poetry reading you
attended; an account of how reading a poem brought a realization
that affected you personally (no instructor-pleasing pieties!); or
an account of an effort to foist a favorite poem upon your friends,
or to introduce young children to poetry. Don't make up any fabu-
lous experiences or lay claim to profound emotions you haven't had;
the result could be blatantly artificial ("How I Read Housman's
'Loveliest of trees' and Found the Meaning of Life"). But if you
honestly can sum up what you learned from your experience, then do
so, by all means.

4. Write an imitation or a parody, as directed in the
"Experiment" on page 237. This topic, and the following topic, may
result in a paper of fewer words than the essay topics, but the
amount of work required is likely to be slightly more.

(Note: This assignment will be too much of a challenge for
some students and not all ought to be required to do it. But those
who possess the necessary skill may find themselves viewing the
poet's work as if they were insiders.) The instructor has to
insist that the student observe the minimal formal requirements of
a good imitation. A convincing imitation of, say, Thomas Hardy can
hardly be written in Whitmanic free verse. Students may be urged
to read whole collections of work in order to soak up a better
sense of the poet. This assignment asks much but the quality of
the results is often surprising. Honestly attempted, such an

exercise requires far more effort from students than the writing of most critical essays, and probably teaches them more.

5. After you have read several ballads (both folk ballads and literary ballads), write a ballad of your own, at least twenty lines long. If you need a subject, consider some event recently in the news: an act of bravery, a wedding that took place despite obstacles, a murder or a catastrophe, a report of spooky or mysterious happenings. Then in a prose paragraph, state what you learned from your reading of traditional or literary ballads that proved useful to you as a ballad composer yourself.

Topics for Long Papers (1,500 words or more)

1. "Concrete Poetry: Vital New Art Form or Visual Trivia?"
2. Leslie Fiedler, the critic and novelist, once wrote an essay in which he pretended to be a critic of the last century ("A Review of Leaves of Grass and Hiawatha as of 1855," American Poetry Review 2 [Mar.-Apr. 1973]). Writing as if he subscribed to the tastes of that age, Fiedler declared Whitman's book shaggy and shocking, and awarded Professor Longfellow all the praise. If you can steep yourself in the literature of a former age (or recent past year) deeply enough to feel confident, such an essay might be fun to write (and to read). Write about some poem once fashionable, now forgotten; or about some poem once spurned, now esteemed. Your instructor might have some suggestions.
3. Write a study of lyrics by some recent or current popular songwriter, showing why you believe they deserve the name of poetry.
4. For a month (or some other assigned period of time), keep a personal journal of your reading of poetry and your thinking about it. To give direction to your journal, you might confine it to the work of, say, half a dozen poets who interest you; or you might concentrate on a theme common to a few poems by various poets.

WRITING A POEM
(Some notes by XJK)

These notes are provided mainly for the instructor who employs An Introduction to Poetry in a creative writing course. Some may be of interest, however, to anyone who in teaching composition includes a unit on writing poems. Such an instructor will probably have firm persuasions about poetry and about the teaching of poets. Instead of trying to trumpet any persuasions of my own, let me just set down some hunches that, from teaching poetry workshops, I have come to feel are mostly true.

In reading a student's poem, you have to look at it with your mind a blank, reserving judgment for as long as possible. Try to see what the student is doing, being slow to compare a fledgling

effort to the classics. There's no use in merely reading the poem
and spotting any influences you find in it--"Ha, I see you've been
reading Williams!" You can, however, praise any virtues you discover and you can tell the student firmly, kindly, and honestly any
adverse reactions you feel. Point to anything in the poem that
causes you to respond toward it, or against it. Instead of coldly
damning the poem's faults, you can inquire why the writer said
something in such-and-such a way, rather than in some other. You
can ask to have anything you don't understand explained. If a line
or a passage doesn't tell you anything, you can ask the student to
suggest a fresh way of wording it. Perhaps the most valuable
service you can perform for a student poet is to be hard to please.
Suggest that the student not settle for the first words that flash
to mind, but reach deeper, go after the word or phrase or line that
will be, not merely adequate, memorable.

The greatest method of teaching poetry writing I have ever
heard of was that of the late John Holmes. Former students at
Tufts remember that Holmes seldom made comments on a poem, but
often would just lay a finger next to a suspect passage and fix the
student with a look of expectancy until the silence became unendurable, and the student began explaining what the passage meant
and how it could be put better. (I have never made the Holmes
method succeed for me. I can't keep from talking too much.)

Most workshop courses in poetry fall into a classic ritual.
Students duplicate their poems, bring them in, and show them around
to the class. This method of procedure is hard to improve upon.
Some instructors find that the effort of screening the work
themselves first and deciding what to spend time on in class makes
for more cogent class sessions, with less time squandered on boring
or inferior material. In general, class sessions won't be any more
lively and valuable than the poems that are on hand. (An exception
was a workshop I once visited years ago at MIT. The poems were
literal, boring stuff, but the quality of the students' impromptu
critical analyses was sensational.) Often a great class discussion
will revolve around a fine poem with deep faults in it.

The severest challenge for the instructor, incidentally, isn't
a bad poem. A bad poem is easy to deal with; it always gives you
plenty of work to do--passages to delete, purple adjectives to
question. The challenge comes in dealing with a truly surprising,
original, and competent poem. This is risky and sensitive work
because genuine poets usually know what they are doing to a greater
degree than you or any other outsider does; and you don't want to
confuse them with reactions you don't trust. For such rare
students, all a poetry workshop probably does is supply an
audience, a little encouragement, and sometimes even an insight.

There are natural temptations, of course, to which teachers of
poets fall prey. Like coin collectors, they keep wanting to over-
value the talents they have on hand, to convince themselves that a
student is a Gem Mint State poet, when a less personal opinion
might find the student just an average specimen, although uncir-
culated. It's better to be too slow than too quick to encourage a
student to seek nationwide publication. It is another temptation,
if you have a class with a competent poet in it, to devote most of

each session to that poet's latest works, causing grumblings of discontent (sometimes) among the other paying customers. I believe that a more competent poet deserves more time, but you have to conduct a class and not a tutorial.

Poetry workshops can become hideously intimate. They are bound to produce confessional or diary poems that, sometimes behind the thinnest of fictive screens, confide in painful detail the writer's sexual, psychic, and religious hang-ups. I have known poetry workshops where, by semester's end, the participants feel toward one another like the members of a hostile therapy group. That is why I believe in stressing that a poem is not merely the poet's self-revelation. It usually helps to insist at the start of the course that poems aren't necessarily to be taken personally. (See in Chapter 2, "The Person in the Poem," if you want any ammunition.) Everybody will know, of course, that some poets in the class aren't capable of detached art and that a poem about a seduction may well be blatant autobiography; but believe me, you and your students will be happier if you can blow the trump in favor of the Imagination. There is no use in circulating poems in class anonymously, pretending that nobody knows who wrote them. Somebody will know and I think that the sooner the members of the class freely admit their identities, the more easy and relaxed and open the situation will be. To know each one personally, as soon as you can, is essential.

As the workshop goes on. I don't always stick to a faithful conference schedule. Some will need (and wish for) more of your time than others, but I like to schedule at least one conference right away, at the beginning of the course. This is a chance to meet with students in private and get a sense of their needs. I tell them to bring in a few poems they've already written, if they've written any. But I make it clear that class sessions will deal only with brand-new poems. At the end of the course, I program another such conference (instead of a final exam), sit down with each student, and ask, Well, where are you now?

Some students will lean on you for guidance ("What shall I write about?"); others will spurn all your brilliant suggestions and want to roar away in their own directions. Fine. I believe in offering the widest possible latitude in making assignments--but in having some assignments. Even the most inner-directed poet can learn something from being expected to move in a new direction. Having a few assignments will discourage the customers who think they can get through any number of creative writing courses by using the same old yellowed sheaf of poems. Encourage revision. Now and then, suggest a revision as an assignment instead of a new poem.

In "Writing a Poem" I offer a radical suggestion: that the students memorize excellent poems. Feeling like a curmudgeon for making this recommendation, I was happy to find some support for it in the view of Robert Bly, who remarks in Coda (June/July 1981):

> I won't even read a single manuscript now, when I visit a
> university workshop, unless the poet in advance agrees to
> memorize fifty lines of Yeats. At the first workshop I

visited last fall it cut the number of graduate-student
writers who wanted to see me from 15 to 2. Next year I'm
changing that to fifty lines of Beowulf.

Bly may seem unreasonably stern, but he and I agree on the value of
memorization. I believe it helps coax the writing of poetry down
out of the forebrain, helps it unite with the pulse. (Bly, incidentally, has sane things to say in this same article about the
folly of thirsting for publication too soon.)
Although knowing something about any element of poetry may
benefit a poet-in-training, here is a list, chapter by chapter, of
material in An Introduction to Poetry that may be particularly
useful in a creative writing class. Certain poems and exercises in
the book may suggest additional writing assignments. For a
textbook wholly devoted to the writing of poetry, see Robert
Wallace's excellent Writing Poems (Boston: Little, 1982).

Chapter 2, THE PERSON IN THE POEM, page 15

Novice poets often think of their poems as faithful diary
accounts of actual experiences. This section may be useful to
suggest to them that, in the process of becoming art, the raw
material of a poem may be expected to undergo change.

Chapter 3, DAVID B. AXELROD, Once in a While a Protest Poem, page
39

Assignment: Write a protest poem of your own.

Chapter 5, ABOUT HAIKU, page 76

Assignment: Write some haiku, either original or in imitation
of classic Japanese haiku.

Chapter 5, Experiment: Writing with Images, page 79

A poetry writing assignment with possible examples.

Chapter 6, HOWARD MOSS, Shall I compare thee to a summer's day?
page 83

Assignment: Choosing a different famous poem, write a
Mosslike version of it. Then try to indicate what, in making your
takeoff, was most painful to leave out. (See also George
Starbuck's parody "Margaret Are You Drug," page 236.)

Chapter 6, JANE KENYON, The Suitor, page 87

Assignment: Write a poem similarly constructed of similes, or metaphors.

Chapter 7, PAUL SIMON, Richard Cory, page 108

Assignment: In somewhat the fashion of Simon's treatment of Robinson, take a well-known poem and rewrite it as a song lyric. Try singing the result to a tune.

Chapter 8, Exercise: Listening to Meaning, page 123

Assignment: After reading these examples, write a brief poem of your own, heavy with sound effects.

Chapter 8, READING AND HEARING POEMS ALOUD, page 135
Assignment: Ponder this section before reading your own poems aloud in class.

Chapter 9, METER, page 147
Assignment: After working through this section on your own, write a poem in meter.

Chapter 10, CLOSED FORM, OPEN FORM

This whole chapter may be of particular value to a poetry writing class. Not only does it analyze some traditional forms, it suggests a rationale for formally open verse and tries to suggest why competent verse is seldom "free."
Assignment: After considering the definition of syllabic verse given in this chapter, carefully read Dylan Thomas's "Fern Hill" (page 369). Work out the form of Thomas's poem with pencil and paper, then try writing a syllabic poem of your own.

Assignment: Ponder, not too seriously, Wallace Stevens's "Thirteen Ways of Looking at a Blackbird" (page 180). Then, as the spirit moves you, write a unified series of small poems.

Chapter 11, Experiment: Do It Yourself, page 200

An exercise in making a concrete poem.

Chapter 14, THE POET'S REVISIONS, page 225

This section may help drive home the fact that poets often revise.

435-450 (text pages)

Chapter 14, TRANSLATIONS, page 229

 Assignment: Consider the translations in this section and
decide what you admire or dislike in each of them. Translate a
poem of your choice, from any language with which you are familiar
or can follow in a bilingual edition.

Chapter 14, PARODY, page 234

 Assignment: Read these parodists, comparing their work with
the originals. Then, choosing some poet whose work you know
thoroughly, write a parody yourself.

Chapter 15, EVALUATING A POEM

 Warning: Although you may care to give "Telling Good from
Bad" a try, this is dangerous matter to introduce into a poetry
writing class. Young poets already tend to be self-consciously
worried that their work will be laughed at. Save this section for
late in the course, if you use it at all.

ON INTEGRATING POETRY AND COMPOSITION

How do you teach students to read poetry and, at the same
time, to write good prose? Instructors who face this task may find
some useful advice in the following article, first published in The
English Record, bulletin of the New York State English Council,
Winter 1981. It is reprinted here by the kind permission of the
author, Irwin Weiser, director of developmental writing, Purdue
University.

The Prose Paraphrase
Integrating Poetry and Composition

Irwin Weiser

Many of us teach composition courses which demand that we not
only instruct our students in writing but that we also present
literature to them as well. Such courses often frustrate us, since
a quarter or a semester seems too brief to allow us to teach funda-
mentals of composition alone. How are we to integrate the teaching
of literature with the teaching of writing? What are we to do with
a fat anthology of essays, fiction, poetry, or drama and a rhetoric
text and, in some cases, a separate handbook of grammar and usage?
Recently, I tried an approach which seemed to provide more
integration of reading and writing than I previously had felt I
attained in similar courses. The course was the third quarter of a
required freshman composition sequence; the departmental course
description specifies the teaching of poetry and drama, but also
states "English 103 is, however, primarily a composition, not a
literature, course. Major emphasis of the course should be on
writing." The approach I will describe concerns the study of
poetry.
Because this is a writing course, I explained to my students
that we would approach poetry primarily as a study of the way
writers can use language, and thus our work on denotation and
connotation, tone, irony, image, and symbol should help them learn
to make conscious language choices when they write. Chapters in
X. J. Kennedy's An Introduction to Poetry entitled "Words," "Saying
and Suggesting," and "Listening to a Voice" fit nicely with this
approach. Further, because this is a writing course, I wanted my

students to have frequent opportunities to write without burying myself under an even greater number of formal, longish papers than I already required. An appropriate solution seemed to be to have my students write prose paraphrases of one or two poems from those assigned for each discussion class.

During the first week of the course, we discussed and practiced the paraphrase technique, looking first at Kennedy's explanation of paraphrasing and then at his paraphrase of Housman's "Loveliest of trees, the cherry now." By reading my own para- phrase, not among the ablest in the class, I was able to place my- self in the position of coinquirer into these poems, most of which I had not previously taught. This helped establish a classroom atmosphere similar to that of a creative writing workshop, one conducive to the discussion of both the poetry in the text and the writing of the students. In fact, while the primary purpose of assigning the paraphrases was to give my students extra writing practice, an important additional result was that throughout the quarter their paraphrases, not the teacher's opinions and interpre- tations, formed the basis for class discussion. There was rarely a need for the teacher to explain a poem or a passage: someone, and frequently several people, had an interpretation which satisfied most questions and resolved most difficulties.

At the end of this essay are examples of the prose paraphrases students wrote of Emily Dickinson's "I heard a fly buzz--when I died." Two of the paraphrases, at 90 and 112 words, are approx- imately as long as Dickinson's 92-word poem; the 160-word third paraphrase is over 75% longer because this student interpreted as she paraphrased, explaining, for example, that the narrator willed her earthly possessions in a futile attempt to hasten death. Such interpretation, while welcome, is not at all necessary, as the two shorter, yet also successful, paraphrases indicate. In fact, I had to remind students that paraphrases are not the same as analyses, and that while they might have to interpret a symbol--as these students variously explained what the fly or the King meant--or unweave a metaphor, their major task was to rewrite the poem as clear prose.

The first paraphrase is perhaps the most straightforward of this group. The author's voice is nearly inaudible. He has stripped the poem of its literary qualities--no "Heaves of Storm," only "the air before a storm"; no personification; the author is only present in the choice of the word "sad" to describe the final buzz of the fly. His paraphrase is a prose rendering of the poem with no obvious attempt to interpret it.

Paraphrase II seems to ignore the symbolic importance of the fly, and perhaps in the very casualness of the phrase "and the last thing I was aware of was this fly and its buzz" suggests the same insignificance of death from the perspective of the hereafter that Dickinson does. More interesting is this student's treatment of the willing of the keepsakes: the formal diction of "proper re- cipients," "standard fashion," and "officially ready to die" sug- gests death as a ritual. Unexpected interpretations like this appear frequently in the paraphrases, demonstrating the flexibility and richness of language, emphasizing the error in assuming that there is one right way to interpret a poem, and sometimes, when the interpretations are less plausible, leading to discussions of what constitutes valid interpretation and how one finds support for interpretations of what one reads.

The third paraphrase, as I suggested before, offers more interpretation as well as a stronger authorial voice than the previous two. The author adds a simile of her own, "as if the winds had ceased temporarily to catch their breaths," and more obviously than the other students uses the fly as a metaphor for death in her final sentence.

I will not take the space for a thorough analysis of these paraphrases, but I think that they suggest what a teacher might expect from this kind of assignment. Clearly, these three students have read this poem carefully and understand what it says, the first step towards understanding what it means. Small group and classroom discussions would allow us to consider these paraphrases individually and comparatively, to point out their merits and weaknesses, and then to return to the original verse with new perspectives.

Most heartening were the comments of several students during the quarter who told me that they felt more confident about reading poetry than they previously had. Though I doubt that my students are any more ardently devoted to poetry now than they were before the course began, they are not intimidated by verse on the page. They have an approach, a simple heuristic, for dealing with any unfamiliar writing. Ideally, my students will remember and use their ability to paraphrase and their ability to use their para- phrases to understand and evaluate what they read when they come upon a particularly difficult passage in their chemistry or history texts during the next three years or in the quarterly reports or technical manuals or journals they will read when they leave the university and begin their careers.

APPENDIX: SAMPLE PARAPHRASES

Paraphrase I

I heard death coming on. The stillness in the room was like the stillness in the air before a storm. The people around me had wiped their eyes dry, and they held their breaths waiting for that moment when death could be witnessed in the room. I wrote a will which gave away my possessions--that being the only part of me I could give away. A fly then flew between the light and me making a sad, uncertain buzz. My eyesight failed and I could not see to see.

Paraphrase II

I heard a fly buzz as I was about to die. The sound of the fly broke the quietness in the room which was like the calm before a storm. The people sitting around waiting for me to die cried until they could not cry anymore. They began to breathe uneasily in anticipation of my death when God would come down to the room to take me away. I had willed all of my valuables to the proper

recipients in the standard fashion. I was officially ready to die,
going through the final dramatic moments of my life, and the last
thing I was aware of was this fly and its buzz.

Paraphrase III

I could feel the approach of death just as I could hear the
buzz of an approaching fly. I knew death was buzzing around, but I
did not know when and where it would land. The stillness of death
was like the calmness that exists between storms, as if the winds
had ceased temporarily to catch their breaths.
I was aware of the sorrow in the room. There were those who
had cried because death was near, and they waited for death to
stalk into the room like a king and claim its subject.
I willed all of my earthly possessions, all that could legally
be assigned to a new owner, in an attempt to hasten death. But
there was no way to control death; I was at the mercy of its
timing. And then like the fly that finally lands on its choice
place, death fell upon me, and shut my eyes, and I could no longer
see.

* * *

Mr. Weiser reported in a letter that, once again that quarter,
he was using the method of poetry paraphrase in his writing course,
and remained pleased with it. "My students," he remarked, "no
longer treat poems as holy scripts written in some mystical code,
but attack them fearlessly." The course had proved fun both for
them and for him, and he felt he was paying his dues to both
writing and literature.

FURTHER NOTES ON TEACHING POETRY

These notes are offered (by XJK) in response to the wishes of
several instructors for additional practical suggestions for
teaching poetry. They are, however, mere descriptions of a few
strategies that have proved useful in his own teaching. For
others, he can neither prescribe nor proscribe.

　1. To a greater extent than in teaching prose, the
instructor may find it necessary to have poems read aloud. It is
best if students do this reading. Since to read a poem aloud
effectively requires that the reader understand what is said in it,
students will need advance warning so that they can prepare their
spoken interpretations. Sometimes I assign particular poems to
certain people, or ask each person to take his choice. Some advice
on how to read poetry aloud is given in Chapter 8. I usually
suggest only that students beware of waxing overemotional or
rhetorical, and I urge them to read aloud outside of class as often
as possible. If the student or the instructor has access to a tape
recorder, it may be especially helpful.
　2. It is good to recall occasionally that poems may be put
back together as well as taken apart. Sometimes I call on a
student to read a previously prepared poem, just before opening a
discussion of the poem. Then, the discussion over and the poem
lying all around in intelligible shreds, I ask the same student to
read it over again. It is often startling how the reading improves
from the student realizing more clearly what the poet is saying.
　3. I believe in asking students to do a certain amount of
memorization. Many groan that such rote learning is mindless and
grade-schoolish, but it seems to me one way to defeat the intellec-
tualizations that students (and the rest of us) tend to make of
poetry. It is also a way to suggest that we do not read a poem
primarily for its ideas: to learn a poem by heart is one way to
engrave oneself with the sound and weight of it. I ask for twenty
or thirty lines at a time, of the student's choice, then have them
write the lines out in class. Some students have reported unexpected illuminations. Some people, of course, can't memorize a
poem to save their souls, and I try to encourage but not to
pressure them. These written memorizations take very little of the
instructor's time to check and need not be returned to the students
unless there are flagrant lacunae in them.
　4. The instructor has to sense when a discussion has gone on
long enough. It is a matter of watching each student's face for
the first sign of that fixed set of the mouth. Elizabeth Bishop

once wisely declared that, while she was not opposed to all close
analysis and criticism, she was against "making poetry monstrous
and boring and proceeding to talk the very life out of it." I used
to be afraid of classroom silences. Now, I find it helps sometimes
to stop a discussion that is getting lost, and say, "Let's all take
three minutes and read this poem again and think about it
silently." When the discussion resumes, it is usually improved.

In recent years, the finest, most provocative essays on
teaching poetry in college I have seen are these:

Alice Bloom, "On the Experience of Unteaching Poetry," Hudson
Review Spring 1979: 7-30. Bloom: "I am interested in the
conditions of education that would lead a student to remark, early
in a term, as one of mine did, that 'I wish we didn't know these
were poems. Then it seems like it would be a lot easier.'"

Alan Shapiro, "The Dead Alive and Busy," TriQuarterly Fall
1984: 62-70. In the main, this is a memoir of a Stanford freshman,
Patty Smith, an early victim of cancer, and the way she approached
poetry. In recalling her and her insightful comments on poems,
Shapiro seeks an answer to a widespread problem: "It never ceases
to disappoint me that the poems I have greatest difficulty teaching
are the ones I care the most about."